"With the core message that the only w: [...] ter citizens of the world, Wilson analyze[...] for important lessons of global significanc[...] [...]ge the world's philanthropic community to rethink patterns of inequitable giving to educational institutions, but he also challenges leadership in higher education to shift mindsets and 're-architect' campus agendas to effectively confront the world's greatest threats before it's too late. The message is timely because the stakes are so high."

—Strive Masiyiwa, founder and executive chairman, Econet Group, and cofounder, Higherlife Foundation

"Wilson astutely mines our shared educational history and renders rich interpretations that are eye-opening and long overdue. This book makes a strong case for nothing less than a re-architecture of both philanthropy and higher education. Its redemptive and refreshing recommendations will inevitably enrich our national dialogue and deepen our understanding regarding the past and future of historically black colleges and universities."

—Darren Walker, president, Ford Foundation

"Traditionally, US philanthropy has favored elite institutions over HBCUs, making these elite colleges among the wealthiest and most powerful institutions in history. Yet many of our elected leaders, typically educated at those institutions, seem among the most hostile to democratic ideals and fan the flames of hate and inequity. John Wilson's remarkable book, *Hope and Healing: Black Colleges and the Future of American Democracy*, persuasively argues how strengthening HBCUs and their character-driven educational model can help our nation meet its current challenges in ways that elite, predominantly white institutions are failing us—and provides a compelling road map for philanthropy to follow."

—Bill Moses, managing director of education, Kresge Foundation

"Wilson's unique experience in higher education—White House liaison to HBCUs, president of Morehouse College, senior advisor to the president of Harvard College, and now training future college presidents at the American Association of State Universities and Colleges—provides an unparalleled understanding of what every college and university can learn from the persistence of HBCUs through unending adversity. He describes in loving detail how these institutions mold young people and makes the case that all of our institutions of higher education should 'elevate, enrich, and scale key elements of the HBCU approach to shaping better citizens.'"

—Freada Kapor Klein and Mitchell Kapor, co-chairs, Kapor Center

"John Wilson's *Hope and Healing* reminds us of the pivotal role that HBCUs have played in pushing the country to fully realize its democratic ideals. From Reconstruction through Jim Crow separatism to the civil rights movement, HBCUs have advanced Black citizenship and continue to do so by disproportionately educating Black scientists, jurists, teachers, and public servants. His arguments make the case for increased investment in institutions that have been at the frontier of social justice for well over a hundred years."

—Mary Schmidt Campbell, president emerita, Spelman College

"There are few scholarly books today that tell the irrefutable story of the history, contributions, and significance of Black colleges to the well-being and prosperity of America. This well-researched work presents a unique lens through which to view the essential role of historically Black colleges in preserving and perfecting democracy in America. It asks whether there can be an American system of higher education today where historically Black colleges can garner the resources to enable them to educate students in physical environments comparable to the Ivy League, while simultaneously offering curricula aligned with the work of the future and the future of work. Of course, they can do this, Wilson argues, if philanthropists and state legislatures right past wrongs and bring these institutions to parity. Run and get this book if you are interested in mind expansion around how HBCUs—few as they are—can be the linchpin to a thriving and inclusive America. I read my copy in one sitting—it was just that compelling!"

—David Kwabena Wilson, president, Morgan State University

"John Wilson brilliantly weaves in seminal historical writings and speeches from Black college leaders to help pose a set of essential questions for those who lead and support HBCUs today. He offers a workbook filled with tough questions that, if answered honestly, will improve the colleges that wrestle with them."

—Walter Kimbrough, president emeritus,
Dillard University and Philander Smith College

"An engaging and illuminating portrait of the history and purpose of HBCUs that makes a powerful case for their indispensable role in American higher education and American life."

—Drew Gilpin Faust, president emerita, Harvard University

"In *Hope and Healing,* Wilson asks us to consider the future of HBCUs and their impact on humanity—but more than that, he asks us to consider how these institutions can create better citizens and offer African Americans an opportunity for 'self-reformation' by adopting a 'growth mindset.' Wilson walks us through the complicated history of HBCUs, but also pushes us to grapple with their destiny. In doing so, he has an insider view that no other can claim—he is a graduate of Morehouse College and served as the venerable institution's president, as well as the executive director of the White House Initiative on HBCUs in President Obama's administration."

—Marybeth Gasman, Samuel DeWitt Proctor Endowed Chair in Education and University Distinguished Professor, Rutgers University

"In *Hope and Healing*, John Wilson candidly connects the history of HBCUs to today's challenges—and to an uncertain future. Through his skilled storytelling, Wilson shares his perspectives and admonitions about this very special part of the American higher education journey. This is a must-read for all who seek to understand, sustain, and grow the powerful and transformative role of HBCUs on our country."

—Richard Legon, past president and CEO of the Association of Governing Boards and member of the board of Spelman College

"*Hope and Healing* will be an excellent handbook for those who want to put HBCUs on a path to reclaim their central role in higher education for African Americans. John Wilson is an ideal spokesperson for the transformation: HBCU student, experienced leader in higher education administration, HBCU policy leader in Washington, and former president of an HBCU. He frames the critical path to transformation by reminding us of the great role these institutions played in the past and how higher education has generally evolved, then points to the new levers for positive change that exists now. I am especially impressed with his focus on the critical role of institutional leadership and stewardship. Wilson highlights and details how discordant leadership and governance have degraded the ability of colleges to deal with headwinds and have failed to embrace opportunities. Transformative leadership and governance are critical. Wilson provides the road map for the path forward."

—Phillip Clay, former chancellor, Massachusetts Institute of Technology

Hope and Healing

Hope and Healing

Black Colleges and the Future
of American Democracy

John Silvanus Wilson, Jr.

HARVARD EDUCATION PRESS
CAMBRIDGE, MA

Paperback ISBN 978-1-68253-804-3

Library of Congress Cataloging-in-Publication Data is on file.

Published by Harvard Education Press,
an imprint of the Harvard Education Publishing Group
Harvard Education Press
8 Story Street
Cambridge, MA 02138

Cover Design: Ciano Design
Cover Image: Miguel Gomez/Shutterstock.com

The typefaces in this book are Adobe Garamond Pro and Helvetica Neue.

Contents

In the spirit of

Ayi Kwei Armah
Genius String Shooter
Best-ever mindset liberator!

In memory of

Eddie "Blue" Weaver
October 2, 1961–February 21, 2017
Steadfast, Honest, True!

In honor of

All the Morehouse students who
attended on my watch, but especially
those six or seven students who met me
outside of King Chapel and told me
the whole truth on my first
Saturday in office.

We are indeed the river, and at the same time . . . the river is more than us—generations more, millions more. . . . For the black river in the United States has always taken on more than blackness. The dynamics and justice of its movement have continually gathered others to itself, have consistently filled other men and women with the force of its vision, its indomitable hope. And at its best the river of our struggle has moved consistently toward the ocean of humankind's most courageous hopes for freedom and integrity, forever seeking what black people in South Carolina said they sought in 1865, "the right to develop our whole *being*."

Vincent Harding
There Is a River, 1981

Malcolm X, the ideological father of the BCM [Black Campus Movement] once reasoned, "You don't stick a knife in a man's back nine inches and then pull it out six inches and say you're making progress." The BCM pulled out the knife several inches. The new ideals, the new racial constitution gave higher education the tools to fully extract the knife and heal the wounds inflicted by over one hundred years of the moralized contraption, standardization of exclusion, normalized mask of whiteness, and ladder altruism. Forty years [now *fifty*] have passed since the demise of the BCM. Has the knife been fully removed? Have the wounds been healed? Has higher education racially advanced? Are we making progress?

Ibram X. Kendi
The Black Campus Movement, 2012

What if America understood, finally, in this 400th year, that we have never been the problem but the solution?

Nikole Hannah Jones
The 1619 Project, 2019

Prologue

I approached this narrative with a mindset informed by three key perspectives. First, I believe America's Historically Black Colleges and Universities (HBCUs) are a threatened national treasure. These institutions stabilized the country by giving critical masses of previously enslaved Americans a pathway to a new future. Many people are aware that most HBCUs were born following the Civil War. But few realize that America's Southern states were once home to well over 300 fledgling operations resembling those that would later survive to be called "HBCUs."[1] The federal researcher who led the 1966 search for signs of lifeless HBCUs referred to his task as "a study of a few dead trees without any definite idea of the total number in the forest." Unsurprisingly, he also determined that most of the 300 institutions closed due to a "lack of financial backing."[2]

From the start, precarity was a normal feature of HBCU life. Modest relief arrived when, as part of President Lyndon B. Johnson's Great Society legislation, Congress used the Higher Education Act of 1965 to officially define an HBCU as "a school of higher learning that was accredited and established before 1964, and whose principal mission was the education of African Americans."[3] There were 117 HBCUs at that time—eighty-one were privately funded, thirty-six were publicly funded, and not one had ever been *sufficiently* funded. The federal institutional and student-based aid provided by the Act eased, but did not erase, HBCU precarity.

The lack of any public alarm when two-thirds of the sector disappeared was predictable in the racially charged, post–Civil War era. For decades after emancipation, it may have been as unremarkable to see stillborn Black institutions on the roadside as it was to stumble upon lynched Black individuals. But the disregard has persisted. Since 1965, seventeen HBCUs, or 14.5 percent, have perished, with no detectable alarm. To the degree that the departed institutions are aptly compared to dead trees, the persistent silence about their fate may indicate, philosophically, that the HBCU trees in America's higher-education forest are the ones that fall without making a sound. But this portends a larger, intolerable outcome. If the country remains deaf to the sound of the next seventeen HBCUs to fall, and the seventeen after that, the eventual disintegration of an important American legacy may be inevitable. Once an HBCU dies, it can never be replaced.

That is why the second perspective—the largely veiled significance of these campuses—is so critical. One of the reasons why the HBCU sector has remained so threatened is because the true value of the institutions has remained so obscure. As a third-generation HBCU graduate, my life and career have convinced me that, in far too many American mindsets, HBCU virtues seem invisible or veiled. Personally, I removed that veil based on my experiences as an HBCU student, trustee, and president. But my experiences as a student and trustee in white higher education have been extraordinarily demystifying and veil-lifting, as well. I am now convinced of the revelatory power of discussing HBCU history in the context of the larger history of American higher education. That contextualization helps to reveal what HBCUs have done to actualize democracy. Minimally, it sheds light on what non-HBCUs have failed to do.

For instance, it is worth asking why the civil rights movement failed to emerge a century before it did. Why was such a movement not launched before the dawn or at the sunset of Reconstruction and led by Ivy League students and alumni, as encouraged by their professors and presidents? Perhaps because so many non-HBCUs drew great institutional wealth from centuries of human enslavement, scores of their alumni could essentially ignore the ensuing persistence of society's stark and systemic injustices. Moreover, a variety of disciplines, from theology to the sciences and social sciences, helped to construct an entire world of thought to justify, sanction, and abide the protracted wrongdoing. Should the graduates of non-HBCUs be blamed if neither their education, nor their religion, nor their definition of democracy inclined them to spend their lives fighting to realize true justice for all Americans? Were those shaped by HBCUs different because they experienced college differently? In what sense?

And why didn't higher education's billion-dollar capital campaign era launch in the early 1970s with huge investments in HBCUs, following the civil rights movement, instead of in the mid-1980s? Why did America's philanthropic community neither facilitate nor reward HBCUs for their signature work to advance American democracy? Was the empowerment of institutions built for marginalized and minoritized communities deemed insufficiently investment worthy? Why? What kind of education fixed such biased viewpoints in the mindsets of so many real and potential philanthropists?

The fixed mindsets of the wealthy aside, given that the earliest yield of American higher education was a "Christian" outlook, how and why did human enslavement last so long? *What brand of Christianity allowed such inhumanity?*

And who were those white northerners whose Christian outlook compelled them to leave their homes and lives to travel south so they could teach in HBCUs? *What brand of Christianity provoked such humanity?*

And what happened to that far more humane Christianity in America? Where did it go? Will it ever return? By contrast, since then, why have so many Americans remained boastful of living in "a Christian nation," while abiding such stark, long-standing, hate-authored inequities and inequalities? Was the Christianity of those who helped to found and stabilize HBCUs a fundamentally different religion from the Christianity of those who made HBCUs necessary? And which Christianity is more evident in an uncertain America wandering toward the middle of the twenty-first century—the aggressive one that cruelly subjugates, the idle one that righteously repudiates, or the engaged one that actively liberates?

The true value of HBCUs can be found in the quality of the citizens they shaped, particularly as compared to those shaped by non-HBCUs. Throughout their history, HBCUs have educated many to have uniquely humane mindsets about what constitutes a meaningful life. Unlike most college graduates in America, countless HBCU alumni have deemphasized the luxury of simply finding a comfortable place in the current system. Instead, many have inclined themselves toward movements to humanize and democratize the system to make it more reflective of America's founding egalitarian principles. Their push for justice was essentially framed as a quest to realize a more perfect union. While HBCU graduates have entered society with competitive skill sets suitable to play the game well, many of their mindsets have uniquely prioritized changing the game itself.

That evokes the third perspective that informs the mindset I bring to this work. Very simply, the world needs better citizens—that is, there is now an urgent need for people who will be devoted to securing the health of the planet as they work to ensure a more egalitarian quality of life for all who inhabit it. To those critical ends, colleges and universities are uniquely situated to play a far more active role, which will likely determine the quality of our future. In my view, meeting today's challenges will require a scaled effort by American higher education to optimize the kind of difference that HBCUs actualized—that is, educating citizens who will compassionately choose the common good over personal gain.

When Dr. Martin Luther King, Jr., said, "The arc of the moral universe is long, but it bends toward justice," he spoke as a man who spent the majority of his life engaged in the effort to bend it. The notion that the arc might bend on its own, King left neither to chance, faith, nor others. He understood the power of human agency as a vehicle for divine prophecy. It matters that an HBCU helped to shape King's mindset. And since the HBCU sector similarly shaped the mindsets of many others, I have chosen in this book to highlight some key aspects of their approach.

I firmly believe every campus community should be guided by a single consequential question: what must we now do to optimize our capacity to shape better citizens?

As a tribute to the HBCU tradition of shaping better citizens, I share a story told by my friend, Ayi Kwei Armah, in his 1979 novel, *The Healers*. Armah, like his protagonist, Densu, personally exemplifies the unique HBCU-like difference. And since that difference is precisely what may save today's world, I also use the story, with his permission, both as an overall theme and as the anchor to this book's final chapter.

The Captive Pigeon

The last day, Saturday, came, the day when the champion for the entire games would be chosen. In ordinary years, the champion was known before the final day. But this year was extraordinary. The way the competitions had gone so far, no one could tell who would be the champion at the end of the day.

Between Appia and Densu the rivalry had been so close. Only the last day's competition could decide who would win the final victory.

The morning was sunny, the air clear. The world was quiet. Everything seemed paralyzed with suspense, waiting for the final competition. This competition was to be in the exhibition of hunting skills. The ancient hunting tools—arrows, spears, knives—were not to be used. Ages had passed since the gun had replaced them.

The first test was simple: the competitors were to shoot bullets at a barrel set twenty tree lengths from the firing line. The first crack of gunshot relaxed the crowd a little, and some began to talk. The tension did not disappear, however. It turned into a sort of eager anticipation, a charge in the air. One youth, Kweku Sipi, failed to hit the barrel. He had to walk away from the line of competitors. The crowd did not even care to notice his shame.

The barrel was moved to thirty lengths. Again, the gunshots blasted the air. Two youths fell out from the line: Buntu and Patu. Forty lengths. One more fell out: Djan.

When there were only five competitors left it seemed no one would miss the target and be dropped—all five shot with consistent skill and care. But at the ninety lengths one, Antobam, shot wide of the barrel. Another, Ampa, missed it at a hundred lengths. By mid-afternoon there were only three competitors left: Anan, Appia, and Densu.

The crowd showed signs of growing impatience, but the judges were patient. They moved the target just a little farther after each round of shots. Each time all three remaining competitors hit the barrel. The crowd was torturing itself with uncertainty.

Then an eager voice shouted: "Bring the birds!"

At the sound of that call a look came over Densu's face as if there was something urgent he needed to tell the judge. He actually took a few steps in the direction of the judge. But before he came close enough to speak to him, he changed his mind and walked away again. He was smiling—a strange smile, as if he were smiling in spite of the pain.

The birds were fated to die. The competitors would have to take turns shooting at them. If a competitor was successful, his bird died. If a competitor failed, his bird was pulled back down, then released for the next competitor to shoot at. The birds were brought. They were young pigeons, each tied at the end of a very long string. At a signal from the judge a bird would be let go. When it had flown as high as the tallest tree nearby, the judge would give the order, and one competitor would fire.

Anan was the first of the remaining three called to shoot. Three guns had been loaded ready for him, and he was quick in their use. He fired all three before the bird had flown the length of the string. The first shot was inaccurate; it missed the bird entirely. But the second grazed its tail and brought a feather spiraling wildly down in the startled wind. The third shot blasted the bird into a plunging mess of blood and bones and feathers.

But the success of the third shot affected Anan strangely. In his behaviour there was no trace of joy or success. His arms shook slightly, and he seemed quite unable to look at the remains of the bird he had killed.

Appia shot next. He wasted just one shot—the first. The second brought down the bird. The bullet had pierced it straight through its body. Then it was Densu's turn to shoot.

Densu picked up the first gun. He stepped aside, leaving the two other guns on the ground beside him. The judge released the pigeon, and it flew. At first it hovered low, uncertainly, quite close to Densu.

Densu aimed the gun. The bird flew into perfect range, but Densu did not shoot. It seemed as if he intended to wait for the bird to fly higher. The flying pigeon rose. Its flight was now much stronger, much more certain now that the shock of sudden liberation had worn off. The bird flew forward, then up. The string holding it blew widely in the wind and formed a giant curve, lengthening still.

The bird had flown past Densu's aim, yet he did not seem disturbed. On his face had appeared a look of the intensest concentration. The judge frowned and looked impatiently at him. But Densu did not fire.

The judge coughed a rasping cough. People in the crowd began to murmur their bafflement. This wave of small noises brought Densu out of his concentration, back to some sense of where he was. He aimed more carefully in the direction of the fleeing bird. A smile relaxed his face as he tensed his fingers to pull the trigger. It was a smile of utter satisfaction, a smile too deep for any watcher's comprehension. Densu let the gun-sight rise to the pigeon. He hesitated a fraction of a moment. The pigeon flew a shade higher. Then Densu fired.

The bird, surprised by the sudden shot in the middle of such a profound silence, faltered in its flight then dropped from the height it had reached, as if the bullet had touched it. But in another moment the pigeon had recovered its speed and straightened out in steep, free flight. For just one more moment it hovered again in the still echoing air. Then it soared high. It soared high into the sky, far beyond the aim of any hunter's weapon.

The judge looked down astounded at the string which had recently held the bird. Left loose in his hand, it was now drifting foolishly back to earth. The judge looked up after the disappearing bird. Then he turned to look at Densu. The silence, the profound silence of the watchers echoed the judge's bewilderment. The judge asked the question agitating every mind there.

"What happened, Densu?"

"You saw what happened," Densu answered. "I missed the bird."

"Deliberately," the judge persisted. "You shot to hit the string, not the pigeon."

"I missed the bird," Densu said again. He did not stay to hear what else the judge would say. Turning away from the scene of competition, he walked towards the river.

When the judge came out of his surprise, he walked over to the prince Appiah where he stood and raised his right arm high above his head, the sign of final victory. He announced the coming night would be devoted to the celebration of Appiah's victory. There would be feasting; there would be songs and dances. And the next dawn would see the birth of a new year.[4]

The Contradictory Thing

Negroes must do a contradictory thing: they must work with all their might against segregation, and at the same time strengthen their so-called segregated institutions as if they expect them to last forever. They must insist that the doors of Harvard and Yale be kept open to Negroes and at the same time build up Howard and Lincoln as if there were no Harvard and Yale.

Mordecai Wyatt Johnson,
Report of the YMCA Commission, 1928

If he is able to survive this catastrophe, he'll come out better than just strong. He'll be wise, in addition to being strong. He'll see the world around him differently.

Ayi Kwei Armah, *The Healers*

The only way to shape a better world is to shape better citizens of the world. Beyond enhancing basic employability, every respectable college campus should strategically aim to equip and incline people to advance the common good. One way to do that is by producing citizens who will actively engage in keeping the planet from growing so warm and human relations from growing so cold. Thus, theoretically, the core business of higher education worldwide should ultimately position each student to develop their whole being while advancing the common good. America's Historically Black Colleges and Universities (HBCUs) have mattered because they embraced that agenda more and better than most other educational institutions.

HBCU graduates have mattered locally, nationally, and globally. But not enough people know that. To multiple audiences today, HBCUs generally seem to matter less than they once did, less than is now apparent, and less than they still must. This book is about why this is so, and how selected Black colleges might model or lead a necessarily scaled effort to shape better citizens to a greater extent and depth than has recently been witnessed or imagined.

In their quest to move to a new mode of mattering, the most formidable obstacle facing HBCUs is the specter of doubt and its power over the human mind. Some minds are made up that HBCUs cannot or will not survive, much less thrive and serve as beacons for other institutions. These doubt-filled mindsets draw, in part, from the wellspring of uncertainty about the value of higher education more generally.[1]

At the very moment when some HBCUs stand poised not only to evolve but to do so in a way that matters more broadly, this is precisely the wrong time for these campuses to have an unelevated value proposition. It is also the wrong time for their real and potential stakeholders to harbor expanding uncertainties about the necessity or benefits of the HBCU sector. It may be, however, the right time to ask some of the hardest questions:

- If these institutions suddenly disappeared, would each of them have to be reestablished? In their current form? Why?
- What constitutes the abiding value proposition of an institution born into a world of extreme racial inequity that still retains some of its visibility and much of its unique power?
- What is the essence of each HBCU's raison d'être that is unauthored by both the barbarous hatred and the radically humane promise that first made these institutions necessary a century and a half ago?
- Have enough HBCUs developed audibly distinctive institutional voices?
- Can they now amplify those voices to effectively contain or render irrelevant this era's infectious uncertainty?

In his 2017 book, *Unequal Colleges in the Age of Disparity*, economist Charles Clotfelter tracked the changes in American higher education from 1970 to 2010. The era's volatility led him to refer to 1970 as "an inflection point."[2] Predominantly white institutions (PWIs) began to diversify, and college-level sports surged in revenue and influence, becoming a generator of institutional prestige.[3] As wealth-based stratification intensified, college leaders grew more anxious about their financial model, and the public grew more anxious about college affordability. When state and federal funding for higher education fell precipitously, the more alert college leaders intensified their quest to amass wealth. So in the 1980s, with institutional class divisions well underway, billion-dollar capital campaigning was born.

Collectively, this was the equivalent of climate change in higher education. And just as climatologists have warned that the poorest countries are the most vulnerable to the earth's extreme weather shifts, economists have cautioned that the poorest colleges are the most vulnerable to higher education's extreme inequity, inequality and volatility. While Clotfelter affirms HBCUs by asserting, "there is probably no more distinctive a group among those that offer bachelor's degrees," he also finds HBCUs falling farther behind on multiple critical measures of institutional competitiveness.[4]

This era of great uncertainty demands that HBCU leaders provide the public with a broader, deeper understanding of why they matter, especially since they have evolved from once enrolling nearly all African Americans in higher education, to enrolling less than nine percent of this group by 2018.[5] Of course, if that change reflects a deliberate, strategic enrollment refinement, then it may be unthreatening. But if it signals a decline in the power of HBCUs to attract students, then it begs a question: how do you manage the uncertainty surrounding your existence when so much of your previously captive audience appears to no longer find you captivating?

INSTITUTIONAL CONSIDERATION FOR THE RECORD: THE UNELEVATED VALUE OF HBCUs

Consider a time when the captivation power of HBCUs was unrivaled.

In 1928, as Mordecai Wyatt Johnson began his thirty-four years in office as the first African American president of Howard University, his former colleagues urgently sought his wisdom. In 1916, Johnson had served as a student secretary of the International Committee of the Young Men's Christian Association, or YMCA. He served for nearly a year before abruptly resigning in protest of the YMCA leadership's tolerance of racism. Nonetheless, he was revered by his African American YMCA colleagues, who continued to value and seek his wisdom. In the twelve years after he left, the racial conflicts worsened and crystallized into a major crisis. Once summoned, Johnson briefly reengaged with the YMCA to offer a timely and timeless resolution.

The YMCA had arrived in America from London in 1852. After launching its inaugural program at the Old South Church in Boston, the organization began to establish associations throughout the country. Predictably, as the movement headed farther south, it soon came into conflict with Southern-style racial apartheid. The younger YMCA members, Black and white, believed the brotherhood imperatives of Christianity to be superior to the segregation imperatives of Jim Crow. Conversely, out of respect for the demands of the Southern racial hierarchy, the older whites preferred to continue to meet separately, as did the older Blacks, but for different reasons.

The African American executives had structured and strengthened an entire Colored Work Department within the YMCA, and by 1925 it employed 132 Black men as secretaries to meet the needs of Black youth.[6] In addition to Johnson, these management positions attracted other well-credentialed men, including Benjamin Elijah Mays, Frank T. Wilson, and Channing H. Tobias. Regarding the conflict, the older African American YMCA officers agreed with the well-motivated Black youths with respect to their recognition of the utter incompatibility between the color line and Christianity. Yet they also realized that this push for full integration would likely come at the expense of their leveraging capacity within the YMCA organization. Eliminating the segregated infrastructure could have yielded a decrease rather than an increase in their power to guide and nurture the younger African American men. It also could have weakened or completely dissolved the multicity apparatus they were still building for Black youths, largely but not entirely in the southeastern region.

Johnson and the African American leaders sought to preserve and bolster their unique outreach infrastructure rather than erode it, as the push for integration would eventually provoke.[7] Recognizing that true equality was not on the immediate horizon, R. H. King, the YMCA's regional executive secretary, ended his letter to Channing H. Tobias, an ally, by saying, "I am chiefly concerned lest we begin to cripple the Colored Department and find ourselves in the position not to go through with something we are attempting for the Colored Students."[8] They deemed it unthinkable to lose their unique approach to nurturing Black youths for citizenship and success in an often hostile world. As high as the generational and racial tensions were, the overall stakes were significantly higher.

Johnson returned amid this crisis. He was challenged to bridge the generational divide within the Black community while simultaneously easing racial tensions with the white community. Exercising wise discernment, he grasped the larger strategic importance of the moment and conveyed this message: "Negroes must do a contradictory thing: they must work with all their might against segregation, and at the same time strengthen their so-called segregated institutions as if they expect them to last forever. They must insist that the doors of Harvard and Yale be kept open to Negroes and at the same time build up Howard and Lincoln as if there were no Harvard and Yale."[9]

Upon hearing this insightful framing, students were understandably calmed and galvanized. They responded, "We are impressed with the truth of Dr. Mordecai W. Johnson's statement. . . . it is in large part upon this philosophy that the Association has proceeded and is proceeding."[10] With this counsel, Johnson had effectively clarified a dual task or quest, privileging both accessing white educational institutions and endowing Black educational institutions.

Regarding access, Johnson charged African Americans to "work with all their might against segregation . . . [and] . . . insist that the doors of Harvard and Yale be kept open."[11] Now, nearly a century beyond that declaration of a dual challenge, it is undeniably clear that only half of it has been met. The doors of Harvard, Yale, and thousands of other PWIs are open, even if the experiences of those African Americans who walk through them are not always fulfilling.

But what about strengthening Howard and Lincoln?

On the surface, there is nothing contradictory about pursuing the dual benefits of opening the doors of Harvard and Yale as if a constitutional America suddenly appeared, while building up the capacity of Howard and Lincoln as if the Ivy League suddenly disappeared. Johnson wanted to secure African Americans' access to unfamiliar campuses while bolstering familiar campuses. He referred to the Howards and Lincolns of the world as "so-called segregated," because he knew they were never segregated. That is, no Black college ever established any policies forbidding access to any racial group. Only the predominantly white institutions were segregated, and quite literally and deliberately so for centuries. As a result, Black colleges were race-based by custom, not rule.

Yet in 1928, Johnson's concept of the "contradictory thing" was bold, if not perilous. To mindsets shaped and conditioned by America's long-standing racial tiering, the aim of securing access to Harvard and Yale might make sense, but why bolster Howard and Lincoln? Johnson dismissed the idea that Black college survival or prosperity was somehow inherently illogical. Even if the Ivy League were to fling open all doors, he thought Black colleges would still be needed. The doors of Harvard and Yale would eventually be opened from without, based on the insistence of HBCU alumni, rather than from within, based on the persistence of ivory tower alumni. The protracted legal and protest activity of these early twentieth-century Black college graduates provoked the opening of American white higher education.

As a result, for roughly fifty years, Harvard, Yale, and thousands of other predominantly white institutions have been steadily admitting critical masses of groups they previously excluded. Most of these institutions have become more diverse and progressive. And while there is much work to be done, that general progress toward full desegregation is strikingly more apparent than the progress toward Johnson's other charge: to strengthen HBCUs with the capacity to last forever. In this respect, there is significant unfinished business, which is among the central challenges considered in this book.

THE ELUSIVE HOLY GRAIL

As a graduate of both Morehouse College and Harvard University, Johnson believed that the world's Harvards and Yales were not so sublime that they warranted neither improvement nor competition. This idea motivated his insistence on a collective quest to build up HBCUs.

Johnson believed in HBCUs. Less than a year before he issued his reharmonizing call to "do a contradictory thing," he made his inaugural address a call for Howard University to produce better leaders for their unfinished country. He saw America as "the experimental crucible" in which to forge a living model of brotherhood that would resound in "all countries of the earth." He charged Howard to guide an America that "has not yet found the power to carry out its own ideals. If thinkers here can discover ways and means of eliciting that power and of bringing it to bear in race relations, they will make a contribution to the sum total of knowledge and to the ongoing of the human race."[12] Not only is a high-stakes commission embedded in the assertion that HBCU effectiveness will yet determine the fate of humanity, but it is also telling that Johnson apparently did not expect such work from the world's Harvards and Yales. In his view, the work of optimizing human harmony was central to the unique HBCU raison d'être.

Interestingly, Johnson had similarly used his student graduation speech at Harvard to insist that solving the race problem would finally place America "in the spiritual leadership of all humanity."[13] Overall, the potential rewards of completing Johnson's contradictory thing more than justified his plea for an aggressive effort. And he was convinced that this special, humanity-focused mission required Howard and other HBCUs to be much stronger.

Unfortunately, Johnson's charge to strengthen HBCUs "as if there were no Harvard and Yale" and "as if they expect them to last forever" is demonstrably unfinished. But what exactly does it mean for institutions to be strengthened as if they might last forever?

Historically speaking, the only thing that has ever reliably positioned educational institutions for sustainable stability, excellence, and relevance is having plentiful endowment. To overlook that basic fact is to render elusive even the loftiest and most insightful vision concerning HBCUs or any other campuses. Endowments can help to ensure the long-term stability, vitality, and sustainability of higher education's most consequential institutions.

The story of HBCUs and endowment will be referenced throughout the book as the pivotal measure of sustainably optimal institutional strength. While no HBCU has ever been sufficiently endowed, a startling exception is the Tuskegee Institute, which remains the singular instance of an HBCU, launched and led by an African American, amassing an impressive, pace-setting endowment relative to the PWIs of the era.[14]

This book homes in on the pursuit of the two universal elements of an ideal campus value proposition. The quest to optimize both institutional character and institutional capital should be the shared aspiration of all colleges and universities. Every institution should aggressively pursue both capital optimization (the resource base to secure a sustainably world-class educational environment) and character optimization (the vision, philosophy, determination, and design to consistently produce purposefully engaged, world-class graduates). Those two virtues position institutions to educate the better citizens the world needs—that is, those who are both equipped to compete and work in the existing world while imagining and working toward a new and better one. Full institutional optimization is the best way to position people to deepen themselves for the dual purpose of self-actualization and advancing the common good. And it is not an overstatement to assert that shaping better citizens by optimizing both character and capital optimization should be regarded as the "holy grail" throughout higher education.

As of this writing, no college or university, Black or white, has ever recognizably optimized both character and capital on the same campus and at the same time. Ultimately, for HBCUs to realize a stabler, more productive future, they must strive and plan for the day when Johnson's contradictory thing is no longer unbalanced. A number of HBCUs have already fruitfully emphasized character and citizenship optimization, as measured by their countless alumni who have devoted their lives to enhancing American democracy. It is difficult to imagine that a sustainable surge in capital investment will not augment their contribution to the common good.

INSTITUTIONAL QUESTION FOR THE FUTURE: HOW CAN CHARACTER AND CAPITAL OPTIMIZATION POSITION US TO SHAPE BETTER CITIZENS?

This study grew out of my career-long quest to identify the most compelling reasons to value, preserve, and bolster HBCUs. That effort has been complicated because many people have consumed an unfortunate pattern of reporting and scholarship that emphasizes long-standing HBCU challenges, including poor governance, deferred maintenance, financial stress, scandals, and a stiffening competition for resources and talent. As a result, HBCUs have been stigmatized as invariably troubled.[15] To the extent that this remains the case, most of the conversations about these institutions will continue to be as limited as they are limiting.

Thus, my primary goal is to spark a new conversation about the future of HBCUs, democracy, and humanity by fundamentally shifting people from a set of conventional, largely unexamined perspectives. I hope to engage philanthropists, policymakers, educators, and prospective students, as well as HBCU-affiliated trustees, presidents, campus communities, and alumni.

Founded just after the Civil War, in one of the most openly racially hostile periods of American life, most HBCUs were surrounded by people who fundamentally denied the humanity of African Americans. Yet HBCU leaders encouraged their students to peacefully enter and repair that same world of hate. With pivotal early assistance from both missionary and industrial partners and philanthropists, HBCUs sought to reform and transform their contradictory world to make it more reflective of truths long affirmed as self-evident.[16] Mostly through their churches, African Americans provided whatever resources they could muster for their own educational efforts.[17] Since support levels typically enabled little more than survival, any pursuit of optimization was improbable.

But even when resources became a bit easier to come by, meeting the challenge of optimizing both capital and character was always impaired by widespread negative HBCU imaging. Rather than being regarded as strivers en route to eventual wholeness, most HCBUs continue to be seen as stragglers en route to eventual closure.

Perceptions matter. Based on the giving and investment patterns that will be illuminated in this book, many potential partners, supporters, investors, and stakeholders seem to see HBCUs as inescapably second-class and unworthy of the support required for optimization. Too many routinely regard HBCUs as separate, unequal, and needy, as if by choice or nature. Their heavy reliance on federal institutional and student aid too easily invites comparisons to welfare-dependent individuals. HBCU leaders too often encounter mindsets with a unidirectional insistence that every unfilled HBCU glass is half empty, rather than half full. It is as if, when observing the miraculous landing of an exhausted bird, having just flown for centuries with one wing broken by bigotry, the observers comment solely on the broken wing and the crooked glide.

Few would find it surprising to learn that negative HBCU perceptions are largely fixed in many American mindsets. No institution can ever optimize capital or character in a world so jaded. Thus, my approach to this narrative is guided, in part, by a need to free HBCUs from the prison of toxic viewpoints. The exit strategy is informed by the kind of mindset shift advanced by Stanford psychologist Carol Dweck.[18]

Dweck described mindsets as self-conceptions, mental structuring, and beliefs that guide and regulate behavior. These may be either limiting, as with "fixed mindsets," or liberating, as with "growth mindsets." Arguing that mindsets drive predictable outcomes, Dweck persuasively illustrates how the growth mindset typically yields positive results, largely because challenges and failure are viewed as opportunities to learn, grow, and improve. Conversely, fixed mindsets yield more negative results, largely because challenges and failures are viewed as exposing one to judgment or condemnation—common among those who believe traits and abilities are fixed.

While Dweck is convincing about mindsets being the axis around which self-concepts turn, I would argue that fixed and growth mindsets can drive more than self-perception. Based on my experiences as an HBCU advocate and leader, I have both observed and felt subject to attitudes akin to those described by Dweck, but along lines that suggest a reversal of what she theorizes. That is, in my experience, mindsets can also profoundly influence or control the perception and treatment not just of oneself but also of "the other" in similarly predictable ways.

Mindsets can influence or drive the conclusions that we draw based on partial observation about who and what possesses or does not possess growth potential, particularly in terms of the assessments made by many key people from the philanthropic community. If key stakeholders like philanthropists, policymakers, and educators have a fixed presumption of HBCUs as inherently unworthy, high risk, or substandard, then the prospects for support or investment are necessarily limited. Over time, that limitation may dictate the same racially tiered outcomes in higher education that are evident in the health and wealth arenas. And mindsets are arguably at the root of the now familiar and crippling set of questions that most HBCU leaders and advocates continue to face.

Candor about the following difficult questions could help to shift some of the mindsets or attitudes people have about HBCUs from "fixed negative" to "growth positive":

Now that the doors of white higher education have been open for decades, why do HBCUs still exist? Why do we need them, anyway? Are they not symbols and vestiges of a bygone racist world? Are they not a contradiction to the American ideal?

Why attend an HBCU, when you can be educated at the "best" universities in the world with first-rate facilities, faculty, and students? Is it not true that HBCUs are long past their prime and are, therefore, attracting only high-need, minimally prepared students? Isn't it true that the very definition of progress and equality includes a healthy transition from all segregated institutions?

These commonplace questions are often posed by people with no detectable inclination to help shape a bright future for HBCUs. But they are also posed by some who would approve in principle of support for such institutions, but who are disinclined to lend such support themselves.

This book is designed to stimulate more growth mindset encounters between the more enlightened leaders of the philanthropic community and the more progressive leaders of HBCUs. The logic is simple. The underlying beliefs, psychologies, and attitudes that many bring to their consideration of HBCUs can be energized and informed by a new growth mindset, causing a fundamental shift in their assumptive base. Their evaluative capacity can become unprejudiced, and their risk assessment more perceptive. Most importantly, their new worldview may yield a different set of conversations, especially in more affluent circles.

Instead of asking why HBCUs should continue to exist, stakeholders with a growth mindset ask which ones can make the best case for an optimized existence, based on their ability to shape better citizens? Instead of presuming innate inferiority, they recognize that, given the right governance, leadership, strategies, and resources, some of these institutions can grow, stabilize, improve, and, again, shape larger numbers of demonstrably consequential citizens. Those with a growth mindset can see that the same forces that fixed the precarity of many HBCUs also fixed the mindsets of those who disparage them. A shift in such thinking could energize and fund the journey of select HBCUs from precarity to optimization.

Yet just as those external to the HBCU community can have either a fixed or growth mindset about them, many stakeholders within the HBCU community face the same choice. This is where Dweck's research finding that "the view you adopt for yourself profoundly affects the way you lead your life" is most relevant. She contends that "it's possible to weave a fixed or growth mindset into the very fabric of an organization to create a culture of genius or a culture of development."[19] When college leaders bring a fixed mindset to their engagement with prospective investors, they typically commit what legendary Morehouse College president Benjamin Elijah Mays called "the sin of low aim." Little do they realize that a leader's excitement and informed ambition can, through the communication of a contagious and courageous spirit of confidence, provoke a philanthropist to provide a grander investment in the hope of attracting a grander return.

In 1928, the president of Straight College, a Black institution, approached a local businessman and philanthropist in New Orleans. Straight was in trouble, so the president requested an emergency grant of $500. The benefactor reportedly replied, "I am favorably concerned about what you are doing. However, if $500 is all you need, I should think your church board could provide it. If you are ever interested in bigger things, you will find me ready to help."[20] It was one of those very rare instances when a leader with an unambitious, fixed mindset encountered a prospect with an ambitious, growth mindset. That prospect was Edgar B. Stern, who became a key donor in the eventual development of Straight College into a considerably stronger Dillard University in New Orleans, Louisiana.

Operating with a fixed mindset is by no means unique to HBCUs, but the stakes are higher. Every fixed mindset on HBCU campuses adds a brick in two proverbial walls—the one separating them from the peak of America's philanthropic marketplace, and the one separating them from the pathway to optimization. Obviously, those two walls are related, if not somehow connected. The pressing need to evolve from a fixed to a growth mindset may be decisive for those HBCUs that have not yet realized measurable self-sufficiency.[21]

Both within and beyond the HBCU community, there is a need to advance and standardize growth mindsets regarding these institutions. It will help to reveal the investment-worthiness of a sector still capable of educating servant leaders and shaping better citizens for the great work of enriching all of humanity with hope and healing.

THE HOPE AND HEALING FRAMEWORK

HBCUs have been responsible for the three eras of transformation, leading to the current, unfinished era:

> Transformation one: Up from illiteracy, 1865 to 1915
> Transformation two: Up from poverty, 1916 to 1969

Transformation three: Up from marginality, 1970 to 2015

Transformation four: Up from precarity, 2015 and ongoing[22]

Contextualized by that timeline, I tell the story of their development in ten chapters, framed by five perspectives.

With the initial perspective, "The Difficult Birth of HBCUs," I use the first chapter, "The Dual Headwinds," to explain my disproportionate focus on Booker T. Washington and W. E. B. Du Bois, two exceedingly consequential leaders. I diminish the prominence of the stereotypes about them ("sellout" vs. "elitist") by clarifying the overwhelming headwinds they and others faced. In the second chapter, "The Literacy Trajectory," I describe how HBCUs performed their first transformation, conquering African American illiteracy.

The second perspective, "The Humane Aspiration of HBCUs," includes chapters 3 and 4, "The Capital Contenders" and "The Character Imperative." I spotlight the ideals and aspirations of Washington and Du Bois, emphasizing their respective approaches to racial uplift and repair.

The third perspective, "The Unfinished Business of HBCUs," includes four chapters. In chapter 5, "The Neglected Agendas," I describe how HBCUs moved African Americans up from both poverty and marginality. Since that success came at a price, I use chapters 6, 7, and 8 ("The Unheralded Value," "The Iceberg Trustees," and "The Risen Tide"), to reveal why and how selected HBCUs will need to sharpen their value proposition, governance, and fundraising in order to finally realize optimization.

The fourth perspective, "The Fluttering Veil over HBCUs," is summarized by chapter 9, "The Re-architecture Ultimatum," in which I provide a snapshot of current HBCU conditions relative to the strongest institutions. I clarify the challenge of the fourth transformation, "up from precarity," at what may be its most critical phase for most HBCUs. They now face their biggest challenge to thrive, just as a toxic mix of threats to the democracy and the climate may normalize disruption and chaos. Each of America's colleges and universities must consider how they will grapple with the re-architecture ultimatum that human survival and wholeness now require.

Finally, perspective five, "The Messianic Promise of HBCUs," frames the tenth chapter, "The String Shooters." By pointing to the new kind of individuals that a re-architecture might ultimately yield, I reveal the meaning of the chapter title, which is based on the story I share in the prologue. I emphasize character development as a way to shape better citizens and a better world.

Each chapter begins with an "Institutional Consideration for the Record," wherein I examine pivotal historical moments rich with current strategic relevance. These immersive field trips to the past are designed to yield important perspectives on the future.

With a later section of each chapter, "Institutional Question for the Future," I shift voices to that of a consultant or adviser. The guidance I offer is largely aimed at the philanthropic community, but also at HBCU leaders and advocates, federal and state policy makers, and all educators. My overarching aim is to offer strategic insights about how selected HBCUs can move up from precarity, and how all of higher education can help to shape better citizens and a better world.

I end each chapter with "For the Mindset," a brief, one-sentence advisory for consideration by all allies who become engaged in this critical work.

The structure underscores my firm belief that strengthening selected HBCUs and other similarly inclined institutions will require a new and elevated partnership between the higher education and philanthropic communities. In the case of HBCUs, I insist that they must be engaged based on what their new wholeness might yet deliver, rather than on what their past brokenness may have failed to deliver.

I have opted throughout these pages to be strategically suggestive, rather than ponderously expositive. My goal is to shift mindsets and launch a new conversation about HBCUs and higher education. Rather than offer the case for an entirely new historiography of HBCUs, I simply want to point to an entirely new way of seeing and, perhaps, embracing them.

Mindful of the world's dire need for better citizens, this project convinced me that the loftiest ideas of the earliest HBCUs leaders remain timeless, and they must powerfully inform and inspire what all current leaders now envision, enact, and build for the sake of generations yet to come.

FOR THE MINDSET

A focused effort to optimize the character and capital at selected HBCUs and other special mission institutions is not a contradiction to American democracy, but rather pursuant to it and reflective of it.

Perspective One

The Difficult Birth of HBCUs

Consider how and why it became contradictory to want to develop your own institutions, while fighting to ensure access to institutions financed, built, and serviced by the commodification of your ancestors. But do not dwell there. Remember this. Only after establishing the educational infrastructure of the New England aristocracy were HBCUs born to face the frightening headwinds of barbarism and hypocrisy. Yet, as these African Americans became literate in the language of their oppressors, they were somehow already fluent in the language of a better destiny for humankind.

This perspective is foundational because a growth mindset about the difficult birth of HBCUs can illuminate how the substantial damage done by yesterday's abiding headwinds remains relevant to the quest to rectify today's inequities and secure humanity's future.

CHAPTER ONE

The Dual Headwinds

No one but a Negro going into the South without previous experience of color caste can have any conception of its barbarism.

W. E. B. Du Bois, *Autobiography*, 1968

Since freedom there have been at least ten thousand colored men in the South, murdered by white men, and yet with perhaps a single exception, the record at no court shows that a single white man has ever been hanged for these murders. . . . The practice of lynching colored people is one of the curses of the south.

Booker T. Washington,
New England Club Speech, 1889

"The healer devotes himself to inspiration. He also lives against manipulation."
"I think I understand inspiration," Densu said. "But manipulation?"
"It's a disease, a popular one. It comes from spiritual blindness."

Ayi Kwei Armah, *The Healers*

Decades before Mordecai Johnson issued his charge to build up Black colleges as if there were no Harvard or Yale, two African American leaders outlined their own lofty expectations. Each envisioned a better world, well beyond that which white supremacist mindsets had so carefully crafted. Yet it is easy to miss the current relevance of many of their ideas if one sees Booker T. Washington as an irredeemable sellout and W. E. B. Du Bois as an incurable elitist.[1] Despite such distortions, it makes better sense to appreciate each for how they thought and worked for the elevation of HBCUs.

INSTITUTIONAL CONSIDERATION FOR THE RECORD: THE HEADWINDS OF BARBARISM AND HYPOCRISY

The following interpretation of each leader is designed to temper the adverse stereotyping of them in order to facilitate a better grasp of their treatment in this book. It will also help to clarify how tragic it is that the best elements of their work remain incomplete.

Why Washington?

In several chapters, I focus on what makes Washington worthy to be included among the most influential educational leaders in American history. Facing headwinds of extreme racial antipathy and outright barbarism, he created, managed, and endowed the Tuskegee Institute, making it as strong or stronger than many of the older and far more advantaged white educational institutions at the time. Yet his accomplishments are touted with caution, because any favorable nod to Washington's leadership is risky. Why? For decades, his image has been distorted by the weight of the more popular scholarship about him. His reputation as an unprincipled compromiser, an accommodationist, and a ruthless power broker was originally shaped by Du Bois. But then an extended roar of disfavor was amplified by historians C. Vann Woodward, his mentee Louis R. Harlan, and most of the civil rights leadership, all of them greatly favoring Du Bois's leadership.[2]

Yet, since this examination is largely about HBCU institutional health and wholeness, Washington is impossible to ignore or dismiss. Starting with only an adviser (Hampton's Samuel Chapman Armstrong), a meager state appropriation, and immeasurable determination, Washington placed Tuskegee among the largest, most successful educational institutions in the South. He became a favorite philanthropic target during America's first Gilded Age, and he left behind an expansive campus with a sizable endowment fund.

Those with mindsets hardened by the conventional, nuance-free condemnation of Washington may find it nearly impossible to appreciate any aspect of his institutional leadership. Thus, I offer a brief perspective on the importance of seeing him anew—that is, from a standpoint neither forged nor distracted by the rich tradition of villainy regarding his race leadership.[3] Instead, consider the world more from Washington's vantage point. Rather than regard him as a leader of his people who happened to serve also as leader of a Black institute, the lens should be narrowed, then widened. First and foremost, he should be viewed as an institute creator and leader who lived and worked in the heart of danger and happened to gain enough broad popularity to serve secondarily as an important national voice for his people.

The brutal racism of the Southern world was never far from Washington, physically or psychologically. He promised to never forget a boyhood memory of seeing his uncle stripped naked and whipped as he cried, "Pray, Master. Pray, Master!"[4] It was, at once, a crushing and defining moment. There were more. When he entered Hampton in 1872, the glow of emancipation and Reconstruction had not yet dimmed. Blacks were being elected or appointed to political office at the national and state levels. Yet this aspiring teacher would graduate from Hampton in 1875 with a classmate who had narrowly escaped being lynched by the Ku Klux Klan for the crime of teaching Black children.[5] By the time Washington traveled to Alabama in 1881 to risk his life in the then-hazardous field of education, the number of Black public servants was greatly reduced by the abandonment of Reconstruction.[6] He launched his career amid the perils of a period that would later be dubbed "the nadir" of the African American experience.[7]

The harbingers grew worse upon Washington's arrival in Tuskegee. He had entered one of the deadliest regions of an anti-Black education war zone. The substantial racist violence by whites in Alabama was largely but not exclusively waged by the aggressive, organized, and barbaric Ku Klux Klan. In fact, a decade before Washington's arrival, the reported increases in lynching, voter denial, political suppression, and a destructive terrorism designed to eliminate Black education all combined to trigger a special probe by a Joint Select Committee of the US Congress in 1871.[8] That inquiry led to what became known as "The Ku Klux Klan Act of 1871." The testimony therein revealed racism-based toxicity in and around Macon County, the site for Washington's new Institute. Numerous witnesses detailed terrorist acts, which included the brutal, consequence-free lynching of countless Black individuals; the murder of sympathetic whites; the burning of Black schools and churches; the forced removal of a white state university president who did not appear to appreciate the profound differences between the Methodist Episcopal Church (North) and the Methodist Episcopal Church (South); and the whipping, removal, or murder of multiple white and Black pastors or elders whose church leadership and perceived objectives were not aligned with the Klan's expectations.[9] The Klan exerted substantial control over Christianity in much of the South. And in their estimation, Black people were equal neither under federal laws, nor according to state customs, nor in the eyes of God.

James Alston, a former Black elected official in Tuskegee who was terrorized and run out of town by the Klan, would later candidly testify during the Congressional inquiry, saying, "They told me they had Jesus Christ tied, and God Almighty, the damned son of a bitch, chained, and they were Ku-Klux."[10] This was Macon County, Alabama, in late nineteenth-century America. Washington had dared to build a consequential Black institution in a place where "barbarism" appeared to have taken up permanent residence.

To assert that Washington faced forms of barbarism may seem like a harsh judgment and label; however, he and others made measured use of that very term, and it aptly describes the destructive racism that gripped his world. Wherever he traveled throughout the South, he was vulnerable to the whims of people who could, with impunity, destroy him and his institution at the slightest provocation. His simplest, most innocent, and well-meaning word or gesture could provoke a murderous response. Indeed, the list of reasons publicly stated by white mobs for why some Blacks were lynched included demanding respect, frightening a white woman, suing a white man, trying to vote, voting for the wrong party, or simply being obnoxious.[11] To stay alive and advance Tuskegee, Washington was forced to constantly make strategic and tactical choices about what to say, how to say it, when, and to whom. And he knew that defying or decrying the supremacist-built ecosystem could be lethal. It was as useless as defying or decrying the weather.

Was Washington too popular to ever be in real danger? He did not think so. Instead, he vigilantly monitored the violence all around him, and once wrote to an ally of his concern that several Southern newspapers "openly advocated my assassination and the destruction of our school property."[12] While the white supremacist violence never invaded Tuskegee, he had to be concerned when the infamously heinous and shocking lynching of Sam Hose in 1899 happened within ninety miles of his campus. The Hose lynching was used by a Georgia congressman to argue before the US House of Representatives for the need to "maintain the supremacy of the Anglo-Saxon race," worldwide, "in the name of civilization."[13] It also led to more extreme violence, as one black man in Georgia was lynched by his neighbors for the "crime" of talking too much about the Hose lynching.[14] Washington had every reason to be constantly concerned about his personal safety and that of his campus community.

Barbarism was the weather.

In fact, the general climate of hatred and violence was largely authored and fully sanctioned by some of the most prominent elected officials throughout the South. For example:

- Joseph F. Johnston, a former Confederate captain in the Civil War who served two separate terms as the governor of Alabama (1896–1900 and 1907–13), stood firmly against industrial and academic education, insisting that "neither improved Negro morals, and that the good that Tuskegee purported to do existed mainly in the minds of northern philanthropists who did not know the real Negro."[15]
- William Dorsey Jelks served as Alabama governor from 1901 to 1907, during the peak of Washington's work to advance Tuskegee, and was an aggressive white supremacist, "widely known for his advocacy of lynching as an appropriate means of disposing of those African Americans accused of rape."[16] But, as Washington and many others were well aware, rape was rarely the motivation for lynching. More often, it was merely a convenient excuse for killing Black people with impunity.
- Tom Heflin was Alabama's secretary of state under Governor Jelks, and then served as an Alabama congressman in 1904 and for the remainder of Washington's tenure at Tuskegee. A devout Christian, he was also known as a "stirring white supremacist orator who proclaimed to the constitutional convention . . . that God put 'negroes' on the earth to serve white men."[17] As he campaigned for Congress, he drew a standing ovation from a crowd when he spoke of lynching Washington, and again later threatened to do so when he was within a mile of the Tuskegee campus.[18]

The verbal vitriol in Alabama was largely echoed by senior elected officials throughout the South, where it created an ideal climate for physical harm to flourish. Several officeholders targeted Washington, seeing him as a disruptor of the Southern status quo, particularly in politics. They had good reason to be concerned.

In 1900, roughly the midpoint of Washington's leadership of Tuskegee, Alabama was 45.2 percent Black. A similarly high percentage of Blacks in Alabama's surrounding states included Florida (43.7), Georgia (46.7), South Carolina (58.4), North Carolina (33), Tennessee (23.8), and Mississippi (58.5). Nearby Louisiana and Arkansas were 47.1 and 28 percent, respectively.[19] It made sense to fear Black political power. And it should be unsurprising that the states with the highest Black representation tended to elect officials who used the most racist language.

In 1901, while in office as the fifty-sixth governor of Georgia, Allen D. Candler said, "I do not believe in the higher education of the darky. He should be taught the trades, but when he is taught the fine arts, he gets educated above his caste and it makes him unhappy."[20]

In his successful campaign to become the US senator from Georgia, Hoke Smith openly expressed the white supremacist view that "the uneducated Negro is a good Negro; he is contented to occupy the natural status of his race, the position of inferiority."[21]

When he campaigned to become the Mississippi governor in 1899, James K. Vardaman's winning platform was to defund Black education, deny the Black vote, and advance white supremacy. Yet he made one "compassionate concession" on race by insisting that white mobs "lynch their victims as quickly and as simply as possible."[22] In 1908, when Washington traveled to Mississippi to speak, Vardaman warned him to stay away by having two Black men lynched and their bodies hung along the train route to ensure that Washington would see them.[23]

It is not clear whether a similar message to Washington was intended when, prior to his March 1912 visit to Lake City, Florida, "six Negro men were quietly and silently hung on a Sunday morning."[24]

Arkansas Governor Jeff Davis declared, "We are not going to have any nigger equality down here as long as we can pull a trigger and there are shotguns and pistols lying around loose."[25]

Furnifold Simmons openly orchestrated a White Supremacy Campaign in 1898, and he was one of the architects of America's most violent overthrow of a Black elected government, when up to three hundred African American citizens in Wilmington, North Carolina, were massacred by over two thousand heavily armed whites. As a show of gratitude, voters elected Simmons to serve in the North Carolina Senate from 1901 to 1931.[26]

Succinctly put, Washington remained under siege not despite his work to educate Black people, but because of it. In 1890, anticipating the surge in racial terrorism that would characterize the decade and stretch well into the next century, Washington offered a Boston audience his estimate that, "Since freedom, there have been at least ten thousand colored men in the South murdered by white men."[27] He later referred to lynching as a "barbarous mode of attempting to administer justice."[28] The barbarism would continue, compelling Washington to track it more formally, a major task for which he eventually hired Chicago-trained sociologist Dr. Nathan Work.

Countless other incidents and scenarios featuring brushes with death and destruction could be listed to further underscore how the threat and reality of racial terrorism defined Washington's existence, posture, and outlook. He spent his life on what biographer Norrell called "a tightrope between candor and survival."[29] How one sees Washington depends on whether and how seriously one views the function and prevalence of the barbarism in his world. Washington should neither be questioned nor judged in the absence of an appropriately candid assessment of the bestiality of those who freely terrorized African Americans throughout the South.

Such assessments are rare, but meaningful.

For example, Ibram X. Kendi cited a revolt by thirty enslaved Africans and two Native Americans who, in 1712, sought their freedom by setting fire to a building in New York and then ambushing and killing those who came to douse the flames. The episode ended after six of the rebels committed suicide, believing it to be the best way to return to Africa, and the remaining freedom fighters were all publicly executed, most by being burned alive. The New York colonial governor who supervised their capture called the revolt the "barbarous attempt of some . . . slaves." Kendi concluded, "No matter what African people did, they were barbaric beasts or brutalized like beasts. If they did not clamor for freedom, then their obedience showed they were naturally beasts of burden. If they nonviolently resisted enslavement, they were brutalized. If they killed for their freedom, they were barbaric murderers."[30]

This is a mindset question. One mindset sees barbarism in the slaveholder, and the other sees it in the enslaved. One thinks it is barbarism to brutalize, and the other to allow oneself to be brutalized. One mindset holds that people are subjugated *because* they are uncivilized, while the other holds that the uncivilized are those who subjugate others. Profoundly different attitudes toward race, and Washington, are embedded in these two mindsets. Why?

An HBCU-friendly growth mindset can see that most of the time Washington spent sounding accommodating, conciliatory, or submissive, he was literally employing a Tuskegee-centric strategy to keep at bay some of the most diabolical barbarism in human history. And that mindset sees Washington not as accepting and exhibiting inferiority, but rather managing and controlling it in its vilest form. The HBCU-friendly growth mindset elegantly frames Washington's "controversial" coping sensibilities and navigational choices as the keys to "forestalling an even greater disaster: the extermination of Southern black people by those who had proven that they were capable of such ethnic cleansing."[31]

Many continue to view Washington as insufferable, largely based on the decades of condemnation heaped upon him by historians and pundits. But it may make more sense to regard him as the first Black educator to live amidst the storm of hate and succeed in founding, managing, and competitively endowing a consequential Black institution.

From that perspective, Washington's career holds important and timeless lessons.

Why Du Bois?

Unlike Washington's central concern with barbarism, Du Bois was primarily concerned about America's headwind of hypocrisy, especially regarding the illusive promise of democracy. Although both headwinds were fierce, while American barbarism constantly robbed people of life, American hypocrisy constantly robbed them of hope.

There is no need to offer a detailed explanation of Du Bois's style. Unlike Washington, he is generally understood to have been an indisputable force for good in the quest to elevate HBCUs and African Americans. Yet the combination of his failed "talented tenth" experiment, his perceived arrogance, his embrace of Marxism, and his eventual departure to Africa may make it easier to miss the overarching humanity of his vision and strategy. From the start, he connected the elevation of African Americans and Africans with the maturation of democracy and the realization of the world's "great destiny." That larger focus is explored fully in the fourth chapter of this book. Here it is sufficient to briefly underscore his thinking about how America's contradictions and hypocrisies were thwarting progress nationally and globally.

Du Bois set the tone for his career-long critique of American hypocrisy when, in 1890, he delivered a commencement address at Harvard University's Sanders Theatre. Entitled "Jefferson Davis as a Representative of Civilization," Du Bois pointed to "something fundamentally incomplete" about the standards of "Teutonic civilization."[32] He described Jefferson Davis as the "typical Teutonic hero," or "Strong man," who symbolized individualism and "the rule of might." The problem was, Davis and those he represented arose to power by "murdering Indians," waging war against Mexicans, "and finally, as the crowning absurdity, the peculiar champion of a people fighting to be free in order that another people should not be free." Citing a betrayal of democracy embedded in "the overweening sense of the I and the consequent forgetting of the Thou," Du Bois brought judgment against America as the premiere "Strong Nation," declaring, "a system of human culture whose principle is the rise of one race on the ruins of another is a farce and a lie." After highlighting that hypocrisy, he ended the speech by declaring, "You owe a debt to humanity for this Ethiopia of the Out-stretched Arm."

Du Bois then spent decades framing his reference to America's debt to humanity as a kind of repentance challenge. His Harvard speech captured the major themes of what would become an outlook on the Western world. He pinpointed America's consistent resistance or hostility to what he referred to as "the idea of common Humanity." In 1899, he described an American pattern of granting "full citizenship in the World-Commonwealth to the 'Anglo-Saxon,'" including the Teuton, the Latin, Celt, and Slav. He saw that "the yellow races of Asia" were half denied, and we admit "the brown Indians to an ante-room only on the strength of an undeniable past; but with the Negroes of Africa we come to a full stop, and in its heart the civilized world with one accord denies that these come within the pale of nineteenth-century

Humanity."[33] As Du Bois saw it, the battle lines were drawn by the mindsets responsible for the ensuing inequities and observable inequalities of the human condition since the rise of the West.

According to David Levering Lewis, during Du Bois's time in Berlin (1892–94), "He resolved to write of the genius, humanity, and enviable destiny of his race with such passion, eloquence, and penetration that claims of African American inferiority would be sent reeling, never to recover full legitimacy and vitality, despite their enormous resiliency."[34] Standing atop the list of such offerings was Du Bois's incomparable *The Souls of Black Folk*, published in 1903. Shortly after its release, the *New York Times* commended the book for viewing the race "not as a dark cloud threatening the future of the United States, but as a peculiar people, and one, after all, but little understood by the best of its friends or the worst of its enemies."[35] As Henry Louis Gates, Jr., described it, of his "twenty-two books and thousands of essays and reviews, no work of his has done more to shape an African American literary history."[36]

After pointing out America's individualism and militarism at Harvard, and her barbarism and racism in *Souls*, Du Bois's eventual critique of capitalism and materialism rounded out the key elements of what can reasonably be called "a noxious American hypocrisy."[37] Like a complex disease, it is a mix of racial conceit, infused with egocentric greed and enforced by military might. Du Bois believed those forces drove America to power and formed a strong headwind to keep at bay those with a different mindset. Du Bois's career was devoted to analyzing and opposing those with mindsets that implicitly justified or excused America's hypocritical conduct.

Citing hypocrisy, Du Bois repeatedly scoffed at the notion of America as a Christian nation. A number of scholars have underscored Du Bois's "lifelong, critical, and often contradictory relationship with religion, and particularly religion as it has historically been used, or rather abused, for Eurocentric-ideological-imperial purposes."[38] In one poignant analysis, Du Bois summarized, "The church has opposed every great modern social reform; it opposed the spread of democracy, universal education, trade unionism, the abolition of poverty, the emancipation of women, the spread of science, the freedom of art and literature, and the emancipation of the Negro slave."[39]

Second, Du Bois, like nearly all other African American leaders, fixated on the power of democracy as ideally defined in the US Constitution, rather than as practiced by those in power. When he launched the *Crisis* in 1910, Du Bois described an editorial commitment to "stand for the rights of men, irrespective of color or race, for the highest ideals of American democracy, and for reasonable and earnest and persistent attempts to gain these rights and realize these ideals."[40] The vision of shaping a true democracy in America was an ally for Du Bois. He made it a theme, especially in the pages of the *Crisis*.

In 1915, he used the publication to assert that "every argument for Negro suffrage is an argument for woman's suffrage; every argument for woman's suffrage is an argument for Negro suffrage; both are great moments in democracy."[41] And although Du Bois was the quintessential "race man," he understood that American democracy would thrive only by actualizing racial harmony. As he once put it, "with a spirit of self-help, mutual aid and cooperation, the two races should strive side by side to realize the ideals of the republic and make this truly a land of equal opportunity for all men."[42] But the headwinds were strong enough to provoke a profound pessimism. Lewis summarized, "vulgar wealth troubled him greatly, but so did vulgar democracy."[43] To Du Bois, democracy was consistently vulgarized by America's narcissistic supremacist tribalism.

Ultimately, Du Bois counted on a critical mass of more talented African American citizens to emerge from HBCUs and, motivated by the loftier values of servant leadership derived from their unique education, realize a better world.[44] But he recognized that white Americans were not the only ones responsible for the headwind of hypocrisy. DuBois saw too many African Americans using their education less to liberate Black lives than to imitate white lifestyles. Therefore, by 1948, he adjusted his theory of change from a reliance on a talented tenth to a guiding one hundredth, saying, "I assumed that with knowledge, sacrifice would automatically follow. In my youth and idealism, I did not realize that selfishness is even more natural than sacrifice."[45] By the time Du Bois decided to spend the late evening of his life in Africa, he already knew that he would not live long enough to see human beings become more inclined toward sacrifice and service than toward selfishness and savagery. And it is likely that he died wondering if that would ever happen.

INSTITUTIONAL QUESTION FOR THE FUTURE: WHAT IS THE BEST WAY TO DIMINISH TODAY'S HEADWINDS IN ORDER TO REALIZE DEMOCRACY?

Like Du Bois, Washington did not live to see the headwind of barbarism vanish. The racism that authored it and the hypocrisy that abided it have inarguably persisted. In fact, the hypocrisy has only intensified, particularly that which Du Bois identified as deriving from individualism, materialism, and militarism. And the resulting headwinds have effectively thwarted the full and simultaneous fulfillment of Washington's dream of capital-enriched institutions and Du Bois's dream of character-enriched individuals.

In 2014, nearly a full century after Washington died, Lisa Cook, a Spelman-educated economist, made a remarkable finding at the intersection of white barbarism and Black mindsets. In what has been called a "groundbreaking paper," Cook examined "the effects of hate-related violence on innovation, and, by extension, real economic activity and living standards," as measured by patents obtained by African Americans between 1870 and 1940.[46] Her findings reveal that as violence against African Americans thwarted democracy, it also depressed the entrepreneurial and inventive activities for which Washington was the most zealous advocate. Based largely on their faith and hope in government, the rule of law, and the arrival of true democracy, patents pursued and secured by Blacks responded positively to declines in violence and negatively to increases in violence.

Cook's research places a firm data foundation under what concerned Washington and Du Bois the most. In her estimation, the ebb and flow of patent applications illuminates the African American mindset about the likely arrival or non-arrival of law and order. She revealed how the tailwinds of hope and healing were overwhelmed whenever the headwinds of America's barbarism and hypocrisy raged. Conversely, when such anti-democracy headwinds subsided, the journey toward a Constitution-based America tended to resume. Interestingly, patent acquisitions reached a peak in 1899, but then plummeted after the Tulsa, Oklahoma, massacre in 1921.[47] More than a century later, they have yet to recover.

In a sense, American history is about which of those winds will ultimately prevail. The anti-democracy headwinds have blown for a long time, perhaps because too few Americans recognize that a democracy based on race and class supremacy rather than equity is, by definition, a broken democracy. That has been difficult to recognize because the underlying forces and sources of supremacist inequity tend to be invisible. And while barbarism and hypocrisy are how inequity's headwinds tended to show up for centuries, inequalities and hypocrisy are how they tend to show up now. The pace and power of the adversarial gales may shift, but, like a mindset, the wind energy is consistent. And that is the challenge that more college campuses need to creatively confront.

The question of how educational institutions can weaken today's headwinds is the focus of the remaining chapters of this book, especially in the "for the future" advisories to the philanthropic community and to higher education leaders in and beyond HBCUs. Come what may, the goal remains the same—to shape the better citizens who will devote themselves to generating a better world.

FOR THE MINDSET

College leaders, educators, and philanthropists should recognize that it is difficult to imagine and work for a new world when so few people understand the headwinds that still gust from the old one.

CHAPTER TWO

The Literacy Trajectory

Overview of Transformation One:
Up from Illiteracy

There is sometimes much talk about the inferiority of the Negro. In practice, however, the idea appears to be that he is sort of a superman. He is expected, with about one fifth of what whites receive for their education, to make as much progress as they are making.

> Booker T. Washington, final major address, October 25, 1915

Unless we develop our full capabilities, we cannot survive. If . . . we simply are trying to follow the line of least resistance and teach black men only such things and by such methods as are momentarily popular, then my fellow teachers, we are going to fail and fail ignominiously in our attempt to raise the black race to its full humanity and with that failure falls the fairest and fullest dream of a great united humanity.

> W. E. B. Du Bois, "The Hampton Idea," 1906

The world around him was the same. Only the way he saw the world was clearer. He now recognized certain people as manipulators. A few he also saw as inspirers. The distinction gave him knowledge of himself he had not had before; he did not like manipulators; he loved inspirers.

> Ayi Kwei Armah, *The Healers*

M ost of the narratives about HBCU beginnings strike familiar themes. They tend to emphasize the pivotal role played by Black churches, Northern white missionaries, and the Freedmen's Bureau in developing the initial infrastructure to educate African Americans. They invariably point to the three decades following emancipation, when thousands of institutions were launched to begin to meet the wide-ranging educational needs of over four million newly freed Americans. They show how these efforts were later bolstered by Northern industrial philanthropists, who had their own priorities—often unrelated to racial equity—for how to shape public and educational policy.[1]

Most Southern state governments provided modest tax-based support for Black educational efforts during the Reconstruction era as part of the process of establishing free public education for all. Predictably, the support was woefully inadequate. They prioritized the educational needs of whites, leaving separate and grossly inadequate choices for Blacks. Even after the Second Morrill Act of 1890 established nineteen land-grant universities for Blacks, the apartheid-like state funding worsened the racialized systemic disadvantages and uneven outcomes.[2]

Most HBCU narratives highlight the danger involved in educating the previously enslaved Americans, given the toxic atmosphere. Prior to 1860, anti-literacy laws were strictly enforced in every Southern state except Tennessee.[3] The idea of educating African Americans had long been deemed abominable because too much was at stake. Many Southern whites logically feared that education would make Blacks less likely to remain subservient and more likely to resist white supremacy. Black lives mattered to them only to the degree that they could be used to continue to generate wealth, advantage, and comfort. So Black education was the enemy. Black codes were used to supplement unchecked vigilante violence to constrain Black freedom and dampen the educational aspirations of Black individuals and institutions.[4] Even with the eventual emergence of the very popular HBCU curricular debate (liberal arts versus vocational) between Du Bois and Washington, too few narratives note that millions of white Southerners favored neither approach, preferring to provide their own "home-school" pedagogy aimed at Black servitude and second-class citizenship.

Understandably, most HBCU birth narratives emphasize the perseverance of their founders in the face of systemic obstruction. Like all American colleges founded before 1861, which had a death rate of 81 percent, the death rate among Black colleges was high.[5] While the number of HBCUs once exceeded 300, the sector had dwindled to a mere 137 by 1915.[6] Few were teaching college-level subjects by that point, but their aspirations far exceeded their capacity. Like the estimated 2,677 pre-college institutions open to Blacks by 1870, most HBCUs were animated by an ambition to eventually provide a first-rate education.[7]

That so many of them endured is noteworthy, and yet, their reptilian survival instinct is just one among many virtues. Although historically accurate, framing HBCUs based largely on their improbable longevity has arguably helped to create mindsets that miss far too much about how transformative they have been.

INSTITUTIONAL CONSIDERATION FOR THE RECORD: THE FIRST HBCU TRANSFORMATION: UP FROM ILLITERACY, 1865–1915

This first transformation is bracketed by the end of the American Civil War and the death of the most dominant figure of that era, Booker T. Washington. While the war ended, the lethal violence against African Americans did not. The postwar Reconstruction period was initially defined by an optimism about the expansion of opportunities for African Americans—at least by law and in theory—with respect to education, politics, and general citizenship. The Emancipation and Reconstruction era gave many Blacks their first chance to pursue a quality of life consistent with the ideals of the nation's founding documents. But the shift toward democracy was short-lived. After roughly twelve years, a brutality and stark inequity that completely contradicted American ideals resurfaced with a vengeance. Southern white supremacists sought to reestablish and harden a racial hierarchy that would fully secure white control over Black lives.[8]

Despite this heinous antidemocratic turn, early HBCU leaders maintained their disciplined focus on winning the war against illiteracy. The passion for education persisted, even as the newly resurgent brutally racist climate choked off opportunities to exercise intelligent and equal citizenship. African Americans understood that no matter the headwinds, literacy was essential for any hope of a better life, individually and collectively. But it was a struggle.

During the two and a half centuries of prewar bondage, reading and writing had been against the law. African Americans who were caught trying to nurture their minds were often met with brutal punishment. The breadth and depth of their passionate quest for education is critical to understanding why HBCUs were so successful in driving the "up from illiteracy" transformation.

The colleges, institutes, and schools built in the immediate wake of emancipation were merely the institutionalization of an already conspicuous African American yearning for education. While the schools benefited from the assistance provided by Northern philanthropists and educators via various denominational and corporate funds, the Northerners had the advantage of building on a foundation of lofty African American aspirations.[9] As historian Heather Williams summarized, "It made perfect sense that someone who had climbed into a hole in the woods to attend school would, in freedom, sacrifice time and money to build a schoolhouse. It rang true that people who waited up until ten o'clock at night to sneak off to classes on the plantation would want to establish schools in the open as soon as they possibly could."[10]

American scholars have not always focused on the agency exhibited in the slave quarter communities. Many white scholars have focused instead on white slaveholders in this context, with respect to both their general outlook and their control over Black lives.[11] Yet ample evidence exists that those who were formerly enslaved "were determined to achieve educational self-sufficiency in the long run with or without the aid of northerners. Their self-determination has escaped the attention of all but a few historians."[12] Narrative approaches that place African Americans at the center of the story are rare.

As more historians have come to focus on pre- and post-emancipation Black agency, it has become clear that the African American drive for education was organic and powerful. Williams points out that:

> Black people emerged from slavery ambitious and determined to direct their own path. Former slaves . . . had created the economic base of southern states, and as free people, they would continue to be fundamental to white American success. However, they intended now to move out of fields and other places of forced servitude and into professions including law and medi-

cine. Education would be essential to their ability to concretize their still ephemeral freedom.[13]

The Black quest for education grew out of the communal aspirations and the secret educational pursuits undertaken during enslavement. As noted by Du Bois, these aspirations, along with the heritage of hidden educational practices, later helped to drive the Southern movement for universal public schooling.[14] Scores of new schools, institutes, and colleges became the venues for Blacks to reset the trajectory of their lives, enrich and expand their possibilities, and invigorate their hope.

The story of the birth and the initial transformational capacity of HBCUs is inseparable from this story. Foundational Black agency, determination, and ambition drove the existence and persistence of HBCUs. The lives that former slaves imagined for themselves would be better than any designed for them by other Americans. After imagining their new lives, learning to read was widely regarded as the next essential step on the journey from dehumanization to self-determination.

Multiple contemporaneous data sources reveal the effectiveness of the war against illiteracy waged by HBCUs. By most accounts, while Black illiteracy exceeded 95 percent in 1860, it declined to between 60 and 70 percent by 1890.[15] By 1910, according to US Census Bureau Current Population Reports, Black illiteracy had declined to 33 percent.[16]

One analysis tracked Black illiteracy relative to the illiteracy rates abroad, which suggests a different angle from which to view the early transformational impact of HBCUs.[17] It revealed that Black literacy, at almost 70 percent in 1910, was higher than that of seventeen countries, including Russia (30 percent), Greece (43 percent), Poland (41 percent), and Italy (52 percent).

By 1920, Black literacy had climbed to 77 percent.[18] In the space of roughly fifty years, HBCUs had served as primary weapons in the largely successful battle against Black illiteracy. Without anything resembling the kind of student federal aid assistance that would arrive much later, they reduced illiteracy rates from 95 percent to 23 percent. They did so in the wake of over two centuries of the systematic use of the law and corporal punishment to deny African Americans opportunities to develop their whole being—one of the most crippling, multigenerational legacies of chattel slavery. The early era of HBCUs features no other outcome more measurably remarkable than the successful war against illiteracy.

Similarly impressive was the humanity of African American aspirations. As they became literate, they demonstrably directed their energies toward repairing, rather than razing, the systems and authors in and of the world that had dehumanized them. By and large, African Americans saw literacy as a gateway to self-determination and an invitation to active American citizenship. The ability to vote was key.

The newly formed HBCUs were clearly bearing fruit. Before Reconstruction's complete demise, "around 2,000 black men had held federal, state, and local public offices, ranging from member of Congress to justice of the peace."[19] Unsurprisingly, at least 83 percent of the African American voters for whom records were available were fully able to read and write.[20] That these leaders were voted into office by an eager and increasingly literate Black electorate is evidence of the early African American investment in the idea and ideals of America. That the leaders themselves used their new roles to focus on reform and not revenge is a testament both to their deep humanity and to their basic understanding of the possibilities of a young democracy.

Yet institutional stability and momentum, especially for HBCUs, remained elusive. Indeed, their very existence would remain rife with uncertainty. Nonetheless, HBCU leaders sought to shape informed citizens who would use the ballot box democratically to assert their wishes, even in the context of the South's one-party Democratic rule.

Again, the population statistics mattered. As early as 1870, Blacks were more than half the population in South Carolina, Mississippi, and Louisiana. They were also nearly half the population in Virginia, Georgia, Florida, and Alabama.[21] The Department of Justice was formed that same year; in theory, it was supposed to help defend the civil and voting rights of those formerly enslaved. In practice, it ended up only frustrating a Reconstruction effort that was already under heavy attack.[22]

Throughout this turmoil, HBCUs never retreated from their disciplined focus on literacy, despite the shifting terrain on which their hopes rested. African Americans understood the Constitution to be on their side. But their interpretation of the founding document was no match for the white supremacists, who had zero tolerance for Black equality. By 1910, when Black illiteracy was down to 33 percent, only 2 percent of Black males in the South were registered to vote, as compared to 83 percent of white males.[23] The leveraging power of literacy had its limitations in a country engaged in full-blown retreat from the core ideals of its Constitution.

In the first few decades of their institutional lives, Black colleges aggressively produced literate graduates to enter a world of shrinking possibilities and growing hate. And all too frequently, their white allies never seemed to be fully committed to a democracy characterized by liberty and justice for all. As a result, they were no match for the passionate enemies of equity. As the deniers of Black progress tended to be more vigorous and active, the allies would often lose their nerve to protect African American rights. HBCU leaders did not have the luxury of naivete. They knew they were largely on their own to survive in a world that their forced toil—and that of their forebears—had done so much to create and fortify.

The early leaders of HBCUs performed an "up from illiteracy" miracle against unimaginable odds. But what if the HBCU emergence story were told using a wider-angle lens? Would a new mindset about these institutions be stimulated by placing them in the context of the larger history of American higher education?

Recent disclosures about the circumstances surrounding the launch of many of the nation's colleges and universities have added depth and precision to the stories that institutions tell about themselves. While adding dimension and texture to our grasp of the overall history of higher education, they can also spark an intellectual and ethical obligation to resituate the HBCU narrative.

INSTITUTIONAL QUESTION FOR THE FUTURE: WHAT ARE THE ELEMENTS OF A REFRAMED RELATIONSHIP BETWEEN HBCUs AND THE PHILANTHROPIC COMMUNITY?

In the first quarter of the twenty-first century, many of America's most prestigious colleges and universities formally announced efforts to examine their historic ties to slavery. On many campuses, the evidence for such connections was conspicuous in their signs, symbols, and archives. Collectively, the institutions began acknowledging and sharing remarkable stories largely inconsistent with the more positive or heroic institutional narratives that preceded them. As impressive as these official inquiries are, they are exasperatingly over-due, since the key themes and evidence have been apparent since American slavery ended.

A sampling clarifies the power of recoloring and reframing elite institutional histories:

- Before formally launching its initiative on the legacy of slavery in 2019, Harvard University commemorated the lives of four enslaved African Americans—Juba, Bilhah, Titus, and Venus—who worked for two of its presidents in the eighteenth century.[24] Present at the commemoration was the late Congressman John Lewis, a hero of the civil rights movement. In 2022, the university released a major report as an initial exploration and rectification of how, "during the 17th and 18th centuries, the sale and trafficking of human beings . . . powerfully shaped Harvard University."[25] Referring to slavery as "integral to Harvard," the report cites the fact that "Harvard presidents and other leaders, as well as its faculty and staff, enslaved more than 70 individuals, some of whom labored on campus."[26]

- In 2015, Yale University's efforts triggered a debate about the potential renaming of one of its residential colleges from Calhoun College to some other name, since John C. Calhoun was among the staunchest white supremacists of the nineteenth century. Not only were three other residence halls at Yale named for enslavers, but Elihu Yale, the namesake of the university, had ties to the East Indian slave trade.[27]

- In 2017, Princeton University, which was founded in 1746, revealed that each of its first nine presidents owned slaves and that one or more slave auctions were held on the campus.[28] After much debate, they also removed the name of Woodrow Wilson—one of the most influential proponents of American progressivism—from its School of Public and International Affairs and from a residential college.[29] Wilson found no apparent contradiction between his progressivism on the one hand, and his overt racism and admiration of the Ku Klux Klan on the other.

- In 2016, Rutgers University, which was founded in 1766 as Queens College, revealed that more than one of its founding leaders had owned slaves, and that they had relied on slave labor to construct the original campus.[30]

- In 2016, after releasing a Working Group Report, Georgetown University, founded in 1789, made plans to pay reparations to the descendants of the enslaved people whom they had owned and sold. The effort to raise the required funding was boosted by Georgetown students, who voted to tax themselves annually as part of their tuition charge.[31]
- In 2020, following the revelation of its ties to slavery, the University of Louisville (Kentucky), founded in 1798, decided to remove from the campus a set of statues honoring Confederate soldiers.[32]

The general themes of these historic connections were best captured and contextualized by MIT historian Craig Steven Wilder, who compellingly detailed how the labor of slaves, and the resultant wealth of their owners, directly and significantly aided the birth, growth, and stabilization of American higher education.[33]

Wilder concludes that the early American academy "never stood apart from American slavery—in fact, it stood beside church and state as the third pillar of a civilization built on bondage."[34] Compared to church and state, the higher education footprint was small and unsteady. Of the 516 colleges founded before the Civil War in sixteen states, financial precarity victimized 412 of them by 1928.[35]

Until recently, most universities avoided revealing how their entanglement with human enslavement measurably elevated their institutional stability and growth trajectory. To the degree that their founders and trustees, along with other campus and alumni leaders, took seriously the imperatives of institutional advancement, they necessarily made strategic alliances with their most affluent contemporaries. Their zeal for growth apparently tended to outweigh any shame they may have felt by receiving funds from the chieftains of an enslavement-driven empire.

Wilder examined the nine colleges established before the American Revolution—Harvard, William and Mary, Yale, Princeton, Columbia, Penn, Brown, Rutgers, and Dartmouth—and explains that "the founding, financing, and development of higher education in the colonies were thoroughly intertwined with the economic and social forces that transformed West and Central Africa through the slave trade and devastated indigenous nations in the Americas. The academy was a beneficiary and defender of these processes."[36] The enslavement of African Americans, in all its stark inhumanity, was material to the Ivy League's wealth, stability, and prestige. More than providing casual or marginal support, Wilder concludes that "human slavery was the precondition for the rise of higher education in the Americas."[37]

Three key aspects of the recent institutional and historical reassessments have the power to help provoke a fundamental mindset shift in today's philanthropic community. Today's benefactors should consider seeing each of them as veils that obscure the allure of HBCUs by shrouding their true history, elevation potential, and investment-worthiness.

AFRICAN AMERICANS AS MIDWIVES FOR EARLY AMERICAN HIGHER EDUCATION

First, philanthropists should consider the implications of the birth stories of America's separate Black and white systems of higher education. Collectively, the new narratives show that even before most of the nation's HBCUs were established, slavery and the slave economy had already undergirded the lofty trajectory of white higher education. The African Americans who founded, led, and enrolled in HBCUs in the late nineteenth century were the descendants of those whose labor, for more than two centuries prior, had involuntarily established, enriched, and serviced the prestigious higher education infrastructure of their persecutors. That fact should never be forgotten or minimized in the mindsets of those who engage HBCUs today.

African Americans literally served as unwilling midwives for the birth of white higher education in America before they were able to focus on mothering their own HBCUs.

In this broader context, it is illogical to hold a jaded view of the relative strength and stability of Black institutions. It is especially nonsensical to disparage the HBCU sector based simply on the wide gap between them and much stronger sectors like the Ivy League. The gap is not rooted in an African American preference for poverty, nor in any pattern of poor decision-making by HBCU leaders. Instead, it is but one of the many inevitable outcomes when countless mindsets are wittingly or unwittingly fixed on a sanitized view of America's past that yields a distorted notion of equality. HBCUs trail the Ivy League and others for reasons scripted by the same authors of the racialized gaps throughout and beyond America's education pipeline.

The gaps are tied to the mindset-defining words of Mississippi Senator Jefferson Davis who, in an April 12, 1860, debate on the Senate floor, argued against a bill to fund Black education. Davis, who would soon become president of the Confederacy, opined on "the equality of the races and whether children are to be put upon the same footing," and called such a policy "violative of every principle of the Constitution of the United States and the history of its foundation."[38] That original hostility to life on "the same footing" not only contaminated generations of mindsets, but it also inclined more people to abide rather than allay racialized inequalities.

When pondering investments in HBCUs, today's philanthropists should consider how the dynamics of American history have broadly authored racialized differences. It was only after their forebears labored involuntarily to put a firm foundation under what would become the leading higher education system in the world that African Americans were free to focus on their own educational infrastructure. Because of that, the overall wealth lag should be an understandable given. In particular, the persistent HBCU wealth lag is inseparable from the sustained capital and convenience that African American labor and servitude generated for those institutions they lag. While there may be other reasons for the sector-based racial gaps (including HBCUs having much smaller alumni bodies, far fewer wealthy graduates, smaller advancement teams, and far weaker connections with America's philanthropic community), they are all largely derived from the long-standing and consequential absence of a level playing field.

Viewing HBCU history from this broader perspective also makes it easier to recognize that when many of the predominantly white institutions began aggressively to integrate in the late 1960s, it was not the first time that African Americans had entered their campuses. It was merely the first time they entered those classrooms as students and eventual professors, rather than merely as builders and eventual custodians.

Nor should today's philanthropists ignore or fail to grasp the full significance of the slave economy as foundational for the subsequent quality of American life far beyond the confines of higher education. African and African American enslavement created and sustained a lofty trajectory for what might be referred to as "the American empire." The twentieth century became both the American Century and the Human Capital Century largely because of the tremendous foundation provided by an economy driven by African American toil.[39]

In 1903, Du Bois famously referred to slavery as "the sum of all villainies, the cause of all sorrow, the root of all prejudice."[40] Eight decades later, Manning Marable pointed to the injuries sustained by African Americans over time and argued that their "underdevelopment was the direct consequence of this process: chattel slavery, sharecropping, peonage, industrial labor at low wages, and cultural chaos."[41] More recent reassessments of the reach and power of America's slave economy provide compelling data that undergird these and similar impressions. Yale historian David Brion Davis pointed to the overall significance of enslavement in 2006, saying not only would "the slaves' value come to an estimated $3.5 billion in 1860 dollars . . . but a more revealing figure is the fact that the nation's gross national product in 1860 was only about 20 percent above the value of slaves, which means that as a share of today's gross national product, the slaves' value would come to an estimated $9.75 trillion."[42] Other scholars have expanded this narrative by describing just how foundational Black enslavement was to America's economic maturation.[43] In fact, they show that if indeed capitalism underdeveloped Black America, it did so as Black bodies accelerated America's rise to power. In 2014, Cornell historian Edward E. Baptist concluded that "enslaved African Americans built the modern United States, and indeed the entire modern world, in ways both obvious and hidden."[44]

Minimally, this larger story should add dimension to those seeking clarity about HBCU challenges. It can also add great texture to those focused on reparations arguments. By force, Blacks erected and financed much of the educational scaffolding others used to live comfortably in a world designed for whites only. New mindsets that take seriously this broader narrative will more likely grasp the importance of realizing the competitive optimization of selected HBCUs.

TODAY'S PHILANTHROPISTS AND THE PRESERVATION OF WHITE SUPREMACY

Second, beyond embracing a new understanding of the origins of the racialized infrastructure differences, today's philanthropists ought to consider the unveiling power of institutional and historical reassessments. As HBCU leaders struggled to keep their institutions alive, they had to prepare their students for a world with increasingly validated hostilities stemming from the scholarship generated by faculty at the older white institutions. The history behind this is compelling.

The value of the slave economy swelled just before the Civil War ended it all. As a relative share of GDP, total slave worth "at the time of emancipation, was close to thirteen trillion 2020 dollars."[45] College creation surged, too. In the thirty years prior to the Civil War, the number of colleges launched in America increased by nearly 300 percent, with college creation pushing west and south.[46] And, as Wilder points out, "this accelerated the politicization of science and the institutionalization of race."[47] The alliances between the leaders of the slave economy and American colleges matured and became mutually beneficial. Beyond providing wealth, naming buildings, and receiving trusteeships, the slave traders and owners were legitimized. Like a permission slip, knowledge was generated, and intellectual theories and cultures were developed to justify enslaving Africans and eliminating Native Americans.[48] White supremacy was implicitly sanctioned by multiple academic disciplines, ranging from science to theology. A poisonous set of ideas about the world's darker races resulted.[49]

That is why the process of becoming literate was fraught. Much of the available knowledge had already been contaminated with ideas consistent with the supremacists' construction of reality. Thus, from the start, the African American quest for literacy was necessarily purpose driven, producing leaders and scholars to counter the Black inferiority narrative. Literacy was the baseline skill set for citizenship, but African Americans also had to be literate in the language of justice and equality. That, too, had a foundation, since an African American tradition of objection had begun long before the first HBCUs were built.

One key example was the self-educated Benjamin Banneker who, in 1791, wrote a letter to Thomas Jefferson about the need to "eradicate that train of absurd and false opinions which so generally prevails with respect to us."[50] Banneker reminded Jefferson of the self-evident truths he had already popularized, and advised Jefferson "and all others to wean yourselves from these narrow prejudices which you have imbibed."[51] In fact, many African

Americans took issue with "that train of absurd and false opinions" and "these narrow prejudices." In 1889, Frederick Douglass spoke at the celebration of the twenty-seventh anniversary of the abolition of slavery in the District of Columbia, and lamented, "At no time in the history of the conflict between slavery and freedom in this country has the character of the Negro as a man been made the subject of a fiercer and more serious discussion in all the avenues of debate . . . against him have been marshalled the whole artillery of science, philosophy and history."[52]

The tradition of objectors also includes Anna Julia Cooper, Ida B. Wells, Alexander Crummell, Booker T. Washington, Mary McLeod Bethune, W. E. B. Du Bois, and scores of other African American activists and intellectuals from this first transformation period. By revealing how racist ideas were eventually interwoven into the curriculum and character of the early academy and pointing to the campus-based production of racist ideas in America, Wilder is locating the hosts, authors, advancers, and legitimizers of a destructive mindset.[53]

Too few deemed it blasphemous for the citadels of higher learning to strengthen, rather than weaken, the toxic headwinds facing African Americans. But it was almost natural that a nineteenth-century academy that had helped to justify the chattel enslavement of human beings would thereafter help to justify their subsequent mistreatment. Enslaving, subjugating, and mistreating people is easier to allow by law and custom if it is based on human differences that are professed in the academies as proven by science and sanctioned by God. It should not be surprising that the all-white campuses were experienced as unsafe, unwelcoming, and potentially damaging places by the handful of Blacks who enrolled in them throughout the nineteenth and early twentieth centuries. Du Bois said of his experience in the 1890s what many students of color could say of their experiences in similar environments more than a century later: "I was in Harvard, but not of it."[54] Du Bois and generations of other African Americans never felt like they truly belonged. Harvard and others were in fact home to scholars who helped to bolster a world of anti-Black racism wherein both African Americans and HBCUs would matter less or not at all.

The presumption of inferiority strengthened the force and toxicity of the headwinds facing HBCU leaders, especially in this first phase of their institutional existence. They had to find ways to survive while preparing their students to function in a world of hatred fortified by academic authority and endorsement. They had to devise ways to attract sizable investments from a philanthropic community with concerns about the cost of disturbing the peace that Southern whites found in a racist status quo.

The more visionary HBCU presidents had to determine how to become eventually strong enough to develop and attract to their campuses the kind of intellectuals who would thoughtfully and definitively debunk the sanctioned hatred. Perhaps fittingly, some of that hateful scholarship was being generated by white scholars working in buildings, rooms, and laboratories named in honor of wealthy slave traders.

Today's philanthropists might consider that the institutional and historical reassessments collectively invite them to a new mindset for understanding HBCUs as the original institutional counterforces to these profoundly un-American developments. The work of many HBCUs to educate people with healthier mindsets about both our American past and our human destiny must now fully shift from being a hidden curriculum to a proud institutional brand.

THE MOVEMENT TO REEXAMINE INSTITUTIONAL ORIGINS

The third mindset shift highlights what triggered the recent institutional assessments. More than anything else, the function of campus leadership is to ensure that institutions have and follow a moral compass. It is not unreasonable to wonder why it took so long for the corrected narratives to emerge. Most of the histories now being rewritten are based on long ignored, yet observable and often self-evident truths about the past. For years, these truths had been minimized and marginalized. Only recently have institutions been morally courageous enough to stop treating their scattered evidence of ties to slavery as if it were somehow unworthy of attention. It is as if they had previously agreed to discount the information, constitutionally, as being only three-fifths true.

To the degree that the crusade of university soul-searching and self-examination can be referred to as a "movement," the leader who heroically paved the way for it all was Dr. Ruth J. Simmons, the first African American woman to preside over an Ivy League institution. In 2003, as she began her eleven-year tenure at the helm of Brown University, she faced a dilemma when Brown was among the universities targeted in a reparations lawsuit brought by Harvard Law School professor Charles Ogletree.[55] In response, she appointed a Steering Committee on Slavery and Justice. Simmons recognized Brown's need for a report to document its well-known ties to slavery. She asked her faculty committee to consider the potential imperatives of reconciliation and reparations, and "to organize academic events and activities that might help the nation and the Brown community think deeply, seriously, and rigorously about the questions raised."[56] That sparked a movement. After Brown published its major report, a slow but steady array of similar initiatives were launched by major universities.[57]

In this context, the key irony is not merely that Simmons, an African American Ivy League leader, triggered the movement. Simmons is also the first HBCU graduate to lead an Ivy League institution. She received her undergraduate education from Dillard University, located in New Orleans. She subsequently received her advanced degrees from Harvard University.

This move by Simmons signified a departure from what might be referred to as the "bystander leadership posture" that has dominated American higher education. College and university leaders have been more likely to reflect and benefit from societal biases, prejudices, or wrongdoing, rather than question, confront, or disrupt them. There were obvious risks in launching this initiative, perhaps the most salient of which was the potential for negative reactions from Brown's donor community. Yet, to the degree that such risks were considered, they were overlooked or viewed as tolerable. That courageous decision by Simmons has yielded benefits well beyond Brown University.

A shining example of what Simmons triggered is the reaction by the University of Virginia, founded by Thomas Jefferson in 1819. Framed as "an institution with slavery at its core," UVA felt compelled to play a leadership role even before they released their official report in 2017.[58] In 2014, they convened other institutions looking to similarly grapple with their history of slavery and racism. What began as an informal consortium of Virginia-based institutions soon expanded into a formal convergence of national Universities Studying Slavery consortium in 2015. As of late 2022, the consortium membership had reached ninety-eight campuses from the US, Canada, and Europe.[59]

Ironically, the Brown effort also motivated Wilder to revive and complete his overarching history. He writes, "I was considering giving up on what then seemed to be too massive an undertaking." But he describes his return to the project as having been inspired by "Simmons's courageous articulation of the academic obligation to pursue truth."[60]

If properly understood, the combination of Wilder's work and the growing number of campus-based confessional narratives should result in more than just an expanding surrender of institutional innocence on the part of many predominantly white institutions. The stories should also add texture and depth to the way we understand the birth and development of both American higher education and the HBCU sector.

HBCUs have not merely survived. They have withstood a challenge that no institution of higher learning should face in any nation engaged in a serious effort to actualize democracy. That challenge was never more intense than in their first five decades when they fought so valiantly to remain sufficiently viable to shape better citizens.

FOR THE MINDSET

A reframed relationship between HBCUs and today's philanthropic community can begin with a new appreciation of how these campuses had to endure what no group should ever have to face in a democracy.

Perspective Two

The Humane Aspiration of HBCUs

Together, Du Bois's insistence on character optimization and Washington's intensity about capital optimization constitute the holy grail of American higher education. Character and capital have never been recognizably optimized on a single campus simultaneously. Yet both leaders saw their respective emphases as essential to perfecting the climate for humanity's eventual oneness. To them, the wholeness of their people was pursuant to the predestined wholeness of humankind.

This perspective matters because a growth mindset about the humane aspiration of HBCUs can illuminate the investment-worthy devotion these institutions have always demonstrated pursuant to a more perfect union.

CHAPTER THREE

The Capital Contenders

There are ten millions of negroes in the United States today. Why not
have somewhere—in the South—at least one large, thoroly [sic] equipped
university where the actual needs of the negro people could be studied
and where such of them as desire to be teachers, doctors, or ministers of
the gospel could be thoroly [sic] equipped for their work?

Booker T. Washington,
"A University Education for Negroes," 1910

Healers are just awakeners of a people who have slept too long.

Ayi Kwei Armah, *The Healers*

One way to reliably develop and annually certify a cohort of better citizens
is to first imaginatively develop and annually renew a better campus.
Educational development and certification are best accomplished in venues
designed and maintained to support these processes. With a better campus,
an institution will find it easier to shape better citizens, and there is no more
compelling reason to provide capital optimization than that.

As the twentieth century approached, for the first time ever, a handful of
men made capital optimization "a thing" in American higher education. This
was a consequential era that featured the creation or significant advancement
of some of the most prestigious universities today, including the University of
Chicago, Stanford, and most of the Ivy League. Considering the stature of
most of these universities at the time, as well as the existence of a philanthropic
community brimming with unprecedented capacity and magnanimity, it is

reasonable to assume that the surges in institutional wealth and stability were predictable. But one leader who set the pace for so many others in this context was anything but predictable.

INSTITUTIONAL CONSIDERATION FOR THE RECORD: AN AGE OF INSTITUTIONAL TRAJECTORY SETTING

In coining the phrase "the Gilded Age," Mark Twain referenced the explosion of wealth and corruption in the last quarter of the nineteenth century. Buoyed by the expansion of the American economy, a larger, stronger educational infrastructure emerged to define a nation destined to become the most powerful in the world. In 1870, at the start of the Gilded Age, there were 563 institutions of higher education, but by 1900, 977 colleges and universities dotted the American landscape. That institutional surge of 74 percent was the platform for a fourfold increase in student enrollment. And even though enrollment shifted only from 1.3 percent to 2.3 percent of the eighteen- to twenty-four-year-olds in the country, it still set the stage for amazing opportunities and outcomes.[1]

America's rapidly expanding and evolving educational infrastructure led to significant technological advances, economic growth, and individual productivity.[2] As basic literacy and numeracy steadily became differentiators in a new work-life readiness ecosystem, the race to educate a better workforce intensified. That set the stage for leadership-driven surges by select colleges and universities. The converging influences of industrial growth, great individual or family wealth, and visionary university leadership helped to redefine fundamentally what it meant for a campus to be "thoroughly equipped."

What distinguished the surging from the nonsurging institutions was the leaders' ability to attract transformational philanthropic investments. The generosity of founding or pivotal donors enabled powerful presidents to conceive or enhance competitive institutions.[3]

One key example is Johns Hopkins University, founded in 1874 with an incomparable level of start-up capital. Although brand new, Hopkins was empowered with "a private endowment free from ecclesiastical or political control, where from the beginning the old and the new, the humanities and the sciences, theory and practice, could be generously promoted."[4] At the time, the gift of $3.5 million from Johns Hopkins, a Baltimore financier, was the largest single bequest that had ever been made to an American college or university. But rather than parrot the undergraduate education he received at Yale, Hopkins's first president, Daniel Coit Gilman, built a research-oriented faculty, modeled after what he revered and admired about Germany's tradition of scholarly leadership, and based on what he experienced during his graduate study in Berlin.[5] Within two decades, his new university was lauded worldwide, motivating Harvard's president Charles W. Eliot to use it as a model for the growth of graduate education at his institution, an elder to Johns Hopkins University by almost 250 years.[6] That innovation was what benefaction afforded when provided to a brand-new but capable leader.

Similarly, with a steady flow of gifts, John D. Rockefeller systematically advanced the early lofty pursuits of the University of Chicago. With an initial gift of $600,000 in 1889, Rockefeller set his sights on world-class excellence from the start.[7] His subsequent giving to the University of Chicago alone grew to approximately $35 million over three decades. The inaugural president, William Rainey Harper, was gifted all the land, buildings, and furnishings necessary to be thoroughly equipped, including, by 1910, a $19 million endowment to keep it that way.[8]

Other prominent examples of philanthropy-based surges in early higher education include the seminal gifts of Ezra Cornell to found Cornell University in 1865, Cornelius Vanderbilt's philanthropy-driven transformation of Central University into Vanderbilt University in 1873, and the conversion of Trinity College into Duke University between 1898 and 1925 by Benjamin Newton Duke and James Buchanan Duke.[9]

Perhaps the most compelling example of a philanthropy-based push toward becoming thoroughly equipped is the rise of Stanford University. Allegedly, following the death of their young son, Leland Stanford and Jane Lathrop Stanford decided that a new kind of university would be the most appropriate memorial. While planning and grieving, the Stanfords selected Cornell-educated ichthyologist David Starr Jordan as their university's leader in 1891. He began his Stanford presidency with fifteen buildings and fifteen professors on a campus of over seventy-eight thousand acres. Based largely on real estate value, Stanford University's estimated $20 million endowment was the largest in American higher education at the time, dwarfing Columbia's $13 million, Harvard's $11 million, and Yale's $10 million.[10] Leland Stanford promised Jordan he had "all the money that could be wisely used" in order to produce "a university of high degree."[11]

At the close of the nineteenth century, the landscape of higher education in America was reshaped in accordance with the wishes of aspiring, greatness-driven university presidents and generous, vision-motivated philanthropists. These partners first visualized and then developed a new kind of thoroughly equipped university.

While some presidents stood on the shoulders of philanthropists to create new institutions, others used the platform provided by their seasoned traditions to elevate their aspirations and approach. Woodrow Wilson's presidency of Princeton University is a prime example of this phenomenon, although it has long been overshadowed by the racism that punctuated his subsequent presidency of the United States.[12] From 1902 to 1910, Wilson set Princeton on a path of "radical reform," aimed at new levels of excellence and distinction.[13] He audaciously believed Princeton could "challenge the supremacy of Harvard and Yale."[14] At the time, Harvard and Yale held endowments of $14.1 million and $6.8 million respectively, while Princeton's endowment in 1902 was $3.8 million.[15] To close that gap, Wilson appealed to his most consequential alumni to help reinvigorate Princeton with funds for a "reconstructed" curriculum, a reorganized faculty, and a new graduate school, law school, electrical engineering school, and museum. When he boldly asserted a need for $12.5 million in 1902, the initial whistles of alumni doubt and derision turned into applause.[16] As a relative share of the nation's GDP, it was the equivalent of a $9.5 billion vision and initiative in 2019.[17] He called it "the Princeton idea," and when his faculty rallied around it, "a spirit of new faith and of high endeavour took hold of the entire institution."[18] While the law school and other elements of his vision never materialized, he did enough to later be described as "the intellectual architect" of today's Princeton.[19]

Nicholas Murray Butler, despite his legendary egocentrism, presided during the dramatic transformation of Columbia University from 1902 to 1945. That is, he led the institution's first significant reach for stature. To the degree that the modern Columbia is recognized as being among the very best universities in the nation and world, Butler's well-publicized ambitions placed it there. He began his presidency with a stated goal of making the university "the intellectual center of this country and of the modern world."[20] He referred to Columbia as "a giant in bonds," and he set out to use his presidency to unshackle it for the fulfillment of its substantial potential.[21] Butler outlined a bold vision for Columbia University's future, featuring systematic debt removal and an enormous expansion of the physical plant, including new buildings for the departments of engineering, chemistry, and philosophy, and for the schools of law and political science. In 1902, Butler announced that the price tag for his vision ranged between $10 million and $15 million.[22] Like Wilson at Princeton, he emphasized alumni giving, although he delayed the creation of an advancement office, which by then had become both common and productive in other major universities.[23] He is said to have raised more than $120 million throughout his tenure. Had he not hoarded the advancement function as much as he did, he might have raised more. Whereas his initial vision was a pricey $15 million in 1902, as he neared the end of his presidency in 1943, he communicated the need for another $50 million to stabilize, strengthen, and secure the institution's future.[24]

Outclassing both Wilson and Butler with respect to the aim of being thoroughly equipped—without the aid of a single transformational gift—was Charles W. Eliot, who presided over Harvard from 1869 to 1909. He was the first president of Harvard who was not also a minister. In addition, he was the first president to set the stage for the eventual education of women, as he launched his presidency saying he hoped the university would "contribute to the intellectual emancipation of women."[25]

From the start, Eliot led with a grand vision and a relentless drive to shift Harvard away from its old colonial mandate to shape and sharpen leaders for the nation's pulpits. A more urban and industrialized world around him was acquiring a taste for graduates with freer, perhaps more cosmopolitan mindsets. Largely in response to that emerging world, he redefined the undergraduate experience. Eliot led the effort to provide undergraduate students with the freedom to choose from a smorgasbord of electives. As a kind of quality control for the new system, he standardized the PhD as the desired credential for all faculty in Arts and Sciences. Eliot quadrupled the student body from a base of 570. He abolished compulsory chapel in 1886. He formed a separate graduate department within the Faculty of Arts and Sciences in 1872, upgraded Harvard's other graduate schools, and launched a new School of Business Administration in 1908.[26]

Most importantly, Eliot focused on enhancing the faculty, which grew by more than fourfold—part of a larger, tenfold expansion of the overall instructional staff—from fewer than sixty to more than six hundred. This enabled him to reduce faculty workloads and shift the emphasis from teaching to scholarship.[27] In the process, he assembled a world-class collection of faculty members, including William James, George Santayana, Josiah Royce, Francis Greenwood Peabody, A. Lawrence Lowell, Albert Bushnell Hart, and Barrett Wendell. They and others educated and graduated hundreds of notable students during Eliot's forty-year term, including Henry Cabot Lodge, Louis D. Brandeis, Theodore Roosevelt, J. Pierpont Morgan, W. E. B. Du Bois, and Franklin Delano Roosevelt.

Eliot's Harvard experienced a dramatic increase in size, stature, and operating costs. The time was right for the first-ever organized capital campaign in American higher education, which was announced by Harvard in 1904.[28] The context was right, too. Eliot knew Harvard's Alumni Association had its share of highly successful and wealthy members. His capital campaign prioritized increasing faculty salaries and endowment while reducing tuition dependency. The goal was set at $2.5 million, slightly exceeding the size of Harvard's entire endowment at the onset of Eliot's presidency. Targeting alumni who could contribute up to $50,000 each, they raised $2.4 million, falling $100,000 short of Eliot's announced goal. Yet the campaign was considered a success, in part because "it was the first time that an institution of higher learning had raised as much as a million dollars at one time."[29]

In his inaugural address in 1869, Eliot set the tone for his tenure by insisting that Harvard must be "the best" in all fields of endeavor. His pursuit of excellence is now legendary.[30] According to one assessment, "Eliot transformed Harvard by relentless cycles of thought, persuasion, and execution; he grew a parochial college into a great university."[31] Upon his retirement, the endowment stood at $22.7 million, nearly an order of magnitude larger than when he began his tenure as president forty years earlier. Harvard was nimbler, both educationally and financially. Eliot had also advanced the authority of its front office as a platform for broader transformation. By the time Lawrence Lowell succeeded Eliot in May 1909, the presidency of Harvard was said to be of "papal prominence in American education."[32]

BOOKER T. WASHINGTON: A CONTENDER FOR CAPITAL OPTIMIZATION

Amid these remarkable contenders for capital, one philanthropy-aided surge is rarely cited.

Based on story arc alone, neither Gilman of Hopkins, Harper of Chicago, Jordan of Stanford, Wilson of Princeton, Butler of Columbia, nor Eliot of Harvard could rival the dramatic leadership of Booker T. Washington, who founded the Tuskegee Normal and Industrial Institute in Alabama in 1881.

Unlike Hopkins, Chicago, and Stanford, Tuskegee's launch was not initially aided by a sizable gift. There was no eager benefactor awaiting Washington's arrival to Alabama with limitless funds to empower a unique pursuit of greatness. Such funding could have enabled Washington to thoroughly equip his institute at a time when education was the only ladder that an underdeveloped and vilified race could use to climb up from illiteracy. Washington also lacked the advantages of a developed educational tradition. He launched Tuskegee in a constant battle to survive.

While other leaders were challenged to leverage their institutional value proposition more fully, Washington had to create, shape, and build one from scratch. He could tap no tradition of giving. In the era preceding Eliot's tenure, "between 1800 and 1860 Harvard received gifts from twenty-eight donors, each in excess of $5,000."[33] And when he took control of Harvard in 1869, the endowment already stood at $2.39 million.[34]

For reasons beyond Washington's obvious disadvantage of having been formerly enslaved, his leadership was a different story altogether. His push to thoroughly equip his institution rivaled that of the other great leaders of his era. And he won the attention and admiration of each of them in the process.

In 1898, the University of Chicago's William Rainey Harper invited Washington to his city and campus for the Chicago Peace Jubilee celebration.[35] For at least two of Washington's many major fundraising speeches in New York City, Columbia's Nicholas Murray Butler sat beside some of the city's wealthiest residents, listening to Washington's wizardry.[36] Washington was an honored, yet controversial guest at the inaugural ceremonies for Woodrow Wilson at Princeton University in 1902. President Gilman of Hopkins was both a critic and admirer of Washington and would later fund

Tuskegee once he left Hopkins and assumed the role of president of the John F. Slater Fund.[37]

Washington toured the fledgling Stanford University campus in January 1903. Although the construction was incomplete, Washington could already see that the buildings would be "the most beautiful and the most complete specimens of a distinctive type of architecture in the United States."[38] As he spoke to a Stanford crowd of two thousand, which included Jane Lathrop Stanford, he must have understood and appreciated what he and the Stanfords had in common—a keen sense of the vital importance of envisioning, prioritizing, and establishing the physical, human, and financial infrastructure required for stability and distinctiveness in American higher education. Interestingly, on that same California trip, Washington met Pomona College president George A. Gates, whom he would later assist once Gates became the president of Fisk University.

In a November 1904 letter to Oswald Garrison Villard, a journalist, editor of the *New York Evening Post*, and founding member of the National Association for the Advancement of Colored People (NAACP), Washington openly admired the Massachusetts Institute of Technology and expressed a desire to see Atlanta University and Tuskegee have a similar prominence and impact.[39] Washington also visited Williams College in 1898 to honor his mentor General Samuel Chapman Armstrong, the founder of the Hampton Institute, whom Washington described as "the Savior of my race."[40] Dartmouth College awarded Washington an honorary doctoral degree in 1901.

But Washington's connection with Harvard's Eliot was qualitatively different from his contact with the other leading educators of his time. Eliot made Washington the first "coloured man" to receive an honorary degree from Harvard University in 1896. Ironically, Eliot presented the formerly enslaved Washington with an honorary master's degree. The two men remained in touch. In a series of letters, Eliot advised Washington on curricular development matters, particularly mentioning Tuskegee's need to ensure that its graduates have "competent mental equipment."[41] When Eliot visited the Tuskegee campus in 1906 for their twenty-fifth anniversary celebration, he underscored the significance of Washington's achievement with several noteworthy remarks.

Speaking to a large crowd that included William Howard Taft, who would soon become the twenty-seventh president of the United States, and Andrew

Carnegie, whose wealth at the time was second only to John D. Rockefeller, Eliot said Harvard was "not as rich after living two hundred years among the people of Massachusetts as Tuskegee is today, after having lived twenty-five years among the people of Alabama."[42] Eliot credited Washington's leadership and vision for his success in securing the attention, affection, and support of some of the most powerful leaders of his time.

In this Gilded Age era of capital contenders, no other transformation could match Tuskegee's narrative arc. After lifting himself up from slavery and illiteracy, Washington was challenged to lift an institution up from the sandy loam of Macon County, Alabama. By leading with a clear vision and a working concept of what it meant to be "thoroly equipped," he did just that.

Upon Washington's 1881 arrival, there was no land, buildings, faculty, students, staff, or supplies. His first small, annual state appropriation was delayed by months. At Washington's death in 1915, Tuskegee had 111 brick buildings on 2,300 Institute-owned acres. That was room sufficient to educate a stable enrollment of 1,537 students from thirty-two states and nineteen foreign countries. Washington alone taught the first thirty-two students, but a faculty of more than two hundred gathered to help memorialize his life. And after starting with no endowment, he left behind an endowment of nearly $2 million.

Beyond the tangible measures of his legacy, Washington left behind an institution with an incomparable trajectory. In 1922, seven years after his death, it would add a liberal arts, college-level curriculum—yet another fundamental advance built on the foundation set by his leadership.

More than any other leader in American higher education's original age of aspiration, Washington should be an enduring symbol of the pursuit of capital optimization, the practical institutional infrastructural stability that shaping better citizens requires.

INSTITUTIONAL QUESTION FOR THE FUTURE: WHY IS CAPITAL OPTIMIZATION ESSENTIAL TO ANY RESPONSIBLE EFFORT TO SHAPE BETTER CITIZENS?

More than a century removed from Washington's death, a closer look at his institutional outcomes may be illuminating for current and aspiring leaders, especially those looking to move up from precarity. In what sense is Washington's context similar to the environment in which today's HBCU leaders are challenged to excel? What strategic mindset facilitated his success in shaping a Black institution with competitive levels of human, physical, financial, and marketing capital? The answers to these and similar questions can inform leaders who are determined to build a campus thoroughly equipped to ensure a bright future.

WASHINGTON'S PHILANTHROPY-RICH CONTEXT

Mark Twain, Washington's friend who witnessed his fundraising wizardry in the first Gilded Age, said, "History doesn't repeat itself, but it often rhymes." The first quarter of the twenty-first century has been described as part of a second, or new, Gilded Age.[43] For a variety of compelling economic and sociopolitical reasons, the comparison is apt.

In his exhaustive analysis of the first Gilded Age, Richard White describes America as "a country transformed by immigration, urbanization, environmental crisis, political stalemate, new technologies, the creation of powerful corporations, income inequality, failures of governance, mounting class conflict, and increasing social, cultural, and religious diversity."[44] Few descriptions could more accurately describe conditions in America toward the end of the first quarter of the twenty-first century. Add to the mix racial strife, which was obviously worse back then, and you have a set of dynamics that, while formidable, did not thwart Washington's success. He made measurable progress toward capital optimization despite a volatile sociopolitical and economic climate, principally by figuring out how to tap surges in extreme wealth for Tuskegee's benefit.

The unprecedented generosity of many new or newly motivated high-networth individuals drove the institutional surges. The contributions were so substantial that "what was given from the new wealth of the 1860s and the following decades overshadowed in magnitude all earlier gifts to higher education."[45] For instance, the $3.5 million investment that launched and endowed John Hopkins "was larger than the total benefactions Harvard had received in 250 years."[46] Several key university leaders successfully captured the attention of the top 12 percent of Americans, who, by 1890, owned 86 percent of all wealth. Or, more narrowly, they connected with those in the top 1 percent, who owned 51 percent of the nation's riches.[47] The abundance of both the industrial and slave economies helped to drive the institutional prosperity surge.

In fact, "the total wealth of the country in 1880 was estimated at thirty billion dollars as against sixteen billion in 1860."[48] That helps to explain why the period from 1870 to 1944 has been described as the "university transformation era" in America. Key philanthropists grew wealthier, major philanthropic foundations were born, and many colleges and universities were advanced.[49] And in that context, Washington was the first to prove the concept that Black institutions were worthy of transformational investment.

The inequality evidenced in that age never fully disappeared. The emergence of Gilded Ages and extreme inequality may be endemic to capitalism.[50] Predictable or not, the first Gilded Age derived wealth from overlapping and successive economies—the old enslavement-based wealth and the new and growing industrial wealth—just as America's second Gilded Age is rooted in multiple economies. The growth dates to the junk bond–based wealth of the 1980s, followed by the unstable internet-based wealth of the 1990s. Both decades helped to set a foundation for technology-driven wealth accumulation, which accelerated in the first quarter of the twenty-first century with help from an economy now driven largely by innovation. Throughout, the gap between the rich and the poor widened.[51]

Some of the most compelling details of the second Gilded Age of inequality were illuminated in a 2019 Federal Reserve study. Citing the mounting evidence of increased wealth concentration since the 1980s, the study illuminates the skewed ownership of an estimated $114 trillion of net assets (real estate, vehicles, mutual funds, pensions, etc.) owned by all Americans by 2018:

- The net worth of the wealthiest 10 percent of Americans is 70 percent of the total household net worth.
- The net worth of the wealthiest 1 percent of Americans is 31 percent of the total household net worth.
- The net worth of the poorest 50 percent of US households is roughly 1 percent of the total household net worth.[52]

The similarity between the two Gilded Ages elevates the importance of what Washington achieved, and points to the challenge and possibilities facing leaders with lofty aspirations.

For example, Washington established a close relationship with John D. Rockefeller, the wealthiest man of his Gilded Age era. He actively engaged the wealthiest people of his time and of all time, including Andrew Carnegie, George Eastman, Julius Rosenwald, Robert Ogden, George Foster Peabody, William G. Willcox, J. Pierpont Morgan, John Wanamaker, Collis P. Huntington, and other Gilded Age tycoons. Most responded quite favorably to Washington's focused and persistent quest for both endowed and expendable funds.

As an indication of the caliber of philanthropic power tapped by Washington, consider that, at around the time of Washington's death in 1915, the wealth of John D. Rockefeller alone was almost at its 1918 peak of $1.2 billion, or the rough equivalent of $340 billion a century later.[53] In 2021, a single HBCU president would need to similarly befriend and receive meaningful gifts from Jeff Bezos, Bill Gates, and Warren Buffett to approximate the Gilded Age access that Washington realized with one relationship. Washington also befriended Andrew Carnegie, who served as a trustee at Tuskegee, and, in 1903, provided what still stands today as the largest GDP-relative philanthropic investment ever made by an individual in a single HBCU.[54]

In neither Gilded Age have other HBCU leaders matched Washington's meaningful and fruitful relationships with those in the upper echelon of Gilded Age wealth. None have received similarly scaled GDP-relative investments. Yet this is precisely what relief from precarity requires.

WASHINGTON'S QUEST MINDSET

Washington should be recognized as a peerless aspirant to long-term health and wholeness for both an institution and a people. He believed Tuskegee needed the kind of capital optimization he saw and admired at universities like Harvard, Columbia, and Princeton. That became his singular focus and he remained energized to realize it. His general quest for capital optimization should be embraced anew, and the most enlightened aspects of his approach should be considered for emulation today.

More than numerous wealthy prospective investors, optimizing capital also requires institutional leaders with a clear and compelling vision, mission, and plan capable of attracting transformational philanthropic investments. That was Washington's quest mindset and skill set. He spent his thirty-four-year tenure ensuring that the Tuskegee Institute would be built to last. From the start, he imagined and set out to realize a thoroughly equipped campus. His board meetings were oriented around that goal, as was his campus management team. To that end, he outperformed the leaders of many respectable white colleges and universities in attracting significant attention and investment. And that is why he was able to amass an endowment of nearly $2 million. It was an impressive foundation upon which future Tuskegee leaders were expected to build with a view toward becoming and remaining thoroughly equipped, especially as the meaning of that term evolved over time.

Washington had a habit of comparing the development and status of Tuskegee to that of peer or aspiration groups, with an emphasis on financial conditions, especially endowment. He studied and often lamented the racial gap in education, and he did not hesitate to compare Black colleges with Harvard, Yale, Columbia, and others.[55] He was not concerned that other institutions were white, older, Northern, or without the disadvantages facing Tuskegee and other Black institutions. Nor did he think aspiring to realize world-class levels of wealth and prominence were inappropriate goals for his race. He thought of Tuskegee and other Black institutions as doing important work for the country, at least as important as any other educational institutions.

To put his aspiration and drive into perspective, table 3.1 shows when many of today's leading liberal arts colleges reached the $2 million endowment threshold, as compared to Tuskegee's $2 million endowment by the end of Washington's presidency in 1915.

That Tuskegee's endowment nearly matched the endowments of colleges like Amherst, Oberlin, Wellesley, Smith, and Swarthmore in 1915 is a testament to Washington's vision and skill. And it is logical to wonder how many unharvested lessons there are in Tuskegee's arrival at a $2 million endowment in a mere thirty-four years, or meaningfully faster than nearly all of the well-known colleges listed.

Washington prioritized endowment growth long before endowment size emerged as the key symbol of institutional stability and health a century later. And, based on that consequential metric, he had a pioneering grasp of what sustainable institutional competitiveness requires in higher education.

As will be illuminated more fully in chapters 7 and 8, when some of today's best liberal arts colleges finally discovered endowment growth as an essential measure of institutional capacity and vitality, they grew their endowments to levels consistent with Washington's original aspiration for Tuskegee and other

TABLE 3.1 Number of years to the $2 million endowment threshold

Institution	Year founded	Year reached $2m	# of years to $2m
1. Tuskegee University	1881	1915	34
2. Pomona College	1887	1926	39
3. Wellesley College	1875	1915	40
4. Smith College	1871	1919	48
5. Swarthmore College	1864	1920	56
6. Carleton College	1866	1925	59
7. Vassar College	1861	1921	60
8. Oberlin College	1833	1912	79
9. Mount Holyoke College	1837	1921	84
10. Grinnell College	1846	1931	85
11. Bates College	1855	1941	86
12. Amherst College	1821	1909	88
13. Furman College	1826	1924	98
14. Bowdoin College	1794	1904	110
15. Davidson College	1837	1951	114
16. Colby College	1813	1935	122
17. Hamilton College	1793	1925	132
18. Williams College	1793	1960	167

Source: Data on the year institutions reached the $2 million endowment level comes from the archives of each institution.

Black institutions. And although they greatly exceeded his pace, they merely caught up with his dream.

FOR THE MINDSET

The philanthropists of the second Gilded Age should provide investments based on what can make the culture of the campus good, rather than on what can make the individuals on the campus great.

CHAPTER FOUR

The Character Imperative

We believe that the Negro people, as a race, have a contribution to make to civilization and humanity, which no other race can make.

W. E. B. Du Bois, "The Conservation of Races," 1897

Damfo was always opening his mind to a future that went far beyond single lifetimes, or even the lifetimes of single tribes and nations. The vision was terrifying even in its hopefulness, but with greater understanding the terror of his own impotence dissolved in the knowledge that if he worked well he would be part of the preparation for generations which would inherit the potency that should bring a people back together.

Ayi Kwei Armah, *The Healers*

In the late nineteenth century, with Booker T. Washington's trailblazing pursuit of capital optimization well underway, W. E. B. Du Bois began his journey to become the next century's clearest, most compelling voice for character optimization. Du Bois's thinking and aspiration bear the most resemblance to the operational definition of character optimization in this book—that is, shaping world-class citizens who are fully equipped to both compete and work in the existing world and, simultaneously, imagine and work toward a new and better one. What each leader may have meant by "better citizens" was simply a matter of emphasis. Washington stressed ripening skill sets, and Du Bois, mindsets. Ultimately, both high-character entrepreneurs and intellectuals were required to defeat the widespread perceptions of Black inferiority.

From the start, Du Bois had an instinct about this. He arrived at Harvard as a student when scholars at several prestigious American universities had already built and embraced a tradition of justifying white supremacy and the enslavement of Blacks. It was uneventful in 1809 when John Wakefield Francis, who would eventually serve as the second president of the New York Academy of Medicine, wrote an undergraduate research paper at Columbia University entitled, "On the Bodily and Mental Inferiority of the Negro."[1] Eight decades later, at the University of Pennsylvania, Yale graduate and eventual president of the American Association for the Advancement of Science, Daniel G. Brinton, described Blacks as being "midway between the Orangutang and the European white."[2] Early in his inaugural leadership of the now prestigious American Sociological Association, Brown University's Lester Frank Ward, still regarded by some as the father of American sociology, built upon Brinton's conclusion.[3] Ward argued "a Negro who rapes a white woman" is attempting "to raise his race to a little higher level." And, as if to justify Southern lynching, he added, "The fury of the white community in which such an act takes place is equally natural."[4] Many in the early American academy were doing their best to help legitimize inhumanity and ignorance.

Harvard, too, had its champions of racial hierarchy. For example, when Du Bois arrived there in 1888, Harvard biologist and geologist Louis Agassiz had recently completed his decades-long effort to put a scientific imprimatur on Black inferiority and systemic racism.[5] As he trained and influenced many people, Agassiz's broad authority and popularity helped to ensure that racism could reside comfortably in the curriculum at Harvard and elsewhere in American higher education. He went on tours, particularly in the Southern states, to satisfy the strong appetite for his polygenist theory. If Blacks and whites had different origins, and Blacks were inferior, then slavery was justified and the Southern way of life, in all of its supremacist brutality, was entirely legitimate.

Agassiz did not disappoint his Southern audiences. In 1847, on one of his multiple visits to Charleston, South Carolina, Agassiz delivered a lecture in which he asserted "the brain of the Negro is that of the imperfect brain of a 7 month's infant in the womb of a White."[6] Such thinking had already been normalized in the American academy, even if it was without the "scientific" theorizing engaged in and authoritatively promulgated by Agassiz.

Du Bois understood the pervasive and persuasive sway of the pseudoscience and pseudotheologies espoused at otherwise prestigious institutions. He was determined to debunk and dismantle it in both the academy and the general public. Reflecting on the challenges he faced as a budding intellectual, he said, "the Negro problem was in my mind a matter of systematic investigation and intelligent understanding. The world was thinking wrong about race, because it did not know. The ultimate evil was stupidity. The cure for it was knowledge based on scientific investigation."[7] To wage that war, African Americans desperately needed the financial and physical infrastructure emphasized by Washington. Without it, they could not actualize the robust intellectual and character infrastructure suitable for ushering in the freedom and wholeness most had only imagined.

From experience and study, Du Bois believed an emphasis on character could be an important HBCU differentiator. In 1948, he contrasted the two institutions that shaped him, saying, "We used to talk much of character . . . at Fisk, we had it dinned into our ears. At Harvard we never mentioned it."[8]

Herbert Aptheker called Du Bois "peerless" as an "expert in the area of the nature, theory and purposes of education; and on the specific subject of the education of black people in the United States."[9] But while Du Bois is understood to be a thinker and writer about what education ought to be generally structured to achieve, he was most often prescriptive and precise about the particular purpose and calling of HBCUs. And much of what he spent his life conveying to HBCUs was rooted in the seminal speech he delivered on March 5, 1897.

Du Bois, then at the dawn of his career, offered a speech entitled "The Conservation of Races" (hereafter "Conservation") at the inaugural meeting of the American Negro Academy (ANA) in Washington, DC.[10] This speech set the tone and framework for his mission-driven lifetime of scholarship, activism, advocacy, and agitation. It also signaled his passion and his subsequent peerless articulation of the purpose of the Black academy. He aimed to do nothing less than to save humanity by prescribing character-enriching institutions and organizations.

INSTITUTIONAL CONSIDERATION FOR THE RECORD: W. E. B. DU BOIS AND THE QUEST FOR CHARACTER OPTIMIZATION

When Du Bois was a young student and budding professional, imagining what he might do with his life, the world around him was swiftly constraining his options. The abrupt end of the Reconstruction era in 1877 accelerated an already aggressive and systematic erosion of Black civil, political, and social rights. That erosion was aided and intensified by extreme violence and an uncompromising "stay in your place" program of white supremacist intimidation. The legion of negative forces converged to form a combative Jim Crow Southern culture, which featured a multifaceted, decades-long barbarous reign of terrorism over Black life. These conditions presented a formidable challenge for Du Bois and anyone else offering ideas about the way forward for African Americans. Having just completed a disappointing two-year experience at Wilberforce University, he had time to think prescriptively about the role of the Black institution, which, ultimately, was the crowning point of his "Conservation" speech.

DU BOIS'S FOUNDATIONAL CONSERVATION

Du Bois argued that Blacks were a distinctive race with a distinctive mission. To fulfill that mission, he thought distinctive organizations were required, or what one might collectively refer to as "infrastructure."

He began his speech with an examination of race differences throughout world history, and he then theorized about the descriptive criteria for determining race. After describing the story of the world as the story of human groups called races, Du Bois calls the "Negro" the "most indefinite of all."[11] Relative to how other racial groups had grown and developed throughout human history, the Negro race had yet to fully emerge from the trauma of racism to recommence their journey to a destiny now beclouded by white supremacy. This was the challenge.

It is not an overstatement to describe Du Bois as, thereafter, spending his life preoccupied with determining how the race could best develop to its fullest potential. He would later underscore that passion in 1940 by referring to his personal reflection on his own life, *Dusk of Dawn*, as "an essay toward an autobiography of a race concept." His embrace of race was a clear point of pride and confidence, rather than either an uncertain or uncompleted point of scholarly analysis.

After defining the challenge in "Conservation," Du Bois then argues that the race has a distinctive mission. Given the choice between developing as a race or abandoning altogether the idea of race, Du Bois insists, "It is our duty to conserve our physical powers, our intellectual endowments, our spiritual ideals; as a race we must strive by race organization, by race solidarity, by race unity to the realization of that broader humanity which freely recognizes differences in men, but sternly deprecates inequality in their opportunities of development."[12] He urged that by the continued "development of Negro genius," conserving and developing the culture, character, and voice of the race, Blacks would finally be able to present a yet ungiven gift to the world. These larger aims were rarely absent whenever he conveyed his vision for the future. Du Bois amplified many of these themes later that year when he published "Strivings of the Negro People."[13]

Finally, Du Bois turned to the infrastructure, or scaffolding, required for the mission. Facing the challenge and change at the turn of the nineteenth century, and with no substantial and reliable white political alliances, Du Bois turned inward. He said, "Weighted with a heritage of moral iniquity from our past history, hard pressed in the economic world by foreign immigrants and native prejudice, hated here, despised there and pitied everywhere; our one haven of refuge is ourselves."[14] The effort to fully realize the race's true character and voice would require a broad institutional infrastructure comprised of numerous and strong race-based organizations designed to affirm and defend the race. He underscores the need for "race organizations," including schools, colleges, newspapers, and businesses.

As for the agenda of these race organizations, Du Bois sounded much like his friend and mentor Rev. Alexander Crummell (founder of the ANA). Both wanted Black people to engage in what Du Bois called, "a vast work of self-reformation."[15] Such an effort would position them to fulfill their destiny of becoming "a peculiar people, to speak to the nations of earth a Divine truth that shall make them free."[16]

DU BOIS, HBCUs, "CONSERVATION," AND CHARACTER OPTIMIZATION

Based on Du Bois's "Conservation," neither the academy (Wilberforce and Atlanta Universities) nor the Academy (the ANA) became key pillars of his prescribed institutional infrastructure. None had evolved to foster "Negro genius" as he imagined. While his move north in 1910 may be logically framed as a switch from academia to activism, it was also a break from the dispiriting experience of being a Black intellectual living in the segregated South, where

Black intelligence was routinely and correctly perceived as being at odds with the reign of white supremacy.

Yet, while Du Bois left Atlanta and campus life, he did not abandon his clear and compelling character-based theory of change. As Lewis put it, "University and college campuses had always been a venue for significant Du Boisian pronouncements, so much so that his presence was unwelcome at conservative institutions such as Hampton and Wilberforce and a source of administrative nervousness at schools such as Fisk and Howard."[17] Focusing almost exclusively on HBCUs, Du Bois prioritized two key agendas—gaining more Black control over HBCUs and ensuring that, thereafter, the character optimization agenda would be pursued.

His first agenda yielded amazing results. Beginning with his own alma mater, Fisk University, Du Bois began to question the motives and style of the whites in leadership at most HBCUs. Du Bois inspired protests at Fisk in the 1920s and 1930s, and helped to stimulate strikes, walkouts, and protests at many HBCUs, including Morehouse, Livingstone, Talladega, Storer, Hampton, and Knoxville colleges. Predictably, the sixfold increase in HBCU enrollments to nearly fourteen thousand prompted more resistance to the stale freedom on many HBCU campuses.[18] His voice emerged at a pivotal agency moment for them. His critique of white HBCU leadership resembled his critique of colonialism in Africa, just as his frequent appraisal of Black HBCU leadership resembled his critique of neocolonialism.[19] He insisted on a more enlightened approach to preparing Black students to challenge, rather than make peace with a hostile world.

The campus rebellions worked. Multiple changes were triggered by HBCU students and alumni, who resisted white paternalism and insisted on the appointment of Black presidents. While Fisk would not appoint its first Black president until 1947, at least eleven HBCUs, including Howard University and Morgan State University, appointed their first Black president within a decade of the rebellions of the 1920s.[20] The restless students also demanded curricular changes. Believing Du Bois, they wanted to learn how to compete and produce in an inequitable world while enriching their mindsets to imagine and shape it into a more equitable one.

Du Bois's "campus control" agenda worked, but he was far less effective with his second, "campus character" agenda. As a public intellectual, he redeployed his core "Conservation" concepts into a mandate for the broader Black institutional infrastructure. And there is ample evidence, particularly in Du Bois's twelve formal speeches on HBCU campuses between 1898 and 1960, that he recognized the difficulties of optimizing character.[21] While Du Bois's definition of the agenda remained consistent, his sense of urgency about it was clearly influenced by changing conditions in and well beyond the HBCU ecosystem. Whether he spoke to graduating seniors, alumni groups, or campus conferences, he consistently pointed to unrealized "Conservation" and HBCU ideals.

Early on, Du Bois emphasized a need for Blacks to fully develop a sense of humanity that had been underdeveloped by enslavement. His themes included striving, identity, and agency.[22] At Hampton in 1906, he affirmed that, "unless we develop our full capabilities, we cannot survive."[23] To his chagrin, HBCUs had not yet followed the "Conservation" mandate to access and embrace their "stalwart originality," or distinctive character. His frustration grew as the lag persisted.

By the time Du Bois spoke at Howard University in 1930, after echoing the "Conservation" call to pursue and exhibit high character, he complained that "the greatest meetings of the Negro college year like those of the white college year have become vulgar exhibitions of liquor, extravagance, and fur coats. We have in our colleges a growing mass of stupidity and indifference."[24] In 1938, at Fisk University, he worried that Blacks were only "half-emancipated," that there was too much parroting of the Northern schools, and that there was insufficient "race loyalty." Du Bois's angst was shared. In 1935, Howard University's Carter G. Woodson complained about what HBCUs were teaching and prioritizing. In frustration, he wrote, "We would close up to seventy-five percent of the so-called Negro colleges and universities and the race would be better off. There would be less miseducation of the youth."[25] In 1938, forty years removed from his "Conservation" statement, Du Bois thought Blacks should only be "under the impression that they are educated."[26]

In the final quarter of his life, Du Bois's "Conservation"-based messaging became more candid than ever. As Lewis assessed, Du Bois had always shown "victim-blaming proclivities," but now it seemed his "years of service to the race entitled him to the privilege of unflinching analysis without the censure of the politically correct."[27] In every speech, Du Bois made it very clear that the HBCUs were failing the "Conservation" test that he had been administering since 1897. He seemed increasingly embittered by the gap between what he had imagined in "Conservation" and what he was observing in the HBCU ecosystem.

Du Bois made a more pragmatic case in 1941 at Lincoln University in Missouri, asserting, "Most men in this world are colored. A belief in humanity means a belief in colored men. The future world will, in all reasonable probability, be what colored men make it."[28] He argued that this "colored world" must come into its heritage. He challenged Lincoln to optimize character, since "that character can only be raised above emotion to planned reason by institutions such as this may become."[29]

Five years later, Du Bois referred to all HBCUs before a Knoxville College audience and wondered, "Are these institutions worth saving?" He made it clear that an affirmative answer to that question was tied to their institutional ability to help illuminate the "distinct and unique culture" of the race.[30] He was frustrated with the entire effort when, in 1948, he returned to Wilberforce, and, before a crowd of over four hundred Black professionals, he offered a far more modest projection of how HBCUs could complete the task of shaping leaders for the world.[31]

For six decades, Du Bois toured HBCUs, only to discover too few signs of his prescribed character optimization on HBCU campuses. As if he believed "character, like oxygen, is most noticeable when it is missing,"[32] when Du Bois did not detect it in the air on his HBCU visits, he used his speeches to serve as the coal mine canary.

Du Bois knew what to seek. His character optimization agenda required an unprecedented convergence of Black intellectuals on a single campus to pursue the project. A gathering of elite intellectuals is precisely what Du Bois had already witnessed and from which he had benefited. While they could not match the superior teaching Du Bois found at Fisk, he wrote with envy about the critical mass of world-class faculty he found at Harvard University when he arrived as a student in 1888.[33] At Harvard, Du Bois saw what education could be, but he also learned a great deal about what education must not be. In each case, his subsequent work at Wilberforce, Atlanta, and the ANA was detectably infused with his dream of a world-class brainpower convergence. Optimizing character was to be the differentiator. But his dream would be repeatedly shattered by a recurrent lack of institutional clarity, will, and resources.

In Du Bois's lifetime, only under the Howard University presidency of Mordecai Johnson (1926–60) would an HBCU converge the intellectuals and curriculum sufficient to pursue a Du Boisian character optimization agenda. And that convergence was quite intentional.

In his 1927 inaugural address, in a section he entitled, "The Destiny of the Negro," Johnson said, "I want my country to conquer all of the inhibitions connected with blackness and all of the fears connected with blackness, but I want the original blackness there, and I want that blackness to be unashamed and unafraid. That day is far off yet, but the existence of this institution tells something about the intent of the American mind."[34] There is obvious common ground between Johnson's proud and fearless embrace of "the original blackness," and Du Bois's insistence on striving for "a stalwart originality." They also shared a belief in "our high destiny."

The faculty who made Howard the renowned "capstone of Negro education" during the Johnson years included: Alain Locke (philosophy), Sterling Brown (literary criticism and poetry); Ralph Bunche (political science); Carter G. Woodson, Rayford Logan, William Leo Hansberry, and Merze Tate (history); Kelly Miller and E. Franklin Frazier (sociology); Dorothy Porter (Black history); Howard Thurman and Benjamin Mays (theology); Ernest Everett Just (biology); Percy Julian (chemistry); Mercer Cook (Romance languages); Lois Mailou Jones (art); and Charles Hamilton Houston (law). For more than four decades, up until the 1960s, the intellectuals who consistently gathered at Howard University bore the closest resemblance to the "Conservation"-style vision that Du Bois and Crummell had crafted.

But it did not last. Many of the best intellectuals, as well as the best students, would eventually be recruited by predominantly white colleges with the superior resources to attract and retain them. Their departures diffused much of the intellectual heft required to contradict the Black inferiority narrative and pursue the "Conservation" vision of a better humanity.

It is unclear whether today's HBCUs can summon the will, courage, and resources to pursue a more lasting version of that Howard University convergence as a way to shape better citizens. What is not at all unclear is the need to try to gather substantial investment to support the undertaking.

INSTITUTIONAL QUESTION FOR THE FUTURE: WHY IS CHARACTER OPTIMIZATION ESSENTIAL TO ANY RESPONSIBLE EFFORT TO SHAPE BETTER CITIZENS?

Du Bois saw a character-intensive education as a pathway to racial wholeness and, thereafter, human wholeness. He listed the need to be "representative in character" as the first requirement of the Academy's success, and he emphasized it in his addresses to HBCUs, insisting that they should, with urgency, "comprise something of the best thought, the most unselfish striving and the highest ideals."[35] In the ensuing half-century, he never lost sight of character as a prerequisite for sustainable change.

Two advisories about Du Bois's character optimization vision are offered here for those leaders who may yet want to operationalize what Du Bois prioritized in their quest to shape better citizens. Each advisory also can also be leveraged for the kind of vision refinement required by institutions seeking to move up from precarity.

DU BOIS'S HUMAN DESTINY MINDSET

Du Bois had what can only be aptly described as a "human destiny mindset." What does that mean and why is it relevant for today's leaders?

He saw the purpose of education in the loftiest terms. In "Conservation," he described human history as racial groups "striving, each in its own way, to develop for civilization its particular message, its particular ideal, which shall help guide the world nearer and nearer that perfection of human life for which we all long, that 'one far off Divine event.'"[36] He concluded that enslavement had disadvantaged Blacks in the quest to make a unique contribution to humanity. Thus, instead of the "self-obliteration" eventually favored by Frederick Douglass, Du Bois insisted on a "race development" effort led by HBCUs.[37]

When he argued that the race be conserved, Du Bois sounded tribal. But any careful reading of "Conservation" reveals Du Bois's race focus as merely an initial, necessary stage in overcoming the injury caused by enslavement. Du Bois articulated a phased process, in which the first tasks were individual and racial wholeness, followed by national wholeness, and ending with human wholeness. There was nothing parochial about his focus on race, nor did he hold a tribal view of the HBCU purpose. From the start, he framed the overarching goal in terms beyond the scope of any college campus, especially

HBCUs. In his view, the goal was to prepare people by giving them the capacity to shape a new world. Not only was that the objective of the human destiny mindset, but it might also be regarded as the primary mission of those who embrace the highest form of national and world citizenship.

College leaders today, especially HBCU leaders, would be well-served to consider a Du Boisian human destiny mindset and approach that privileges more explicit ties between the educational experience they provide and the most pressing needs of humankind. There is a persistent need to shape campus infrastructures, curricula, and cultures to yield graduates who are willing and able to transform the world, rather than merely conform to its largely inequitable systems. That underscores the current relevance of Du Bois's prescribed character-driven approach to educational development. He based it on his diagnosis of a world in dire need of substantial repairs that are not unfamiliar today, including racism, systemic inequities, and structural inequalities. He wanted HBCUs to embrace their special mission and lead the rest of higher education, accordingly.

Yet the lack of progress troubled Du Bois. Seven decades after offering his "Conservation" prescription, he saw a questionable embrace of his recommended agenda, in spite of his direct insistence on it as the singular pathway to a new world. At Hampton in 1906, he cited the need to "raise the black race to its full humanity," and warned that a failure to do so would preclude the realization of "the fairest and fullest dream of a great united humanity."[38]

Du Bois did not have the fixed mindset other leaders seemed to hold about the scourge of segregation. He certainly objected to racial barriers, but he was relatively unruffled by them, at times regarding them as an advantage. When the legal battle against separate schools was in its infancy, Du Bois saw beyond the unjust isolation and prioritized finding "competent and intelligent teachers." Just as leaders today could devote more attention to the arc of their institutional agenda or mission, he redefined the problem as one of mindset, advising, "Instead of our schools being separate schools, forced on us by grim necessity, they can become centers of a new and beautiful effort at human education, which may easily lead and guide the world in many important and valuable aspects."[39]

So often, his messaging pointed to the connection between education and the desired condition of the world. At one point, he challenged "the Negro

College" to shape "the world of our dreams."[40] At a later point, he described it as educating "a new and redeeming generation of men."[41] He expected HBCU work to be far more consequential than many of their leaders may have felt equipped and resourced to make it.

In an essay about Du Bois's "messianic vision," or mindset, Vincent Harding wrote, "The genius of Du Bois is that he was able to take his personal responses to the color line and turn them into matters of ultimate significance—matters of personal, racial, and human destiny."[42] Harding elaborated, "For much of his life Du Bois saw the black people of the nation as critical transformers and redeemers of the destiny of the world . . . his deepest hopes and convictions . . . stretched over the boundaries of humanity."[43] Indeed, Du Bois challenged HBCUs to accept that broader mandate, once telling a Fisk audience to become "the sort of Negro University which will emancipate not simply the black folk of the United States, but those white folk who in their effort to suppress Negroes have killed their own culture—men who in their desperate effort to replace equality with caste and to build inordinate wealth on a foundation of abject poverty have succeeded in killing democracy, art and religion."[44]

Clearly, Du Bois never thought African Americans were the only ones who needed to be elevated. He simply thought they needed to be elevated because they were uniquely qualified to elevate the rest of humanity. Instead of his HBCU focus being a contradictory thing, it was merely the first essential step toward redeeming humankind. And that is what made it both timeless and investment worthy.

DU BOIS AND A GATHERING OF ELITE INTELLECTUALS

It was national news, in 2021, when Howard University recruited to their faculty both Nikole Hannah-Jones and Ta-Nehisi Coates. Both renowned journalists, she won a Pulitzer Prize and was named a MacArthur "genius," and he won both National Book and National Magazine Awards. The hires brought new attention to Howard and all HBCUs, triggering stories about a potential "new day."[45] But rather than awakening a new day, the move renewed an old strategy.

Du Bois and others understood that the best way to position Blacks for "the realization of that broader humanity," was by converging elite intellectuals. They aimed to generate and convey new knowledge using unique approaches unlike the supremacist norms of many white campuses. Du Bois first imagined doing that at Wilberforce, and he joined others in a resource-free attempt with the ANA.[46] In his most robust effort, an attempt to launch a world-class laboratory in sociology at Atlanta University from 1897 to 1910, he never received sufficient funding and, thus, remained stymied by precarity.[47]

Well before the arrival of Mordecai Johnson, Howard University professors tried to converge noteworthy intellectuals. In 1901, Howard sociologist and ANA member Kelly Miller tried to convince his university leadership to subsidize and partner with the ANA, thereby providing the multiple benefits of stabilizing the Academy, posthumously honoring former Howard faculty member Crummell, and adding intellectual heft to Howard. Miller's proposal was rejected by the Howard trustees. Similarly, in 1919–20, Howard's white president and board denied attempts by Carter G. Woodson and William Leo Hansberry to establish Black history courses, and an effort by philosopher and Rhodes Scholar Alain Locke, who simply wanted to offer a course on "interracial relations." Trustee curricular control was the norm at that time, and it would not begin to abate for nearly three decades.[48] Nor did it seem to matter to the board that the Black intellectuals whose curricular choices they denied had each been trained at Harvard.

The mindsets of those in the paternal HBCU trustee community tended to be the impediment then, but which mindsets are similarly obstructive now?

The persistence of skewed giving patterns may indicate that some of the mindsets in America's philanthropic community, perhaps unwittingly and driven by tradition, remain unable or unwilling to consider HBCUs as investment worthy. Nonetheless, HBCUs must continue to generate investment-worthy, character-rich initiatives for the same reasons they always have—because it is the right thing to do. And they have.

In a sense, a number of HBCUs have tried to push toward excellence by converging clusters of consequential intellectuals one program at a time. Echoing Du Bois' strategy of inviting top sociologists to join him in researching and seeking to solve "the problem of the color line,"[49] leaders today could construct what is referred to as "academic steeples." By attracting and stabilizing a critical mass of intellectuals in a given field, they can deliberately and methodically make a tangible difference in society. Accordingly, from a leadership standpoint, a transformative theory of change or development would require each president to construct at least one such steeple during their leadership tenure. After several years, perhaps spanning several presidential eras, once you build enough steeples, you could end up with a cathedral—or with the thoroughly equipped university imagined by Du Bois at Atlanta, planned by Washington at Tuskegee, and attempted by Johnson at Howard.

Howard University's recent hirings are a highly visible example of the kind of "center of excellence" or steeple strategy tried by several other HBCUs, with varying degrees of success. Examples include the Race Relations Institute at Fisk University (1942–2005), the Women's Research and Resource Center at Spelman College (ongoing), and the Juvenile Justice Research Institute at Florida A&M University (ongoing). But none of these initiatives has yet benefited from the high-end funding that today's first-rate, prestigious programs tend to enjoy. That is, none has been built on multiple endowed faculty chairs for the program's anchor professors; state-of-the-art space, if not a donor-named building; and a sizable endowment to cover operations, seed research, substantial student brainpower, and the building's physical maintenance, all in perpetuity.[50]

Steeple construction in higher education in the post-2015 era has become more expensive than ever before, requiring hundreds of millions of endowed dollars. This is what true competitiveness requires. And it is precisely what too many institutions like HBCUs are without. Serious, conscious, and aggressive efforts to construct stable steeples may in fact be quietly underway, but, if done the right way, they cannot remain quiet. With a wise approach, they will have the power to enhance the brand and elevate the stature of the entire institution as they materially change the world.

Most of the same racial health, wealth, education, and employment gaps illuminated by Du Bois and his team a century ago have persisted in the first quarter of the twenty-first century.[51] Since enslavement-borne gaps remain unclosed, and a truly robust character-centric education remains untried, HBCU leaders, joined by others, should at least explore the current relevance of building Du Bois–like character-centric steeples to meet the needs of the post-2015, up from precarity era. The presence of a critical mass of well-supported and highly visible HBCU-based intellectuals may inform and alter the mindsets of those skeptics who may now be jaded about the HBCU value proposition.

Perhaps Howard University will be able to build a state-of-the-art steeple around Hannah-Jones and Coates. Such an effort remains long overdue, broadly relevant, greatly needed, and highly likely to be perceived as investment worthy. And the only reason to do it is to produce better citizens.

FOR THE MINDSET

Campus leaders and philanthropists should recognize how character-driven campus steeples and cultures can equip more students with a Du Bois–like human destiny mindset, thereby inclining them to measurably advance the common good.

The Unfinished Business of HBCUs

Early in the twentieth century, a trio of complementary agendas swirled throughout the HBCU community—HBCU character optimization, HBCU capital optimization, and desegregating white higher education. The African American focus on desegregation as a way to move up from poverty and marginality undervalued the other vital work envisioned long ago. African Americans and others simply overlooked the HBCU optimization imperative, leaving it stranded as the most far-reaching unfinished business of the entire era.

A growth mindset about the unfinished business of HBCUs can create a better context for remedying their lack of optimization and improving their lusterless branding, trusteeship, and fundraising.

CHAPTER FIVE

The Neglected Agendas

Overview of Transformations Two and Three: Up from Poverty and Marginality, 1916–1969–2015

There is no black academic journal; no major black intellectual magazine; no major black periodical of highbrow journalism; not even a major black newspaper of national scope. In short, the black infrastructure for intellectual discourse and dialogue is nearly nonexistent. This tragedy is, in part, the price for integration—which has yielded mere marginal black groups within the professional disciplines of a fragmented academic community . . . black intellectuals have little choice: either continued intellectual lethargy on the edges of the academy and literate subcultures unnoticed by the black community, or insurgent creative activity on the margins of the mainstream ensconced within bludgeoning new infrastructures.

Cornel West, "The Dilemma of the Black Intellectual," 1985

He felt in himself a natural, increasing urge to fly far from manipulators, seeking only to be with inspirers. Yet all the life around him belonged to the manipulators . . . force, fraud, deceit: these were the chosen methods of most of them. That this was the way of the world Densu had come to see with increasing sharpness.

Ayi Kwei Armah, *The Healers*

When HBCUs were less than a half century old, three Black leaders offered strategic guidance about the best way to complete the transformation of the race in an era dominated by the color-line problem. All three recognized the protracted nature of the required work. Each stressed the need to optimize HBCUs for their unique mission to shape better citizens and a better world.

The first of the three, Du Bois, was the clearest thinker about the HBCU mission. In his foundational "Conservation" speech, he insisted on the creation of "race organizations," calling them "necessary for our positive advance" and "absolutely imperative for our negative defense."[1] His emphasis on character was pursuant to "the greater ideals of mankind," and he expected that HBCUs would shape the kind of citizens who would reflect those ideals.

The second of the three, Washington, was also remarkably clear about what he thought an infrastructure required. Twenty days before he died in 1915, he addressed a gathering of the American Missionary Association (AMA) in New Haven, Connecticut.[2] As he had done repeatedly, he stressed the need to endow Black institutions. This time, he cheerlessly pointed to the chasm between the endowments of two white universities, Chicago and Columbia, and all Black colleges combined. Washington barely concealed his worry as he summarized for the AMA gathering the remaining educational infrastructure gaps between the races. He pointed to the fact that Blacks were 11 percent of the American population but received less than 2 percent of the nation's annual educational investment. He lamented that far too few of the Black children in the South were attending school, and he highlighted institutional racial disparities in property, annual expenditures, and educational facilities. Then, as if exasperated, he closed the speech by conveying a critically important mindset shift of his own. He said, "at the present rate it is taking, not a few days or years, but a century or more to get Negro education on a plane at all similar to that on which the education of the whites is."[3]

For a man with such a reliable, if not predictable optimistic posture, this was a startling slouch. It is unclear why Washington shifted from expecting to realize educational parity in his lifetime to seeing the struggle last generations into the future, extending to or beyond 2015. Even as his death, in 1915, marked the end of the first HBCU "up from slavery," or "up from illiteracy" transformation, Washington died expecting African Americans to spend the next century emphasizing capital optimization and, with capital provided by Black businesses, endowing an HBCU-centric educational infrastructure. He felt the quality of the infrastructure mattered more than anything else in the quest to shape better citizens.

The third leader, Mordecai Wyatt Johnson, also recognized the basic human need for a safe and secure haven for maturation, which is why he and his fellow Black secretaries in the YMCA argued against an approach to integration that would instantly dissolve their Colored Work Department into the larger association. They had worked very carefully to build powerful venues of support, reaching more than twelve thousand Black college and college-age students.[4] They defended their department as a nurturer of young leaders, even though it seemed, as Johnson called it, "contradictory." In 1928, he urged others to do the same "contradictory thing." He saw a need to access Harvard and Yale (an inclusion agenda), while strengthening Howard and Lincoln as if Harvard and Yale did not exist (an HBCU infrastructure agenda). He, too, was confident about the ability of HBCUs to shape better citizens.

Two of the three agendas, character and capital, focused on the Black educational infrastructure, as did Johnson's "strengthen Howard and Lincoln" agenda. The inclusion agenda was about removing the barriers to a whites-only educational infrastructure that had been largely built by the profits and labor of the slave economy. Progress on all three agendas, particularly by the end of either Du Bois's color-line century (1900–2000) or Washington's gap-closure century (1915–2015), would largely rely upon the mindsets of African Americans, private philanthropists, and America's strongest democracy advocates.

INSTITUTIONAL CONSIDERATION FOR THE RECORD: TWO MORE TRANSFORMATIONS AND TWO NEGLECTED AGENDAS, 1916–2015

After HBCUs prepared the newly freed African Americans for productive citizenship by leading a scaled literacy effort, they drove the African American rise from poverty and marginality. Those two transformations were a logical result of African Americans gradually assuming more control over their own lives and institutions.

The Du Bois–led rebellions disrupted the HBCU ecosystem in the 1920s and 1930s, forcing changes in the purposes of leadership, trusteeship, curricula, campus culture, and alumni activities. As Wolters put it, "Whatever the intentions of the founders and patrons of the black colleges may have been, many black students and alumni of the 1920s were engaged in a deliberate effort to establish institutional bastions for the assault on segregation and white supremacy."[5] Many of them shifted the infrastructure to be more aggressively purpose driven. Yet a number of HBCU leaders, Black and white, resisted this progressive movement early on, as they remained wary of how lethal it could be to disturb Southern sensibilities.[6] The appearance of using their campuses to prepare disruptors of the Southern status quo still had the power to provoke barbarism. But despite their intense conflicts, HBCU leaders and their protest-minded students also had common ground. Everyone agreed on the need to broaden HBCU curricular offerings beyond the conventional practice of educating teachers and preachers. Late in their first fifty years, a critical mass of these institutions finally began to expand their academic agenda by shaping students for careers in law, science, medicine, and business. And that set the stage for mitigating both poverty and marginality.

OVERVIEW OF TRANSFORMATION TWO: MITIGATING POVERTY, 1916–1969

HBCUs mitigated poverty by systematically educating America's first Black middle class. Its emergence justified the fears of racist Southern whites who were convinced that education would make Blacks unfit for second-class citizenship. But the process took time. Only 4.6 percent of gainfully employed Black workers held white-collar jobs by the end of the 1920s, perhaps largely because only four thousand Blacks had graduated from college by the start of the first World War.[7] Yet HBCU enrollment then increased sixfold, from 2,132 students in 1917 to 13,580 students by 1927.[8] That increase eased but did not erase the financial burden facing most of these institutions. It also expanded the number of African Americans qualified to play new roles in American society. And they kept coming. Black enrollment grew for the next two decades, including HBCU attendees nearly doubling from 1954 to 1966, with those in college-level courses also surging by 1,700 percent.[9]

It made sense that the number of Blacks in poverty began to decline. While the poverty rate among Black families was 87 percent in 1940, it dropped to 47 percent by 1960. President Lyndon B. Johnson's War on Poverty (1964–73) helped reduce Black poverty another seventeen points by 1970.[10] Although half of the collegiate African Americans were enrolled in predominantly white institutions by 1964, HBCUs incubated much of the ambition-driven energy of Black college-goers, as evidenced by having prepared most of the key leaders and foot soldiers of the civil rights movement.

Notably, the productivity of HBCUs in the 1940s through the 1970s provided the earliest high-profile talking points for clarifying and amplifying their value proposition. The flow of new Black professionals enabled the United Negro College Fund (UNCF), a fundraising and advocacy agency of the private HBCUs, to add dimension to its "A mind is a terrible thing to waste" campaign. In the early 1970s, UNCF leaders began to market HBCUs with a series of perception-enhancing facts about the institutions. They touted HBCUs as the source of "more than half of all black elected officials in the United States, 75 percent of the country's black Ph.D.s, and 85 percent of the country's black doctors."[11] Various HBCU advocacy agencies have expanded and evolved that list over the last fifty years, typically as an appeal to those who might invest, yet often without revealing the concrete data that might substantiate the more recent productivity claims.[12] Thus, in addition to enriching the American republic with these and other professionals, and enhancing it with activists for civil rights, the HBCU-dominant transformation of Blacks up from poverty was an effective rebuke to the doubters and deniers of Black brainpower.

OVERVIEW OF TRANSFORMATION THREE: MITIGATING MARGINALITY, 1970–2015

The strategic decisions made by many African Americans in the last half of the twentieth century evolved from mindsets formed in its first half. Not only was Du Bois prescient in pointing to "the color line" as the defining problem of the century, he also wisely highlighted the critical need for HBCUs to be consequential in solving that problem.[13] He expected a talented tenth of African Americans to prioritize that as an HBCU agenda. But too few of them embraced his idea of it, and the twisted roots of mindset development within the Black middle class helps to reveal why.

Once the enrollment in HBCUs began to surge in 1917, the tiny cohorts of new HBCU graduates found jobs and quickly constituted a middle class large enough for E. Franklin Frazier to begin writing about it in 1925.[14] Frazier would make a career of analyzing and critiquing this growing sector, especially in terms of how their social psychological pain tended to be triggered by their estrangement from the white world.[15] For decades, he observed a class of previously excluded people bent on being accepted and welcomed into mainstream America. Their determination to be included made sense. African Americans had admirably defended the country in two World Wars, and, just like other Americans, they aspired to live higher quality lives. But separate had never been equal, especially in the education arena. And for millions of Americans, Black and white, it was axiomatic that only a higher quality education would yield a higher quality life.

But the African American quest to be included was driven by more than a mere desire for quality. By the time Frazier wrote his signature book, *The Black Bourgeoisie*, in 1957, he had spent more than three decades observing and analyzing the choices made by middle-class African Americans. His book featured a compelling critique of their general mindset. He concluded that among the consequences of the Black middle class's futile quest for "White status" was "a quasi-pathological character" provoked by their marginal and unequal existence.[16] As Black leaders fought to realize an egalitarian America, Frazier described an unhealthy outlook among a class of people engaged in a frustrating, decades-long quest for acceptance.

To be fair, their determination to be included resembled a mindset reflective of America's then-emerging culture of aspiration.[17] Like so many other Americans at the time, African Americans eagerly sought opportunities to have productive careers. Through the 1960s, the HBCU campuses, increasingly under both Black presidential control and Black student pressure, became incubators for the leaders of a civil rights movement to desegregate and, thereby, strengthen America. In the context of higher education, that meant utilizing an inclusion mindset to fight a war to end exclusion.

Thus, even if very few African Americans were aware of Johnson's two quests, their mindsets and behavior were less indicative of a duality than a strong preference. To the degree that Black leaders saw themselves as choosing agendas, they minimized the HBCU agenda. They emphasized closing the gap between America's founding, equity-inspired principles and her suffocating, inequitable culture, habits, and systems. In the mindsets and values of many Blacks, being able to attend PWIs was more important than strengthening HBCUs. It was as if they thought African American access to white higher education would always be limited and attendance in Black higher education would always be limiting.

The protracted fight to end marginality featured the NAACP's key legal victories in the 1936 case of *Murray v. Maryland* and the 1954 case of *Brown v. Board of Education of Topeka, Kansas.* Each helped to stimulate the major legislative victories of the 1960s. Even as Black pride and Black power were asserted, they were generally asserted within the context of a respectability-saturated struggle to be included.

Ironically, in the final year of his life, among the reasons why Dr. Martin Luther King, Jr., became very unpopular, especially among liberals and the Black clergy, was his growing doubt about the merits of the intoxicating quest to be included.[18] King had one mindset when he stood by the Lincoln Memorial Reflecting Pool in Washington, DC, in 1963 to share a dream that he described as "deeply rooted in the American dream."[19] But his mindset had shifted by the time he stood at the Riverside Baptist Church in New York City in 1967 when, in his "Beyond Vietnam" speech, he fundamentally questioned America's identity. He was profoundly skeptical about the quest to simply be included in an American empire that appeared to him to be "approaching spiritual death," as long as she was beholden to "the giant triplets of racism, extreme materialism, and militarism."[20] Not many others in the movement had similarly shifted from a poolside mindset to a Riverside mindset—a shift widely understood to have cost King his life.[21]

King's death in 1968 also helped to trigger a surge in Black enrollment on campuses where Blacks had previously been excluded or tokenized. The college-attending rate of Blacks aged eighteen to twenty-four had been 7 percent in 1960, but it more than doubled to 15.5 percent by 1970, and tripled to 22.6 percent by 1976.[22] HBCUs were without the physical or instructional capacity to handle that kind of surge. And because they were also without the resources to compete for the best Black minds, what had often been referred to as "the Black brain drain" was well underway. For example, in 1967, Blacks represented a mere 2.3 percent of the students enrolled in Ivy League institutions, but their percentage doubled by 1970 and tripled by 1974. Similarly, the Black presence more than tripled in "other prestigious" institutions during that same period, with new and sizable surges in Black enrollment on many predominantly white campuses in September 1969.[23]

A wider-angle view of this evolution reveals that Washington's century began with over 90 percent of the African Americans in higher education being educated inside of HBCUs, but it ended with over 90 percent being educated outside of HBCUs (see chapter 9).

In retrospect, Johnson's inclusion agenda was a quantitative success. And, unfortunately, diversifying white institutions featured more than simply the recruitment of the top Black academic students. They also targeted the top Black faculty and athletes, who might otherwise have found their way to HBCUs.[24]

What could be described as a final phase of the inclusion agenda is the movement to go beyond mere diversity to focus on the quality of the experiences of Blacks and other minoritized students on campuses where they had been previously excluded. Once the new African American presence began to jell in the 1970s, campus-based racial incidents, ranging from violence to microaggressions, increased dramatically. It worsened as "the conservative Reagan era of the 1980s seemed to open a Pandora's box of racist behavior on college campuses, all designed to denigrate African Americans."[25] By 1988, the campus racial climate warranted a *Frontline* focus on the PBS network. A 1990 Report from the National Institute Against Prejudice and Violence estimated that nearly a million American college students were victims of ethnoviolence annually.[26] Later, in 2001, the Department of Justice produced a report showing that campus racism had persisted, and the physical and emotional safety of students from groups previously excluded remained questionable.[27] Racial strife in white higher education continued to prove disruptive on multiple campuses, eventually warranting a 2014 independent film, *Dear White People*, which became a Netflix series in 2017.

Almost fifty years after the Black presence in white higher education began to stabilize in the early 1970s, the perceived intractability of campus racial unrest began to stabilize in American popular culture. The diversity was sustained, the challenges persisted, and many white institutions bolstered their inclusion and belonging initiatives, ostensibly to improve the campus experiences for all students.

THE NEGLECT OF AN HBCU INFRASTRUCTURE AGENDA

Even if unfinished, the inclusion quest clearly benefited from all the focus it received. By contrast, Du Bois's character agenda suffered. He expected HBCUs to help provoke the "utter disappearance of color discrimination in American life and the preservation of African history and culture."[28] The history and culture agenda was to be campus based, which was almost impossible while enduring institutional precarity. Du Bois's grasp of that predicament provoked his fruitless suggestion that African Americans provide "not a tenth, but a quarter of their income to support education."[29]

And that is why the capital optimization agenda is so key. HBCU fundraising and endowments are examined more closely in chapters 8 and 9. For now, it is worth considering Tuskegee's endowment growth relative to those it had outperformed by 1915. Figure 5.1 reveals that, after most of the top liberal arts institutions of 2015 took an average of nearly a half century longer than Tuskegee to reach the $2 million endowment mark, they each now dwarf Tuskegee and all other HBCUs a century later.

Beyond their average endowments exceeding $1.2 billion, nearly 75 percent of the institutions listed have completed capital campaigns of more than $400 million. By 2015, no HBCU had yet sustainably benefited from such transformational levels of philanthropic support.

The next three chapters will outline some of the things HBCUs can do to improve their prospects. But since a bright future for HBCUs will likely require a new mindset in much of the philanthropic community, several key issues deserve focus.

INSTITUTIONAL QUESTION FOR THE FUTURE: CAN A REEXAMINATION OF THE ROOTS OF AMERICAN PHILANTHROPY STIMULATE SELF-EXAMINATION BY TODAY'S PHILANTHROPISTS?

The institutional resource gap widened, in part, because HBCUs have not yet attracted and sustained a flow of the sizable philanthropic investments that are now a norm in competitive higher education circles. From the start, HBCUs received smaller transactional gifts, rather than scaled transformational

FIGURE 5.1 Tuskegee endowment relative to others by 2015

INSTITUTION	# OF YEARS TO $2M	2015 ENDOWMENT
1 Williams College	167	$2.4B
2 Amherst College	88	$2.2B
3 Pomona College	39	$2.1B
4 Wellesley College	40	$1.9B
5 Swarthmore College	56	$1.8B
6 Grinnell College	85	$1.8B
7 Smith College	48	$1.8B
8 Bowdoin College	110	$1.4B
9 Vassar College	60	$983M
10 Hamilton College	132	$856M
11 Oberlin College	79	$832M
12 Carleton College	59	$785M
13 Colby College	122	$746M
14 Mount Holyoke College	84	$700M
15 Davidson College	114	$683M
16 Furman College	98	$631M
17 Bates College	86	$262M
18 **Tuskegee University**	34	$120M

| | 1800 | 1850 | 1900 | 1950 |

Sources: Data on the year institutions reached the $2 million endowment level comes from the archives of each institution. Data for 2015 endowments is from the *Chronicle of Higher Education Almanac* (Washington, DC: Chronicle, 2016), 54–55.

investments. The relatively meager private giving to HBCUs can be explained in part by a history of negative perceptions about their investment worthiness.

HBCU leaders and advocates bear the primary responsibility for addressing the skepticism many seem to have about their value proposition and investment worthiness. But since the problem may also lie in the mindset of the beholder, it makes sense to consider what mindset advice to the phil-anthropic community might make a meaningful difference in the prospects for the movement of selected HBCUs up from precarity. Investing to enable optimization is very different from giving to enable survival.

HBCUs are unlikely to conquer precarity without an evolution in the mindsets of the most consequential members of America's philanthropic com-munity. Thus, for their consideration, these three perspectives are designed as mindset shift advice, the goal of which is to trigger a new conversation between key leaders of HBCUs and American philanthropists.

THE NEED TO GRAPPLE WITH THE BIRTH DEFECT
OF AMERICAN PHILANTHROPY

If it is true that "a change in perspective is worth 100 points of IQ," then today's American philanthropists might consider a new perspective on the protracted patterns of giving set by the benefactors who preceded them.[30] A new perspective on the past and future impact of philanthropy may add a new strategic intelligence to their current decision-making. Two key perspective shifts warrant serious consideration.

First, today's philanthropists should reconsider the origins of the nation's philanthropic enterprise. It has been said that America was born with a "birth defect" called slavery.[31] For reasonable people, it is self-evident that two and a half centuries of human enslavement and terrorism have helped to yield lasting effects in the quality of American life. As of 2023, it remains the case that African Americans were enslaved (1619–1863, or 244 years) for longer than they have been free (1863–2023, or 160 years) in America. Moreover, a subsequent century of Jim Crow laws worsened an already un-American set of racial disparities in health, education, employment, housing, wealth, and life expectancy. In fact, most American adults agree that "the legacy of slavery affects the position of Black people in American society today."[32] Yet, not unlike America's congenital malformation, the earliest philanthropy to-ward higher education was similarly defective at birth. Regarding the impact of slave economy wealth and the origins and early advancement of American higher education, Wilder asserts:

> In the decades before the American Revolution, merchants and planters became
> not just the benefactors of colonial society but its new masters. Slaveholders

became college presidents. The wealth of the traders determined the locations and decided the fates of colonial schools. Profits from the sale and purchase of human beings paid for campuses and swelled college trusts. And the politics of the campus conformed to the presence and demands of slaveholding students as colleges aggressively cultivated a social environment attractive to the sons of wealthy families.[33]

Since the mindsets at the foundation of American philanthropy were apparently shaped by slave economy instincts, how likely is it that those original mindsets continue to cast a long shadow of influence over the subsequent decision-making of philanthropists? The institutional racial gaps in higher education have likely persisted and widened solely or largely because of the long shadow associated with that original birth defect. Could today's philanthropists be the unwitting heirs of that tradition? Might they now consider a set of creative ways to shift their giving from being a driver of gap expansion to being a driver of gap closure?

Charitable donations to all colleges and universities in fiscal year 2015 totaled a record $40.3 billion. As has annually been the case for decades, the already wealthy top twenty institutions attracted $11.56 billion, or 29 percent of the total.[34] A mindset shift by today's philanthropists, based on a reconsideration of what may be inherited tendencies, may help to elevate the $316 million raised by all HBCUs in 2015, which was less than 1 percent of the overall total.

Today's philanthropists need to pause and consider their own responsibility for the tradition of depressed giving to HBCUs over time. More than likely, the box holding or imprisoning HBCUs was originally constructed by America's first philanthropists, or by those who made African Americans the commodities of their transactional mindsets so long ago. Seeing HBCUs exclusively in the same transactional terms today simply preserves that history. Alternatively, grasping the transformational capacity of select HBCUs and then investing in them accordingly, can, at once, help to create a new future while countering and rebuking the toxic racial inequities that yet persist.

THE NEED TO INTERROGATE AMERICA'S POPULAR HBCU-FREE DEFINITION OF PROGRESS

A second reason why HBCU leaders have tended to encounter transactional rather than transformational thinking relates to the definition of progress shared by many Americans. It is not unusual for some of the most well-meaning white Americans to wonder aloud why HBCUs continue to exist more than fifty years after Blacks became eligible to be admitted by the previously segregated institutions where they qualified for admission. Therefore, they ask, why has the appearance of desegregation not yet provoked the disappearance of HBCUs? Moreover, why invest in HBCUs, if it is only a matter of time before many or most of them will eventually close or be absorbed into larger, more solvent institutions?

In other words, they see the very existence of HBCUs as an anachronistic or contradictory thing.

This mindset was quite evident in the immediate aftermath of the 1954 *Brown* case. As a compelling pivot toward desegregation, that consequential decision created profound doubts about the sustainability of all race-based educational environments. While so many people in the country were focused on the social implications of the decision, HBCU leaders became immediately concerned about its philanthropic implications. In fact, HBCU officials had every reason to be shaken by John D. Rockefeller Jr.'s comments in response to *Brown*. According to one of Rockefeller's associates, upon hearing about the decision, he said, "We won't need the United Negro College Fund or any of the member colleges. That means I won't have to serve on the board anymore and we won't have to raise any money anymore."[35] By extending a family tradition of HBCU support, Rockefeller had been one of the biggest donors to the UNCF. Yet if it was that easy for such a close ally to abandon the entire HBCU cause at the first sign of desegregation, what chance had HBCU presidents with the rest of the philanthropic community?

The head of the UNCF and president of Tuskegee, Frederick D. Patterson, described Rockefeller's response as "a wave," or a common view among Northern white donors.[36] Thus, UNCF leaders could not be faulted for suspecting that their attempts to engage wealthy white Americans might now become both discouraged and discouraging. To an aspiring HBCU world, this was a potentially catastrophic form of philanthropic climate change. If HBCUs were perceived as unworthy of significant support, their leaders had no chance at enhancing their competitiveness. And if the very existence of HBCUs was incompatible with how many donors defined "progress," how could HBCU leaders then convince them to continue providing any support at all, much less make the coveted shift from smaller incremental transactional gifts to scaled multiyear transformational investments?

Marybeth Gasman referenced "the stigma placed on all-black environments in the post-Brown era," to explain the presumption, in and beyond the philanthropic community, that HBCUs were inferior.[37] The test of HBCU investment worthiness would soon come when the UNCF tried a larger scale campaign in 1962, more than two decades before major capital campaigning became a norm in American higher education. Even after adjusting down from the $100 million they originally imagined raising, the effort failed. Morehouse College president Benjamin E. Mays assessed the failure, saying, "Even with the prestige of President John F. Kennedy behind the effort, the Presidents of thirty-three United Negro College Fund colleges could not get anyone to head a drive to raise a hundred million dollars for all of these colleges. The goal we had to accept was fifty million, and we raised only thirty million. The University of Chicago recently raised a hundred and sixty million dollars in three years. The Negro is truly the invisible man."[38]

While the *Brown* decision was a major victory for the inclusion agenda, it also revealed a stunning superficiality in the donor community's commitment to the vitality and longevity of HBCUs. The tension between Johnson's inclusion agenda and his HBCU agenda gradually became frighteningly clear. If too many Americans, Black and white, saw the two as contradictory, then HBCUs would be truly disadvantaged when donors chose between the two. HBCU leaders had to imagine and anticipate that white donors might eventually prefer to help their own predominantly white alma maters to become more diverse rather than fund the dreams of a Black college.

As it turned out, the sluggish pace of integration kept most donors from an immediate, *Brown*-related abandonment of HBCUs. But it is also true that the scaled investments to HBCUs, which *Brown* made much harder for many to imagine, were never realized within Washington's century. It is not unreasonable to think that the lingering HBCU-free definition of progress held by many philanthropists will continue to hurt these institutions.

Today's philanthropic community is challenged to consider HBCUs as a legitimate and special class of institutions, worthy of a boost in capacity and value. The pathway to deciding to invest might resemble the logic behind their decisions to invest in other institutions with unique identities, different voices, or special missions. Such institutions include Brandeis (Jewish), Notre Dame (Catholic), Liberty (evangelical), and Brigham Young (Mormon), as well as campuses like Wellesley (women) and Hampden-Sydney (men). Today's HBCU leaders are challenged to develop and convey an alternative and compelling definition of progress, in which select HBCUs not only still exist, but become much stronger and far more consequential in shaping a new and better world. The move from transactional gifts to transformational investments will likely depend on both challenges being met. The goal of shaping better citizens should never be lost.

THE NEED FOR PHILANTHROPISTS TO SHIFT THEIR VIEW FROM THE HBCU FOREST TO THE HBCU TREES

A third reason why transactional private giving has been the typical outcome of HBCU engagements with philanthropists is tied to the unfortunate way in which many people persistently misperceive these institutions as an amalgam. That is, many donors and observers view and treat HBCUs as a whole, rather than as a sum of separate and separable parts. They only see HBCUs as a forest, rather than seeing or engaging with the individual HBCU trees that dwell in America's diverse higher education forest.

This misperception matters, and it can be especially costly because the publicity about HBCUs has traditionally been largely negative. As a result, many individual HBCUs must face the tougher task of overcoming what often ends up being negative and sweeping judgment against the entire sector. An analysis of how the mainstream media portrays HBCUs concluded, "Perhaps the most serious problem with media coverage is the tendency to report the direst circumstances at HBCUs and then portray these circumstances as the norm. . . . The notion that HBCUs 'never measure up' or are a 'lost cause' permeates the media narrative, and as a result, the general public, the higher-education community, and even some African Americans have negative perceptions of HBCUs."[39]

Blurring the distinctions between Black institutions is akin to blurring those between Black individuals. Both blurrings can have negative consequences. Just as stereotyped inferiority helps to widen academic achievement gaps, often to the disadvantage of women and minorities, the stereotyped inferiority of all HBCUs in the mindsets of donors may still be helping to widen the wealth gaps between institutions.[40] What is often a more impressive truth about individual HBCUs can be rendered inaccessible by the volume of negative stereotypes about the group. A pattern of unflattering HBCU publicity can confirm the instincts of a philanthropist who is already disinclined to provide a transformational investment.

This is not entirely the fault of the American media. One decades-long disadvantage that individual HBCUs have is the blurring impact of having been *collectively* marketed and sold to America's philanthropic community *as a forest*. There is little question that the UNCF was a timely, desperately needed, and effective agent for the sustenance of HBCUs, at and long after its launch in 1944. There is indeed a cogent argument that can be made for the persistence of the forest-style fundraising of both the UNCF, for privately funded HBCUs, and the Thurgood Marshall College Fund (TMCF), for publicly funded HBCUs. But an unfortunate by-product of that consolidated approach is to condition the mindsets of the wealthy to think of HBCUs collectively, rather than individually. That is problematic, since the value proposition that matters most is that of the stand-alone HBCU trees, or institutions, as contrasted with the entire HBCU forest.

Forest-style fundraising is, empirically and by definition, incremental. The multibillion-dollar gift has not yet arrived in higher education, nor is it likely to target a consortium. If it did, it would have to be in the tens of billions of dollars to make a real difference. Apart from the $40 million gift from Apple to TMCF in 2015, no real meaningful movement from the transactional mode occurred between 1915 and 2015.[41] Whenever it finally happens, it will be most consequential at the institutional, or tree level, rather than at the forest level.

And that is why the next three chapters offer mindset advice on what individual institutions can do to attract the kind of transformational investments that can measurably close the resource gap. Beyond amplifying an investment-worthy value proposition, HBCUs must also optimize both their trusteeship and their advancement capacity.

FOR THE MINDSET

Philanthropists should shift their transformational investments to institutions that are already excelling at shaping better citizens, and to those with aggressive plans to do so.

CHAPTER SIX

The Unheralded Value

The Negro Academy ought to sound a note of warning that would echo in every black cabin in the land: unless we conquer our present vices, they will conquer us.

W. E. B. Du Bois, "The Conservation of Races," 1897

Those who learn to read the signs around them and to hear the language of the universe reach a kind of knowledge healers call the shadow. The shadow, because that kind of knowledge follows you everywhere. When you find it, it is not difficult at all. It says there are two forces, unity and division. The first creates. The second destroys.

Ayi Kwei Armah, *The Healers*

From the start, HBCUs have had a low signal-to-noise ratio—that is, the noise of their vices has tended to be louder than the signal of their virtues. People have known more about their deficiencies than their efficiencies, leaving them either devalued or undervalued. This has obscured their measurable ability to shape larger numbers of better citizens, relative to non-HBCUs.

When considering HBCUs, those with a growth mindset will tend to focus more on their virtues. They will understand that, while many HBCUs have characteristics in common, they are not all the same. Recognizing that, they will be both quicker to grasp what these institutions have endured and more open to imagining how they might realize their full potential, thereby optimizing their outcomes. Regrettably, those with mindsets formed and fixed by conventional narratives will focus more on HBCU vices. Tending to blur institutional distinctions with stereotypes, they will be quicker to define HBCUs by their faults, and they will be inclined to wonder aloud why they should survive. Mindsets drive whether Black lives, individually or institutionally, matter.

What has been the unheralded value of HBCUs?

At their best, these distinctly American institutions have been a productive and valuable sector of the world's strongest and most diverse system of higher education. HBCUs owe their birth to the rawest forces of human will and determination. They owe their survival to the truest forces of human duty and devotion. They are peerless examples of the power of patriotism, since a multiracial team of Americans worked together to create and advance an educational response to the devastating national crime of chattel slavery. Largely resulting from those efforts, HBCUs became the primary agencies for the transformation and elevation of a previously dehumanized race confined, by law, to a multigenerational dungeon of illiteracy. These institutions authored three African American transformations—up from illiteracy, poverty, and marginality. In the process, they nurtured a movement that continues to challenge America to finally *become* America. That HBCU work remains immensely unheralded and incredibly unrewarded.

What have been the unwarranted hardships of HBCUs?

At their worst, based on a small set of poignant and relative circumstances, if American higher education were a city, HBCUs would resemble the rougher, underserved side of town. Many of the same forces that successfully dehumanized Black individuals also ensured the precarity of Black institutions. And while many HBCUs have performed well, they have remained a largely separate and unequal sector. Most have small endowments and enrollments, preserved, in part, by small advancement and admissions teams. Many faculty are underpaid and overworked in facilities where deferred maintenance is not uncommon. These and related conditions form a stubborn HBCU precarity that has generated an abiding, multifaceted competitive disadvantage.

MINDSET AND PERCEPTION

The general question of whether some HBCUs can be regarded as a select class or whether they remain clustered in an underclass is a consequential mindset choice—a choice that is also false and imprecise. HBCUs can and should occasionally be appreciated as a group, given their collective historical role in American society. Yet, while many continue to share virtues and values at the group level, as highlighted in the previous chapter, any transformational investment they attract will arrive based on their value at the institutional level.

This suggests that each institution's leadership team should ask a set of logical questions. For instance, what makes our college or university distinctive? What is virtuous and therefore magnetic about our institution? What value proposition could our institution identify, clarify, and amplify to sustainably shift the mindsets of potential investors? Is there an unheralded value somewhere inside of our institution that is somehow waiting to be recovered, uncovered, or discovered? And could that unheralded value become the core of a new case statement for the pursuit of an investment-rich future?

These and similar questions require institutions to probe and clarify their own essence, character, and purpose. Within the campus communities that thoughtfully explore such questions lies the substance for completing the statement, "If we did not exist, here is why we would have to be invented . . ." In a sense, this was Du Bois's fondest desire for HBCUs. He wanted them to be the primary agencies for completing the same "vast work of self-reformation" and "striving" he carefully outlined at the start of his career.[1] Du Bois believed that African and African American character was destined to be imparted as a gift to the world. He thought this important work would justify their existence and underscore HBCU's investment worthiness.[2] If Du Bois is correct, and there is yet a unique, unheralded, or undiscovered value that HBCUs have yet to fully realize, then it is the world's loss if HBCUs disappear en masse.

But this has happened before. An entire set of Black institutions with a distinctive approach was lost, in part because their leaders were unable to clarify and leverage their value proposition for the right investors at the right time. Nor was there a concerted effort to recover that which was lost. And since the disappearance of a unique Black enterprise with unheralded value has happened before, it is worth illuminating some of the lessons for their relevance to HBCUs today.

The persistent precarity of HBCUs suggests that their fate in the first half of the twenty-first century could soon resemble that of Negro League Baseball (NLB) in the last half of the twentieth century. Given that, some key NLB lessons deserve consideration.

INSTITUTIONAL CONSIDERATION FOR THE RECORD:
THE DISAPPEARANCE OF A UNIQUE BLACK INSTITUTION

Black professional baseball was no insignificant operation in America. Launched in 1920, it became a $4 million annual business by 1944. It surpassed the talent convergence and rivaled the drawing power of white professional baseball. Some NLB teams drew twenty to fifty thousand fans to each game.[3] NLB leaders managed to shape a different world with its own virtues and vices. While the enterprise had voice and the players had pride, the League could not clarify, amplify, and leverage enough of its distinctive value to escape precarity. Nor could they match the stable lifestyle and influence of Major League Baseball (MLB). As a result, the League gradually moved toward final closure in 1960.

Two forces played a meaningful role in the League's demise, and they might inform the strategic thinking of HBCU leaders today.

QUALITY-OF-LIFE DIFFERENCES

First, although the League was victimized by the same presumption of Black inferiority that victimized many Black institutions and individuals at the time, there were stark, practical differences between MLB and NLB life. Those resource advantages and better conditions clearly motivated much of the African American quest for MLB entry. The better salaries, facilities, schedules, and management resulted in a better overall lifestyle.

Among the players who were drawn to the more well-appointed MLB lifestyle was Jackie Robinson, who became a major critic of the gap between the two leagues. Ironically, just before he started with the NLB's Kansas City Monarchs, Robinson served as athletic director for Samuel Huston College, an HBCU located in Austin, Texas. His time there was as brief as his tenure with the Monarchs, for whom he played not even one whole season before joining the Brooklyn Dodgers in 1947. Within the first year of his MLB debut, Robinson candidly exposed many of the League's troubles in a June 1948 *Ebony* magazine cover story, "What's Wrong with Negro Baseball?"[4] He offered a long litany of deficiencies, including sloppy umpiring, low salaries, corrupt leadership, uncomfortable buses, cheap hotels, and poor team budgeting. While Black ballplayers would eventually discover that MLB life was not ideal, Robinson felt it provided relief from the taxing deficiencies of NLB life.

Unsurprisingly, the differences between MLB and NLB lifestyles echo many of the stark, wealth-driven differences between HBCUs and many PWIs. Also unsurprisingly, drawn by those differences, many African Americans preferred accessing the Harvards and Yales, rather than bolstering the Howards and Lincolns.

MINDSET DIFFERENCES ABOUT INSTITUTIONAL WORTH

Second, a number of African Americans were uncertain about the value of their own institutions. Two seemingly contradictory mindsets gained traction. Representing one mindset was Mal Goode, a pioneering Black reporter who covered baseball and became the first Black correspondent on network television news in 1962. Goode opined on the racial gaps in sports, journalism, and society. In addition to seeing the resource gap, he emphasized the psychological angle on the League's demise at the start of MLB integration, saying, "We gained something, but we lost something, too. But what we gained was the greater. We got our self-respect, and you have to be black to understand that."[5] With that comment, Goode represented a point of view shared by many other African Americans who believed the self-respect available in the Negro League was, like the lifestyle, subpar or insufficient, compared to MLB conditions and self-respect. In this mindset, the end of segregation would immediately dissolve the League's reason for being, and this could be seen as an entirely logical and desirable outcome.[6]

Conversely, other African Americans thought the League had established its own unique value proposition, making it worthy to last for decades, perhaps forever. They saw better baseball being played by men with more speed, skill, power, and charisma. When NLB and MLB teams played exhibition games, the NLB teams typically won, and they embarrassed the MLB teams "with disturbing frequency."[7] The distinctive play excited a swelling fandom and made the League's disappearance especially difficult for some. Novelist John Edgar Wideman, holding a viewpoint opposite that of Mal Goode, said, "Losing institutions that have that long a life and play that crucial a role in the community . . . it's very worrisome. . . . What was contained in those institutions was not simply a Black version of what white people were doing, but the game was played differently."[8]

Highlighting each mindset, William C. Rhoden argues that the death of the League was tragically symbolized by two men: Rube Foster, known as "the Father of Black Baseball," who built it using Black wealth, and Jackie Robinson.[9] Like others, Foster anticipated integration, just based on the NLB quality of play, but "his theory was that the league's strongest teams would be absorbed intact, not picked apart like a carcass by so many buzzards."[10] He continued:

> The two men represented the same general ideals: integration and empowerment. But Robinson did not realize the complex effects of segregation on black and white communities, and failed to balance the goals of integration and empowerment. In the end, he achieved one without the other.[11]

Robinson symbolized integration, which succeeded. Foster symbolized Black institutional empowerment, which was never optimized, perhaps because it was perceived by far too many people as a contradictory thing. Many Black players followed Robinson, but a great deal of Black talent was abandoned, as was a unique approach to the game.

The two mindsets about institutional worth are key in understanding perceptions of the HBCU world. Some have a version of the fixed, Goode-Robinson mindset that sees HBCUs as poor imitations of PWIs, instantly rendered obsolete once desegregation began its sluggish entry into America's reality. Others, having a Wideman-Foster growth mindset, recognize that HBCUs generally originated a fundamentally distinctive approach to education that is worthy of longevity. But, as with the NLB, the arrival of integration in American higher education was somehow positioned as substitutional for the cause of HBCU empowerment, rather than supplemental to it. A bright future for these institutions depends on the ability of their leadership to fruitfully engage and expand their growth-mindset allies worldwide in order to finally shift the gaze of their aspiration to the empowerment of select HBCUs in all of their organic uniqueness.

THE LEAGUE-LEVEL HBCU VALUE PROPOSITION

A final analogy between the NLB and HBCUs involves the optimal location of their essential worth. The NLB value proposition had three tiers—the league, the teams, and the individual players. For comparison purposes, the league is the equivalent of HBCUs as a group, each team is the equivalent of a stand-alone HBCU, and the players are akin to the most talented HBCU faculty, students, athletes, or staff. In their pursuit of marketability, HBCUs and their advocates have, over time, maximized the focus on the league level, minimized the focus on the institutional level, and been victimized by an external focus on the individual level. This persistent pattern has been ruinous for HBCUs.

Nearly every HBCU can lay claim to the league-level value proposition. It is grounded in the protracted role of HBCUs in positioning Blacks to build a better America while emerging from the gloomy past authored by America's lesser angels. From the start, HBCUs assumed an institutional posture that made them different from all other colleges and universities, before or since. The arc of the original HBCU value proposition was bent toward the realization of freedom and justice for all, which means it privileged an America that would no longer be disjointed from its founding principles, but reflective of them. Thus, HBCUs, by definition, were premised, created, and functioned in accordance with a deeply and uniquely American DNA.

With few exceptions, the antebellum colleges cannot lay claim to such a tradition of intentionally educating graduates to realize democracy for all.[12] How could they? After emancipation, most HBCU graduates toiled for more than a century to transform a world that was shaped or abided by the graduates of these colleges and their similarly segregated counterparts.[13] HBCUs were obviously producing people with very different mindsets about what constitutes a meaningful or successful life. Their earliest leaders knew their graduates would not have the same options as other college graduates, so they had to prepare and commission them differently. In those initial and subsequent leadership, pedagogical, and campus differences resides the shared, foundational, and league-level value proposition of HBCUs.

HBCU graduates led the push for full American citizenship. As the institutions matured, they more openly shaped mindsets to help transform the nation toward a freedom that had been broadly preached but not yet practiced as self-evidently true.

This transformative freedom quest prioritized servant leadership. As early as 1875, when Booker T. Washington graduated from the Hampton Institute, he and his thirty-eight classmates received a culminating mandate to "Go out, boys and girls! Bear aloft the banner of your Institute. Don't be satisfied until in every one of these southern states there is a Hampton. Don't be so mean as to go out and use these advantages for yourselves: use them for your people."[14]

Similarly, as Du Bois moved toward his commencement from Fisk University in 1888, his "sense of mission was fully evident in his senior year. Fisk was basic training for combat, and Fiskites were to provide the officer corps."[15] Countless HBCU students were bolstered with racial pride to counteract the racist disparagement throughout society. They were also commissioned to "uplift the race," and counteract the persistent Jim Crow–style second-class citizenship that awaited them.

Through much of their first century, these valuable and affirming HBCU-based calls to duty resided mostly in what Ben Snyder would later describe as the "hidden curriculum."[16] That is, rather than being openly outlined on any syllabus, they were the nonacademic expectations, truths, insights, and values that were effectively infused into the culture or fabric of the teaching and learning experiences. They functioned as encouraging guideposts for student success, especially beyond the classroom. In the case of HBCUs, these signals were initially hidden because they were dangerous. As Jelani Favors points out, "With Black colleges assuming a nonthreatening posture and the notion of higher education evoking momentary civility from aggressive whites, it appeared that no community, southern or otherwise, found reason to annihilate Black college campuses or lynch faculty and administrators who seemingly kept Black youths in step with the white supremacists' agenda."[17] In other words, they veiled their mission-driven character and messaging in order to manage and keep at bay the reign of racial terror that surrounded many HBCU campuses.

Logically, the partial lifting of this veil was yet another benefit of the Du Bois–led campus rebellions of the 1920s and 1930s. Not only did the protests help to shift the complexion of the leadership from white to Black, and the culture of the campuses from extremely restrictive to just very restrictive, but it also eventually shifted the largely hidden curriculum to a more open one. Black students, young alumni, and several key intellectuals became similarly impatient with some of the new Black leaders from the 1930s through the 1950s. A particularly poignant example of this came from the Lincoln University–educated Langston Hughes, who visited fifty HBCUs and generated an assessment that symbolized the frustration of many.[18] In 1934, he summarized his two-year tour of HBCUs and explained, "To set foot on dozens of Negro campuses is like going back to mid-Victorian England, or Massachusetts in the days of the witch-burning Puritans."[19] Hughes thought the HBCU leadership focus on conduct was clearly at the expense of deepening critical student thought, and he concluded, "American Negroes in the future had best look to the unlettered for their leaders, and expect only cowards from the colleges."[20]

In addition to Hughes and Du Bois, scores of Black students, intellectuals, and alumni activists opined openly and negatively about suboptimal and repressive conditions at HBCUs. The many voices and stories often revealed a generational tug of war between educating to abide or fight the color line.[21] The 1960s ended that phase of the tug of war. Multiple Black college campuses became boot camps, preparing students to fight in a new movement for justice. So, it was logical that "by the end of the summer of 1960, over 70,000 students had taken an active part in disruptive civil rights demonstrations."[22] Some of the key leaders of this movement are listed in table 6.1.

As Favors put it, "Black colleges produced a wave of foot soldiers unlike anything the burgeoning movement had ever seen. The explosion of student activism in 1960 was no accident or anomaly. It was indeed a development long in the making."[23] Most of the people who quietly and openly led the gradual transformation of American society from the 1950s through the 1970s were HBCU students and graduates.

They used sit-ins, speeches, marches, occupations, boycotts, and numerous other forms of protest and nonviolent civil disobedience to call attention to the disjuncture between American ideals and American life. They risked their careers and lives to improve the life chances for others, if not for themselves. Beyond those listed above, tens of thousands of others, Black and white, have remained anonymous and unheralded, but were no less brave.

The greatness and goodness of HBCUs was wrapped up in the steady production of civic-minded graduates. These outcomes have been fundamental to the general HBCU identity.

Unfortunately, HBCUs continue to be unheralded for their virtuous, decades-long tradition of using their various curricula and culture to incubate a movement designed to finally shift America beyond its birth defect–borne hobble. For reasons grounded in this broad value proposition, HBCUs should be widely regarded as a cohort of uniquely American institutions. But, as vital as it is, this league-level value proposition should never be confused as the primary driver of individual HBCUs on the pathway to optimization.

TABLE 6.1 A sampling of HBCU key alumni architects of a new America

HBCU Attended	Leader	Year Graduated/ Attended
Alabama State University	Fred Shuttlesworth	1951
Alcorn A&M College	Medgar W. Evers	1952
Benedict College	Septima P. Clark	1942
Fisk University	Nikki Giovanni	1967
Fisk University	John Lewis	1967
Fisk University	W. E. B. Du Bois	1888
Fisk University	Ida B. Wells	Classes, 1884
Fisk University	Diane Nash	1956
Hampton Institute	Booker T. Washington	1875
Howard University	Zora Neale Hurston	1918–1924
Howard University	Ossie Davis	1935–1938
Howard University	Edward Brooke	1919
Howard University	Andrew Young, Jr.	1951
Kentucky State University	Whitney M. Young, Jr.	1941
Lincoln University	Langston Hughes	1929
Lincoln University	Thurgood Marshall	1930
Morehouse College	Martin Luther King, Jr.	1944
Morehouse College	Julian Bond	1957
Morehouse College	Lonnie King	1969
Morgan State University	Earl G. Graves	1958
Morris Brown College	Hosea Williams	1947
North Carolina A&T University	Jesse Jackson	1961–1964
North Carolina Central University	Julius Chambers	1962
Shaw University	Ella Josephine Baker	1927
Shorter and Philander Smith Colleges	Daisy Lee Gatson Bates	Classes, 1940s–50s
Spelman College	Marian Wright Edelman	1960
Spelman College	Alice Walker	1965
Tuskegee University	Lonnie Johnson	1973
Virginia Union University	Charles Sherrod	1958
West Virginia State University	Katherine Johnson	1937

THE UNHERALDED INSTITUTION-LEVEL VALUE PROPOSITION

Value proposition ambiguity beneath the league level is the central reason for the NLB demise, and it represents the biggest threat to individual HBCUs today.

When Wideman asserts, "In those institutions [teams] . . . the game was played differently," he is pointing to what might have been regarded as the most important asset or value proposition—the one at the team level, rather than at the League or individual level. Wideman wisely recognized that the core value was in the artistry of the team play, which yielded handsome re-sults. Rhoden described it as "the fast-paced, daredevil, 'Africanized' style of play that became the league's resonating, rousing signature . . . characterized by exciting, daring base running, spikes-first slides into second base, and bun-ting for base hits . . . a showcase of this Black style of ball, distinguished by nonstop rhythm."[24]

The NLB teams died largely because the value of NLB team play was never optimized, elevated, or leveraged. And none received a transformation-enabling investment.

This failure to optimize the institutional value proposition continues to sting HBCUs. It provokes a default focus either at the league level, where the League suffered from MLB resource comparisons, or at the individual player level, where MLB leaders focused. The MLB focus on the individual NLB superstars (Jackie Robinson, Larry Doby, Dan Bankhead, etc.) ignored the power of the NLB game. Similarly, the leaders of predominantly white colleges and universities focused on recruiting the best individual HBCU faculty, ath-letes, and students, and with the same effect. They pursued the HBCU players but disregarded the HBCU game.

So, how might HBCUs elevate and leverage their institution-level value proposition?

INSTITUTIONAL QUESTION FOR THE FUTURE: HOW CAN DEMOCRACY-ENRICHING INSTITUTIONS SECURE INVESTMENTS SUFFICIENT FOR OPTIMIZATION?

Drawing upon the foundational HBCU value proposition, each HBCU must determine the specific differentiating features of its own institutional value proposition. The campus-level value is grounded in whatever distinguishes one institution's approach to educating students from that of others. It is often indicated by the achievements of their alumni, which explains the HBCU pride about the impact of the graduates listed in table 6.1.

Building on the foundation set by the earliest graduates, the HBCU output has continued to feature innovators and pioneers, such as Tuskegee University's Lonnie Johnson (engineer, inventor), Tennessee State University's Oprah Winfrey (entertainment pioneer), Morehouse College's Spike Lee (pioneering innovator in film) and Paul Judge (innovator in cybersecurity), Spelman College's Stacey Abrams (innovator in Southern politics), and Howard University's Kamala Harris (vice president of the United States). If appropriately leveraged, stories like these will form the new and robust institution-based value proposition that can help some HBCUs to finally emerge from precarity and uncertainty.

Colleges and universities are known by the fruit they bear. Over time, how each institution prepares citizens to make a life and a living constitutes its value to humanity. Choices made by the institution's leaders will establish patterns and themes in the lives of their graduates. Leadership choices will also convey an institutional identity and image to various campus stakeholders, especially among those who consider enrollment or investment. The stakes are not trivial.

Given that all HBCUs are heirs of this shared foundational value proposition, how might each campus go about clarifying their more vital institutional value proposition?

Two critical priorities will help to position the leaders of HBCUs and other aspiring institutions for a more promising future, based on sharpening their institutional value proposition enough to galvanize their real and potential stakeholders. Like growth mindset stimulants, they are designed to provoke discussions among the leadership teams of each institution about their value proposition and their signal-to-noise ratio. At least one recommended pathway to a compelling answer is provided, while recognizing that each institution will choose its own approach and arrive at its own set of answers, drawn largely from their institutional history and trajectory. The aim here is to be suggestive in motivating each campus community to grapple with a single, pivotal question:

What would be lost, and to whom would it matter, if our HBCU disappeared?

DEVELOPING A CLEARER, INVESTMENT-WORTHY VALUE PROPOSITION

As measured by a long history of scarce contributions from donors in the highest echelon of the philanthropic marketplace, the value proposition for most HBCUs is insufficiently clear, compelling, or financed. The billion-dollar capital campaign era was publicly launched by Stanford in 1985–86, but only in the post–George Floyd era have HBCUs received a critical mass of eight-figure gifts.[25] It seems apparent that much of the giving came not as a result of institutional solicitations based on an optimized value proposition or extended cultivation, but from a more general recognition by the donors of a need for philanthropic balance, especially in the context of intensified racial strife.[26] Decades ago, such scaled investments became the norm for many of the non-HBCUs that now compete for the sharpest academic and athletic talent. While there is good reason to celebrate this new philanthropy to HBCUs, there is also good reason to wonder whether some of the individual HBCUs can now use a sharper institutional value proposition to deepen, expand, and sustain such investments. Can they now leverage their campus-based values, attract other investors, and ensure that this is not merely a brief, newsworthy moment for HBCUs collectively, but a new era for some, institutionally?

How might an institution clarify, develop, and embrace a more unique and investment-worthy value proposition?

First and foremost, decades of accreditation in American higher education have helped to standardize and harden much of the structure and substance of what is offered by roughly three thousand US four-year colleges and universities. Thus, in a higher education industry marked by a consistent sameness, harnessing a unique and investment-worthy value proposition is an intimidating project for most leaders. Only certain mindsets are intrigued by both the question and the quest.

The mindsets of those in senior leadership will determine the quality of each institution's response to the industry's sameness. Some leaders understand the importance of it but are fixed in their lack of imagination about how to respond. Other leaders have an abiding concern about it, preferring to use a growth-mindset campus culture to constantly clarify their distinctions for their real and potential stakeholders. Of course, a third mindset causes some institutional leaders and cultures to remain as unconcerned about their sameness as they are about their relative precarity and invisibility.

The advice herein is for campus leaders who are inclined to see the stubborn sameness not as the weather they must accept, but as the mystery they must solve. This is the kind of drive that invites and enriches institutional leaders and cultures with a "differentiate or die" mindset, wherein the competition must be outpaced, or a "blue ocean strategy" mindset, wherein the competition must be made irrelevant.[27]

Mindful of the overall higher education forest, with three thousand other trees, and the smaller HBCU forest, with roughly one hundred trees, one way for an HBCU to determine what constitutes its investment-worthy uniqueness is to use an institution-wide process (including internal and external stakeholders) to carefully outline what the participants think constitutes the campus's current comparative or competitive advantage. What identifiers do people now use to grasp the institution's identity and importance? That process can yield a combination of attributes like:

- We have a powerful mission and tradition.
- We operate with a values-driven liberal arts philosophy.
- We offer unique programs (in depth, breadth, and quality).
- Our curriculum can meet current and projected workforce demands.
- We have a robust, nimble IT infrastructure and state-of-the-art facilities and equipment.
- We offer a small, family-style environment where everybody knows your name.
- We keep costs low.
- We enroll overlooked students (due to race, class, or family challenges).
- We nurture our students better.
- Our four-year and six-year completion rates are exemplary.

Whichever general or specific qualities are surfaced by this exercise in institutional self-examination, Rowena Patton, an expert in value proposition clarification, recommends strength-testing it with two rules.[28] The first, she calls "the 80 percent rule." Very simply, if 80 percent or more of your competitors are also providing that which you tout as your value proposition, then it can be considered as a given, and therefore should be eliminated from the list.

This highlights the downside of the predominant HBCU forest image, which has succeeded in blurring the HBCU trees. When you sell the forest for nearly eight decades, as the UNCF and many other HBCU advocates have done, it is hard to blame major philanthropists if they have dull instincts about attaching themselves to a tree. Because HBCUs are widely perceived as a collective, the average American would logically adopt a "seen one, seen them all" perspective. Even African Americans, and particularly HBCU insiders, would find it hard to generate a list that is truly unique.

On January 19, 2017, UNCF CEO and president Michael Lomax reposted an op-ed entitled, "Six Reasons HBCUs Are More Important Than Ever."[29] His list included these attributes:

- Outsized impact, low cost = "best buy" in education
- Meeting the needs of low-income, first-generation students
- Lower costs narrow the racial wealth gap
- Campus climate fosters success
- Addresses the nation's under- and unemployment crisis
- HBCUs offer a true value/values proposition

Not only would many or most of these attributes be familiar and touted by many community colleges, where a third of the African Americans in postsecondary institutions are being educated, but they are also what HBCUs have in common, which is Lomax's point. The value proposition exercise is about what makes each institution unique, rather than what makes the sector unique. The overarching HBCU transformation narrative remains key, but each institution should clarify its connection to it. That can be done simply by touting their own noteworthy graduates who have been servant leaders in the effort to establish a truer America.

In addition to touting the institution's distinguished alumni, here are other attributes that can offer more unique, investment-worthy brand distinction:

- The noteworthy faculty who shaped our distinguished alumni citizens
- Our ability to graduate students with minimal debt
- The breadth, depth, and quality of our program offerings

- Our uniquely coordinated institutional vision, philosophy, and values
- The quality and size of our physical infrastructure
- Our students can see critical masses of senior faculty and staff who look like them

Rather than discredit any of the HBCU associations, this assessment is meant to challenge each campus to go well beyond what the UNCF and TMCF tend to tout as general, league-level HBCU value descriptors, and to convey a new and unique way to see themselves and to be seen by current and potential stakeholders. Taking seriously the 80 percent rule requires it.

The second way to test the merits of your list of institutional qualities is to administer Patton's "so what?" rule. Are your proposed value proposition attributes of interest to stakeholders, be they students or donors? Is there a real market for what you are offering? How magnetic is each attribute? Why would students be drawn to experience it? Why would donors be drawn to bolster it?

Letting the world know that you have a curriculum that can teach students to help end oppression is an attribute that will appeal to some. But it may be just as appealing to tout a curriculum that also offers a unique approach to coding, thereby positioning each student for high-end employability, which might enable them, individually, to stop being oppressed. If what you tout is insufficiently clear, compelling, and specific, it is also unlikely to be appealing. Nor is it likely to be valued and bankrolled by a critical mass of investment-savvy donors.

In the case of each attribute, once you clearly establish that you are offering what most of your competitors do not or cannot offer (the 80 percent rule), and it is clearly valued by a critical mass of your real or potential stakeholders (the "so what?" rule), then you are ready to leverage your unique value proposition for substantial enrollment, partnership, and investment.

ACTIVELY MAINTAINING A HIGHER SIGNAL-TO-NOISE RATIO

Every institution has a signal-to-noise ratio (SNR), but only some presidents and boards realize the importance of remaining disciplined and vigilant about monitoring and managing it. Not only is this a critical variable, indicative of an institution's health and trajectory, but it ought to be regarded by trustees as a core basis for the annual evaluation of the president. This is especially true for HBCUs, which have rarely enjoyed the benefit of the doubt from most traditional American media outlets.

As mentioned in the previous chapter, Marybeth Gasman and Nelson Bowman published an analysis of media portrayals of HBCUs in 2011, and they pointed to the American media's "tendency to report the direst circumstances at HBCUs and then portray these circumstances as the norm."[30] They also recognized another important pattern, saying, "The notion that HBCUs 'never measure up' or are a 'lost cause' permeates the media narrative, and as a result, the general public, the higher-education community, and even some African Americans have negative perceptions of HBCUs." In other words, they found substantial noise already contaminating the news environment in and beyond higher education. This often loud "white noise" has the obvious potential to diminish any signal that individual HBCUs might develop.

The negativity lingers like a toxic fog and, similar to the persistence of higher education's sameness, functions as the weather that must be endured for many HBCUs. This is not an unusual phenomenon in America. When HBCU alumnus Jesse Jackson campaigned for the US presidency in 1984, he became frustrated with the consistent negative spin in the national media coverage of his campaign. At several points, based on a growing frustration with the press, he quipped, "If I were to walk on water, the headline would read, 'Jesse Can't Swim!'"[31] His message was a clear parallel to the HBCU experience. HBCUs have walked on water with their three transformations, but the widespread perception is, "HBCUs can't swim." Gasman and Bowman indicate that even with opportunities to focus on the HBCU signal, the press has tended to focus on the HBCU noise. Only by making journalists more diverse and responsible can the broader, contextual toxicity be remedied. In the meantime, each HBCU must do what it can to ensure that its institutional signal is not only louder than its institutional noise, but also louder than the constant blare of the weather-based noise, as well. The adoption of a signal-to-noise ratio management capability can only help.

But what is signal-to-noise ratio management in higher education?

Ratios are fractions, and, in this case, the numerator is your institutional signal, and the denominator is your institutional noise. The total value should be far greater than one, and can only be less than one if your campus noise is louder than your campus signal.

This chapter began by comparing signal to virtues and noise to vices. From Harvard University to the smallest community college, every institution must contend with both. The optimization challenge is to amplify the signal while simultaneously reducing the noise. Success is realized when, in the general press, the positive news stories about your institution sustainably overshadow the negative news about your campus.

What exactly is being counted to calculate this ratio? Sources of institutional noise include headlines and other media attention focused on controversies such as no-confidence votes in leadership, student protests about campus conditions, misspending, embezzlement, sexual assaults and rape culture, governance scandals, deferred maintenance, frequent lawsuits, etc. Sources of institutional signal include media attention or reports about awards to faculty, prestigious scholarships and fellowships to students, substantial alumni giving, consequential research programs, distinctively productive departments, transformational investments that demonstrate investment worthiness, campuswide involvements in community service and community outreach, etc. The simple advice is to perform an SNR audit every quarter, if possible, and certainly every year. If the positive news stories about your campus do not outnumber the negative news stories, preferably by a count of more than five to one—giving you an SNR of at least five—you have significant work to do.

Every campus leader wants their signal to be strong enough to inform, inspire, and incentivize the institution's real and potential stakeholders, partners, and investors to become and remain engaged in a constant effort to build institutional value. Achieving an SNR greater than five should be the fundamental objective of any presidential tenure.

FOR THE MINDSET

Campus leaders who can both firmly grasp and sustainably curate their uniquely relevant institutional value can attract the multiple forms of investment sufficient for the journey to character and capital optimization.

CHAPTER SEVEN

The Iceberg Trustees

The day I joined the board in 1970, Joe said to me, "Our job is to make this institution financially impregnable." Those were his exact words.

Gardiner Dutton about Joseph Rosenfield, *Money* (magazine), 2000

Although I have lost count of the number of HBCU vacancies and recent appointments, suffice it to say I believe the number of vacancies is far too high in proportion to the number of HBCUs as a percent of the total number of colleges and universities. The situation is so dire that some presidents are not in office long enough to be officially inaugurated.

Charlie Nelms, open letter to HBCU trustees, August 6, 2021

There's power in healing work. But it isn't personal power. It cannot satisfy an individual's craving for self-importance. It's a real power that has nothing to do with our small, selfish dreams. It's the power to help life create itself.

Ayi Kwei Armah, *The Healers*

In the quest to realize the sustainable institutional competitiveness required to shape better citizens, governance is more important than any other force in the higher education ecosystem. Presidents matter because their work determines the quality of an institution's journey toward a destination. But boards matter because their work determines the quality of an institution's journey to a destiny. Presidents matter because one or several of them can exert the kind of leadership that will close any wide and measurable gaps between an institution and the best in the industry. But boards matter because trustees and trustee culture have everything to do with why such gaps open in the first place. Presidents matter because they must decide what mix of students, faculty, staff, and resources will optimize the institution. But boards matter because they must decide what mix of trustee bylaws, practices, membership, and resources will optimize the presidency. More often than not, presidents speak from the stage, and boards speak from the balcony. If boards do not do their jobs, they can, wittingly or unwittingly, make it impossible for presidents to do theirs.

Most people do not realize the importance of governance, precisely because trustees tend to operate in the background. Their gatherings and proceedings are among the least visible of all the stakeholders of most institutions. Yet, though unseen, their decisions tend also to be the most consequential. Few are aware that failed presidents, especially a pattern of them at the same institution, are a primary indicator of irresponsible governance. Yet boards are not commonly viewed as key enablers or retardants of both presidential and institutional success. Boards are rarely specifically targeted for praise, criticism, or overhaul. That means boards can be the functional equivalent of hypertension, a barely detectable silent killer. When left untreated for too long, an eroding quality of institutional life eventually becomes terminal. More than any other factor in the higher education ecosystem, healthy governance matters.

Failed and short-term presidents are not unique to HBCUs, but they are far too commonplace in the sector. One informal but compelling analysis showed that between 2010 and 2016, there was "an average of 11 new presidents each year for the 78 four-year HBCUs, with the high point being 15 in 2015," and amid a national average of 6.5 years in the presidency, "for the 49 HBCU presidents hired between 2010 and 2014, the average tenure was only 3.3 years."[1] Ironically, Washington's beloved Tuskegee had long been the picture of presidential stability, with five presidents in the 129 years between 1881 and 2010. Yet from 2010 to 2021, the Tuskegee trustees made eight separate decisions about who would lead Tuskegee University in the Office of the President until the board's next appointment decision.[2]

Fortunately, or unfortunately, the only force capable of remedying these trends is the same force that caused them. For that reason, HBCU trustees are among those who might benefit by remaining aware that many lives are at stake when they make governance decisions, as one mindset-enriching example clearly illustrates.

WHEN POOR TRUSTEESHIP CAN BE LETHAL

On April 15, 1912, more than fifteen hundred people lost their lives when the *Titanic* sank. The tragedy was rooted in the mindsets of those in governance. The British regulators with the relevant governance responsibility failed miserably by not ensuring that ships invariably had enough lifeboats. Whether their negligence was borne of a preference for leaving room for deck chairs instead of lifeboats, a desire to avoid the cost or inconvenience of last-minute adjustments, a baffling fealty to outdated regulations, or a combination of these and other reasons, a governance failure was cited in numerous assessments.[3] As it turned out, even with a ship touted as "unsinkable" as it set out on its maiden journey, lifeboat requirements mattered. And that meant vigilant, state-of-the-art, healthy, and optimized governance mattered.

Any institution can unexpectedly encounter life-threatening icebergs. Writ large, icebergs symbolize both the anticipated and unanticipated threats that the trustees exist to help avoid. Trustees who are attentive to real and potential icebergs are engaged in the best kind of governance. Alternatively, when governance is lazy, demonstrably outdated, blind to institutional risks, or suboptimally focused on inconsequential matters, the institution will only totter and suffer, perhaps eventually unto death. In short, when trustees focus on any industry's equivalent of deck chairs instead of its icebergs, they are engaging in the worst kind of governance. This is what the oversight malfeasance involving the sunken *Titanic* shows. It also points to how critical it is for boards to adopt an iceberg mindset, rather than a deck chair mindset.

The relatively recent instances of high HBCU leadership turnover are one key indicator of the governance challenges facing many HBCUs. But powerfully clear warning signs about deck chair governance in HBCUs were flashing at least a half century ago.

In 1967, the Ford Foundation funded an analysis of the caliber and effectiveness of governance at fifty private, "senior" HBCUs.[4] Authored by two former HBCU presidents, Samuel M. Nabrit and Julius S. Scott, Jr., the study was designed to assess "the quality and vitality of the boards" and the "thrust and relevance of the institutions." Based on the views of 1,255 HBCU trustees from fifty boards, the state of HBCU trusteeship in 1967 was troubled. Dominated by clergy, the majority of the trustees were over age sixty, and no board had student or faculty representation. While African Americans held 58 percent of the board seats, the authors determined that "the power of these boards is concentrated in the hands of the white membership; they make the policies and choose the presidents."[5] Although "most trustees regard finances and investments to be their primary responsibilities as board members," many developed "little capability in raising money or in investment policy." Others took "advantage of their positions to profit at the expense of the colleges or use their influence to assist their friends." Almost 70 percent of the members annually contributed $200 or less to their institutions, and only five percent gave more than $1,000 annually. The analysis revealed an "almost universal . . . lack of clear perceptions of role-functions and obligations."[6]

Although Nabrit and Scott refrained from making any summary judgments about the overall quality of HBCU governance, their findings clarify that its condition and trajectory in 1967 were not aligned with a meaningful quest for optimization. They cited the HBCU presidents' interest in developing ways to educate their trustees, referring to the need to close an "intelligence gap." They said, "The reading of board members seldom includes the scholarly Negro journals or the professional journals published by higher education agencies." Nabrit and Scott were careful to note that, "With only one exception, the institutions we studied are not related to the Association of Governing Boards."[7]

Then and since, the Association of Governing Boards (AGB) has served as the nation's peerless resource for strengthening higher education governance. In the half century since Nabrit and Scott made their assessment, the AGB has sharpened and refined its ideas about what constitutes sound governance, including developing a special focus on HBCUs. Precisely at the end of Washington's gap-closure century in 2015, AGB officials recognized that HBCUs were "at an inflection point," and the quality of their future would be dependent on "strong governance, strategic leadership, and robust financial health."[8] With funding from the Kresge Foundation, they announced a competitive initiative to strengthen HBCU governance by offering consulting and diagnostic services to HBCUs. AGB's analysis of general HBCU governance conditions revealed a need to improve board committee structures, trustee orientation and education, partnering between the board chair and the president, board self-examination, and strategies to yield financial stability and sustainability. Published in 2019, the AGB's recommendations about next steps bore a striking resemblance to those offered by Nabrit and Scott in 1967.

While all of this may point to a general lack of HBCU governance sophistication, or the predominance of deck chair trusteeship, it is not true that HBCUs have never benefited from iceberg trusteeship.

INSTITUTIONAL CONSIDERATION FOR THE RECORD: TWO UNLIKELY INSTITUTIONS THAT USED ICEBERG TRUSTEESHIP TO OPTIMIZE GOVERNANCE

When a president and trustees decide to focus on endowment, they are, to a degree, selflessly and strategically placing their leadership and governance responsibility to meet the anticipated needs of future generations on par with meeting the needs of the current campus community, however dire. They make a bold statement about their long-term confidence in an institution's relevance and effectiveness when they choose to spend a nickel out of every dollar at a time when dollars are scarce. The endowment focus is also indicative of their belief in the sustainability of the institution's value proposition.

In the illustrations below, governance was optimized at two very different institutions. The institution's leader drove the effort in one case, while the board chairman led in the other case. Both reveal how institutions without the advantages of location, a recognizable brand, and scores of wealthy and engaged alumni can make significant progress toward eliminating precarity.

A Principal Equates Effective Governance with Enlarging Endowment

Long before the AGB was born in 1921, and before Harvard's iconic President Charles Eliot relied on an Episcopal bishop to lead what has been referred to as higher education's first modern capital campaign in 1904, a Black institution optimized governance, primarily by focusing on eliminating precarity.[9] To them, that meant prioritizing financial sustainability through endowment growth. Booker T. Washington was a leader who was not chosen by a trustee board. Instead, with early assistance from Hampton's Samuel Chapman Armstrong, he chose his trustees and, together, they convinced an emerging philanthropic community to invest in and endow a Black institution founded and run by a formerly enslaved African American man.

To be sure, no other revenue source included the same potential elasticity as philanthropy. Federal aid was not yet born, and tuition revenue was not yet an option. While Washington's students were enormously eager to learn, they were also overwhelmingly penniless and illiterate. Thus, it was strikingly illogical for Washington and other Black leaders of his era to privilege long-term benefits over near-term needs. Nonetheless, he prioritized endowment throughout his tenure at Tuskegee. In Washington's view, endowment would provide Tuskegee with self-sufficiency and independence. He personally craved both, dating back to his five-hundred-mile walk from West Virginia to Hampton, Virginia.[10] He knew Tuskegee needed to be invulnerable to the whims of Southern whites, which meant he could not become overly reliant upon the annual state appropriation provided months after his arrival.[11] They were the same state officials who repeatedly overlooked the terrorist lynching of African Americans.

Washington's decision to make July 4, 1881, the Institute's official founding date was also a symbol of his determined quest for self-sufficiency and independence. It is why he amended the Institute's incorporation documents to explicitly require the formation of a trustee board to help build up "an endowment fund."[12] Washington saw and envisioned things to which people with immediate needs are typically blind. He saw endowment as the best foundation for a race struggling to become self-sufficient.

In 1890, only nine years into his leadership tenure, Washington received the first endowment fund contribution.[13] Thereafter, he worked so hard to raise expendable and endowed funds that his declining health motivated his Boston-based friends to fully finance a trip to Europe by the summer of 1899. Two important developments followed that trip. First, his wife, Margaret, began connecting the endowment pursuit with her husband's mortality. She wrote to a friend, "If only he could get an endowment at this time of his life, how much longer he might live. The whole thing fills [me] with terror."[14] Second, the trustees echoed that sentiment by highlighting how endowment growth could free Washington to spend less time on the road fundraising and more time on the campus educating and leading.[15]

The quest also revealed what would become a deep-rooted and durable racial skew in American philanthropy. Although the missionary philanthropists worked hard to help ensure that the newly freed Americans were educated, no Black institutional support was sufficient to erase or diminish the leadership's long-term worry about survival. That difference was highlighted when Boston's Edward Austin died and bequeathed over $1 million to charity, including $500,000 to Harvard, $100,000 to the Massachusetts Institute of Technology, and $30,000 to Tuskegee. In response, "Edward P. Clark of the New York Evening Post wrote [to Washington] that the bequest should have been reversed, with Tuskegee receiving $500,000 and Harvard $30,000."[16] But that was and remains the tendency of American philanthropy.

That fall, Washington planned his first organized endowment campaign. He launched the effort with an event held on December 4, 1899, at the concert hall of New York City's Madison Square Garden. Among the reasons for its success was the convergence of people with substantial wealth and influence. The crowd of two thousand included J. Pierpont Morgan, C. P. Huntington, Jacob Schiff, Robert C. Ogden, W. H. Baldwin, Jr., and Mr. and Mrs. John D. Rockefeller. Former President Grover Cleveland had agreed to preside, but illness forced him to merely send a supportive letter announcing that he had secured an endowment gift of $25,000.[17] The endowment goal was set at $500,000. At the top of the meeting, the Tuskegee endowment stood at $62,253, more than half of which had arrived the year before. By the end of the meeting, the endowment exceeded $150,000.[18] With a milestone goal of reaching $250,000 before the end of 1900, the campaign was off to a great start.[19]

It is not clear when Tuskegee's "Committee on Investment of the Endowment Fund" was officially launched, but they were rewarded for their focus on fundraising. With Washington, they amassed $227,000 by 1901, short of the pace they sought, but clearly headed toward the $500,000 goal. It was a pivotal year for Tuskegee, principally because Washington's autobiography, *Up from Slavery*, was published and quickly became a best seller.[20]

The philanthropic community was especially intrigued by Washington's story. They thought his approach could advance the education of Blacks in the South without being too disruptive to the status quo built by racism.[21] His book was intentionally written and marketed for the benefit of his Institute and his race. As Washington wrote to his publisher, whatever he published "will have for its main advantage the bringing of this institution before a class of people who have money and to whom I must look for money for endowment and other purposes."[22] In fact, a number of Tuskegee's donors were directly motivated to give after reading *Up from Slavery*, including H. H. Rogers, of the Standard Oil Company, and Andrew Carnegie. According to one assessment, "*Up from Slavery* has brought more money to Tuskegee than all the other books, articles, speeches, and circulars written by Mr. Washington himself and the many others who have written or spoken about him and his work."[23] For Washington and Tuskegee, the book was the equivalent of a modern-day capital campaign case statement.

By 1903, following another similar gathering in New York, the Tuskegee endowment received $600,000 from Andrew Carnegie, its largest investment ever.[24] Carnegie, Ogden, and Baldwin would eventually join the Tuskegee board, which, on Washington's watch, also included Julius Rosenwald, William G. Willcox, William J. Schieffelin, and President Theodore Roosevelt.

By the time Tuskegee celebrated its twenty-fifth anniversary in 1906, it had grown to 1,600 students being prepared for 37 industries, 156 faculty, 83 buildings on 2,300 acres, 880 alumni, and an endowment "in the neighborhood of $2,000,000."[25] The anniversary gathering included some of America's wealthiest and most influential philanthropists and leaders. Beside Ogden and Carnegie, the crowd included William Lloyd Garrison, Lyman Abbott, and Oswald Garrison Villard.

Comments by Harvard's Charles Eliot highlighted Washington's extraordinary progress. He said, "the oldest and now largest American institution of learning was more than two hundred years arriving at the possession of much less land, fewer buildings, and a smaller quick capital than Tuskegee had come to possess in twenty-five years."[26] Then, referring to what is typically called an "unrestricted endowment," Eliot elaborated, saying:

> This evening I have received another impression from your Principal. He said that the great need of Tuskegee, today, was a considerable sum of money, which could be used at the discretion of the trustees, to fill gaps, to make improvements and to enlarge and strengthen the different branches of the institution. Now I should not find it possible to state in more precise terms the present needs of Harvard University. The needs of these two institutions, situated, to be sure, in very different communities, and founded on very different dates, are precisely the same.[27]

This was high praise for Washington from Eliot, a man widely regarded, then and now, as among the most consequential university leaders in American history.

By 1907, Washington delivered an address in Brooklyn, New York, in which he expressed a desire to "increase the endowment fund to at least $3 million."[28] That high aspiration was typical of Washington, yet it was rare for any college leader at the time, Black or white. And he won key outside supporters in his quest to endow Tuskegee: Mark Twain helped Washington raise endowment funds for Tuskegee, as did US presidents Cleveland, McKinley, Theodore Roosevelt, and Taft.[29]

Beyond his passion to enlarge Tuskegee's endowment, Washington was a statesman who regarded endowment as essential for all HBCUs. He advocated for larger endowments at other Black institutions, including Fisk University, Lincoln University, Hampton, and Wilberforce.[30] Throughout his tenure, he prioritized those twin ideals—self-sufficiency and independence. Both were tangibly present when, less than eight months before his death, he contacted Howard University professor Kelly Miller, writing, "I very much hope that the trustees of Howard University will find a way to increase its endowment from year to year to such an extent that the Institution will not be so wholly dependent as it is now upon the good will of Congress."[31]

At Washington's death in 1915, Tuskegee Institute's sizable endowment made it nearly as strong as Hampton, and stronger than all the other Black colleges, as well as most of America's other colleges and universities at the time. Yet after thirty-four years, while the Institute was more thoroughly equipped than most, it was far from being as thoroughly equipped as the founder aspired. In his final report to the trustees, Washington described an annual budget of nearly $290,000 and an endowment of nearly $2 million, for a healthy endowment-to-expense ratio of nearly seven, as he raised $100,000 per year.[32] Not only was the Tuskegee endowment over 7 percent of Harvard's endowment of $28.4 million at the time, but it was also 80 percent of the endowment Charles Eliot had at Harvard when he took office in 1869, when Harvard was 233 years old.

As a crowning indicator of Washington's ambition, he used that final report to not only call trustee attention to over $158,000 in "urgent needs," emphasizing scholarships and buildings, but he also stated his desire to boost the Tuskegee endowment to $5 million. As a calibration, an announced quest to add $3 million to any endowment in 1915 is the equivalent of a GDP-relative quest for $1.4 billion in 2015.[33] Clearly, Washington knew he had enough wealth among his trustees to be successful without any external input. And in addition, his board's philanthropic connections were as impressive as their individual wealth. It is worth noting that, had Washington lived, his likely success in such an effort would, to this day, remain the largest trustee-aided drive in HBCU history. Washington announced the equivalent of a billion-dollar-plus capital campaign a century before billion-dollar capital campaigning was popularized in American higher education.

A Board Chairman Equates Effective Governance with "Financial Impregnability"

Ironically, as the Ford study on HBCU governance was being conducted in 1967, a different revolution was getting underway on a campus amid the cornfields of America's Midwest. The revolution was led not by the leader of the campus administration, but by the leader of its board of trustees. Joseph Frankel Rosenfield was a 1925 graduate of Grinnell College in Iowa. He was so enamored of his student experience at Grinnell that he made it his lifelong priority to strengthen the institution to an unprecedented degree. After stabilizing a successful law and business career in Des Moines, worthy of being referred to by the *Des Moines Register* as the "Patriarch of Iowa Business," he joined the Grinnell board in 1941.[34] At the time, Grinnell's endowment totaled $1 million. With Rosenfield's encouragement, the board decided to focus on the sole mission of growing the endowment. His fruitful, singular focus helped to earn him the role of board chairman from 1948 to 1952, and he continued as a trustee long after that.

On October 29, 1967, with the Grinnell endowment totaling $10 million, Rosenfield traveled to campus to hear a speech by a visiting Rev. Dr. Martin Luther King, Jr. King's delayed arrival allowed Rosenfield to get to know a then-unknown young businessman named Warren Buffett.[35] Inspired by King's speech, "Remaining Awake During a Revolution," the two men developed a close friendship and decided to work together to bolster the Grinnell endowment. Buffett joined Grinnell's board in 1968, as did Grinnell alumnus Robert Noyce, founder of a company soon to be known worldwide as Intel. Rosenfield convinced the board to secure a significant early phase stake in Intel, Berkshire Hathaway, the Sequoia Fund, and Freddie Mac. They also bought a television station and made other daring moves, eventually placing the Grinnell endowment on a very impressive trajectory.

Gardiner Dutton joined the Grinnell board in 1970, at a time when Rosenfield had distilled the board's collective purpose to one thing: making Grinnell College "financially impregnable."[36] Becoming financially impregnable meant ensuring that any campus need or challenge for which funding is the answer shall be provided forthwith. The Grinnell trustees collectively affirmed that campus leadership would never be without the required financial wherewithal to realize their fondest educational desires. A lack of imagination might be a problem, but never a lack of money. In other words, financial impregnability is the perfect antidote to institutional precarity.

The singleness of mind worked. On Rosenfield's watch, the endowment grew by three orders of magnitude in six decades. From its $1 million value in 1941, it reached $10 million in 1967, and $100 million in 1983. By the year 2000, when Rosenfield died, the endowment of the largely unknown midwestern college exceeded an astonishing $1 billion. Grinnell was then touted as being the wealthiest private college in the country, as measured by endowment per student. And while other institutions were building their endowments with the help of major capital campaigning, involving broad and continuous giving from friends, old and new, Grinnell's achievement was borne of a disciplined governance focus on financial impregnability. Smart investing was a far more productive strategy for them. For instance, when Grinnell launched a capital campaign in 1995 to try to raise $75 million over a seven-year period, its invested endowment funds grew by more than twice that amount in the first two years of the campaign. Between 1980 and 2015, when the Grinnell endowment increased forty-fivefold, a mere $69 million, less than 4 percent of the growth, stemmed from gifts.[37]

Grinnell College did what any tuition-driven, underresourced, ambitious institution could hope to do. They surged toward financial impregnability without the benefit of a visible institutional brand, Division 1 sports, a large and leverageable research portfolio, scores of wealthy and generous alumni, an amazing fundraising track record, transformational gifts from nonalumni friends, or being located near a major business hub. Like most other non-limelight institutions, they never received a gift of more than $5 million, and the only gift provided to Grinnell by Warren Buffett was advice.

By far the key differentiator for this small liberal arts college was enlightened trustee board leadership—that is, Grinnell was ushered to a new echelon of institutional security by a man whom *Forbes* magazine once referred to as "the guardian angel on Grinnell's Board of Trustees."[38] Once Rosenfield used a single decade to focus the Grinnell board on a single aim, the stars aligned to converge the right people, ideas, opportunities, and outcomes.

Grinnell's success was celebrated widely, but a concern was raised in 2006, when a Grinnell physics professor, Mark B. Schneider, openly wondered whether and when an endowment might be too big, and whether "there must be at least some rough ideal value for an endowment."[39] Schneider argued that an institution's endowment-expense ratio is a better measure of their optimal endowment size, rather than the conventional endowment per student. He was more concerned about the ideal endowment size to sustain institutional competitiveness. How big did the endowment need to be to realize the coveted impregnability without inviting or provoking mission drift? Schneider concluded that "an ideal endowment would provide a third to a half of the operating budget, and the endowment-expense ratio would be in the range of five to 10."[40]

Schneider became concerned about Grinnell's endowment size in 2003, when it reached nearly $1.1 billion, and the endowment ratio neared fourteen. Yet, when the end of Washington's gap-closure century arrived in 2015, Grinnell's endowment exceeded $1.8 billion. Schneider's concerns aside, with an endowment-expense ratio north of twenty, Grinnell was more financially impregnable than Rosenfield ever imagined. And they got there using an approach that any HBCU with enlightened governance could have emulated long ago and can yet pursue in what is now the first decade of the second gap-closure century.

INSTITUTIONAL QUESTION FOR THE FUTURE: WHAT ARE TWO KEY INDICATORS OF ICEBERG TRUSTEESHIP?

In 2018, the AGB determined that optimal governance in higher education involves "three key essentials for all governing structures: ensuring that boards have the best people serving on them, that boards address the right issues, and that board members engage in the right manner to add value."[41] Since governance is why many presidencies are broken and many presidents fail, it makes sense that the journey to institutional health starts with addressing defective governance.

In cases where boards are just forming or reforming, a foundational principle for selecting rightminded trustees is to ensure that all candidates understand the difference between iceberg and deck chair governance. While deck chair trustees are inclined to constantly meddle in campus management, iceberg trustees focus on avoiding whatever might obstruct the institution's journey to optimize character and realize financial impregnability. Deck chair trustees threaten the institution's ability to survive, while iceberg trustees maintain a disciplined focus on how the institution can thrive. Deck chair trustees are responsible for broken presidencies and failed presidents. As self-less fiduciaries, iceberg trustees make the presidency safe for high-performing presidents, confident that consecutive first-rate presidential appointments are the only way to position the institution for optimizing character and impregnability. And whereas deck chair trusteeship is largely responsible for the findings of the Ford Foundation's 1967 HBCU governance study, only iceberg trusteeship can offer last rites to such misguided and costly governance.

Boards that are dominated by iceberg trustees tend to prioritize a key pursuit and a key practice.

Iceberg Trustees Prioritize the Pursuit of a High Endowment-Expense Ratio (EER)

Operationally, iceberg governance maintains a disciplined focus on building endowment, particularly in relation to expenses. A healthy endowment enables the financial impregnability required to optimize character, thereby positioning the institution to shape better citizens. The story of Grinnell's emergence from financial precarity to peerless financial impregnability is instructive for iceberg trustees. Grinnell's campus leaders are now free to pursue whatever educational agenda they desire, since their board and board culture have afforded them that rare privilege. Their sustained discipline regarding impregnability yielded a remarkable 2021 EER of twenty-three. That means the only force capable of keeping Grinnell College from the holy grail of optimizing character is a lack of will or imagination.

Again, noting that an EER toward the top of the five-to-ten range constitutes institutional competitiveness, which HBCUs have a sufficiently competitive EER to position them for financial impregnability? Figure 7.1 reveals the simple answer: not one—yet.

The wealth gap that troubled Washington in 1915 would have troubled him more in 2015. And based on the critical role played by his Tuskegee

Figure 7.1 The top ten HBCUs by endowment-expense ratio, 2015

1	Spelman College	3.90
2	Dillard University	1.70
3	Xavier University	1.60
	Morehouse College	1.60
	Hampton University	1.60
6	Tuskegee University	0.78
	Clark Atlanta University	0.78
8	Howard University	0.70
9	Fisk University	0.64
10	Claflin University	0.57

Source: US Department of Education, National Center for Education Statistics, Integrated Postsecondary Education Data System, spring finance component (2015), retrieved from https://nces.ed.gov/ipeds/datacenter.

trustees, he would correctly suspect that HBCUs had not been well served by optimized, iceberg governance.

Washington found good cause to focus on endowment since, throughout his tenure, the expected family contribution of those he enrolled was zero. That same rationale for HBCU boards and presidents to emphasize endowment persists to this day, since, as of 2015–16, 58.2 percent of African American college students come from homes with an expected family contribution of zero.[42] Also, since 2011, more than 70 percent of the full-time, first-time students enrolled in HBCUs have received federal Pell Grants, which is another clear indication of the limited family wealth of HBCU students.[43] Under those general circumstances, all HBCU trustees continue to have every reason to be at least as passionate about endowment as the earlier boards of both Tuskegee and Grinnell.

Financial impregnability is about being prepared for icebergs. The wealth disadvantage of African American families has always been an iceberg. But other potential icebergs include a market crash, stiff competition from other educational providers, decreases in federal aid, demographic shifts, and a global pandemic. The sizable endowments at the heart of financial impregnability can buy both the time and expertise required to move past nearly all icebergs without damage. The ability to avoid threats and seize opportunities is what iceberg governance is all about. And it requires trustees to use a telescope more than a microscope—that is, to see and interpret emerging signs, patterns, and trends, and to nimbly act to preserve the privilege of shaping better citizens. Alternatively, when trustees habitually function as if using a microscope, they cannot possibly focus on an institution's destination or destiny. This underscores the outlook imperative of optimized, iceberg governance.

Iceberg Trustees Prioritize the Practice of Leading with Peripheral Vision

Iceberg governance happens when trustees are attentive and responsive to the right things. It is about both the sharpness and the range of trustee vision. In fact, any institution in a competitive industry is unlikely to realize meaningful strategic advantages without having an appropriate amount of peripheral vision.

George Day and Paul Schoemaker have generated a defining body of work on peripheral vision, which they variously describe as an institution's perceptive ability to avoid being blindsided by "high-impact competitive events" in their industry or environment—or, "the hidden opportunities *and* threats that can profoundly impact your enterprise."[44] They cite a number of early-stage, often veiled opportunities and threats that can be difficult to detect, analyze, and manage. That is why trusteeship with good peripheral vision is mission critical. For any college or university, this capacity is key. But for those HBCUs that face financial precarity, it is urgently important.

As revealed in the previous chapter, unlike most other sectors of American higher education, HBCUs must constantly contend with the white noise of undignified publicity. And it is also true that individual HBCUs are often barely visible because multiple audiences continue to groupthink them. Putting peripheral vision to good use is more difficult when you are barely heard or seen. It is as if HBCUs are seated together in the dimly lit section of the loud cafeteria of higher education. The risk is clear. Over time, their voices can become harder and harder to hear over the competition, and their eyes can grow accustomed to the gloom. The risk is heightened if HBCU trustees find it harder to hear or heed the message of HBCU-relevant coal mine canaries.

But that is the function of trusteeship. And it is easier to realize enlightened governance with the aid of peripheral vision.

The fact that 1965 became the first year when the majority of African Americans were enrolled in non-HBCUs had been explicitly signaled a decade earlier by Thurgood Marshall, just after announcement of the *Brown* decision. Marshall warned HBCUs and the UNCF "to find another sales talk."[45] He was right. Not unlike Rockefeller's reaction to the *Brown* decision, Marshall quickly sounded an alarm because once the US Supreme Court made desegregation the law of the land, he saw an immediate threat to the core marketability of HBCUs. At that time, the decision may have seemed like a faint or blurry indicator at the periphery of HBCU life, but, in Marshall's peripheral view, it was worthy of immediate attention and strategic adjustment. He saw an iceberg.

What does it mean for HBCUs to have peripheral vision nearly seventy years later? If a set of HBCU leaders took a "strategic eye exam," to diagnose, evaluate, and sharpen their peripheral vision, as Day and Schoemaker recommend, what threats and opportunities might their improved early warning system reveal?[46] Just three examples will help to underscore the danger of having institutional or governance blind spots in the increasingly volatile and hypercompetitive industry of American higher education.

The first example highlights a nonobvious threat that is emerging with increasing momentum and is the equivalent of a weapon aimed at a standard HBCU virtue. A great deal of research has substantiated the general perception that "HBCUs create a warm, nurturing, family-like environment which helps to facilitate Black students' self-efficacy, racial pride, psychological wellness, and optimize academic development and persistence."[47] Call it "the belonging advantage." Many HBCUs tout their campuses' ability to provide to each student a sense of belonging reliably and almost effortlessly, as if it is embedded in their institutional hardware, rather than in the software. It constitutes the unique magnetism or appeal of many HBCUs and is an oft-stated reason for attending.[48] Thus, HBCUs should pay close attention to the increasingly prominent and substantive efforts by predominantly white institutions to bolster a sense of belonging in individuals from the groups they previously excluded, ranging from people of color to the LGBTQ community. If the seekers of this new capacity succeed in a convincingly powerful way, it will dull the luster of a long-standing HBCU competitive advantage. While good for America, these efforts ought to spur HBCU leaders to think innovatively about their core value proposition.

Second, again mindful of the core "belonging advantage" of most HBCUs, their leaders should strategically consider the power and popularity of online education and see it as an opportunity zone. Online education first gained meaningful traction in the 1980s and, by 2019, the market was nearly $188 billion globally.[49] It is expected to range from $319 billion to $350 billion by 2025.[50] And that estimate was offered before the global pandemic of 2020 and 2021, which forced countless educational environments to invent or enhance online platforms, which have now become mainstream. Yet the online enterprise still has an unsolved riddle, which could represent a golden opportunity for HBCUs.

The online industry's unfinished business leaves room for significant growth and differentiation. In particular, no online provider has yet clarified and stabilized a "high-touch" experience in the context of online education. This absence could easily be regarded as the holy grail in the sector and, as a long-standing unmet need, it is a direct match for what has been a longer-standing HBCU strength. The challenge for the more advanced HBCUs is to translate their much touted and noteworthy "other-mothering" capacity and technique into the online context in a way that will yield tangible, measurable, and distinctive outcomes. Doing so could differentiate them and position an HBCU strength as an accelerant at the forefront of a still-surging online enterprise.

Finally, a third force on the horizon could represent a threat or an opportunity, depending upon the mindsets of HBCU presidents. In the spring of 2021, the Biden administration took major steps toward making a community college education affordable or free. The goal is to eventually lower the nationwide access hurdle. Because of their accessibility and price point, community colleges have always been perceived as high enrollers of students who might otherwise attend HBCUs. In fact, while community colleges have enrolled at least a third of the African Americans in higher education since 1986, HBCUs have enrolled under 10 percent of them since 2009.[51] The last time HBCUs enrolled more than a third of the African Americans in higher education was in 1968–69.

To perceive the free community college policy as a threat on the horizon is to envision only increased enrollment disruption at HBCUs. And if those free community colleges use their new federal funding to launch or enhance retention and belonging initiatives to improve the experiences of Blacks and other minority and minoritized students, they will justifiably be regarded as a bigger threat, requiring a smarter HBCU strategy.

On the other hand, those HBCU leaders with a growth mindset and peripheral vision are more likely to recognize the free community college movement as an opportunity around which to strategize. While some HBCUs now have articulation agreements with community colleges, this is an ideal time to strategically increase, broaden, and deepen those agreements, with a goal of becoming a "preferred destination HBCU" for community college transfers. With African American annual enrollment in community colleges averaging over 925 thousand students since 2009, and with a relatively poor transfer rate for them and other minority students, it is almost irresponsible to not see it as an arena in which to form mutually beneficial partnerships.[52]

FOR THE MINDSET

Not only should iceberg trusteeship be coveted by every aspiring educational institution, but it should also be the threshold litmus test that philanthropists use to clarify and ratify investment worthiness.[53]

CHAPTER EIGHT

The Risen Tide

Great universities, then, are the products of high aspirations and the human talent, will, and material resources to realize them. As many universities in the twentieth century have discovered, often much to their chagrin, great ones are not easy to build and, once built, not easy to surpass or supplant. For while ambition is cheap, the best students and faculty, outstanding facilities, and deep endowments are anything but cheap and are correspondingly hard to come by.

James Axtell, *The Pleasures of Academe*, 1998

There was no precedent then of rich white folk amply endowing a colored institution and there were no rich Negroes.

W. E. B. Du Bois,
"The Future of Wilberforce University," 1940

Just remember this while you sleep: in this world there are those who thrive, and there are those who don't. Those who thrive, thrive because they respect power. They see where it comes from, and they take care to place themselves beside it, never against it. . . . But Densu had no desire to go in their direction.

Ayi Kwei Armah, *The Healers*

In 1946, when Dr. Benjamin Elijah Mays was only six years into what would become a legendary twenty-seven-year presidency of Morehouse College, he restlessly observed that "all of the 82 private [Negro] institutions put together would have less than one third the endowment of Harvard."[1] At the time of

Mays's assessment, Harvard's endowment was a pacesetting $138.7 million. Those might have been the halcyon days of relative college wealth, however. Since Mays's lament, instead of such gaps being narrowed by the march of progress toward equity, they have widened by what can only be described as a steadfast allegiance to inequity. By 2015, the combined endowments of all 102 HBCUs, at $3.48 billion, totaled less than 10 percent of Harvard's endowment of $37.62 billion. Harvard used long-standing inequity-borne advantages and excelled at becoming stronger on pace with the second major rise in the tide of the nation's wealth.

The surge in philanthropic giving to American higher education, which began in the last quarter of the twentieth century, happened for logical reasons. Just as the skyrocketing wealth of a small percentage of individuals drove unprecedented university investments in the first Gilded Age, the second Gilded Age featured similar surges in private wealth and shifts in income distribution, beginning in the late 1970s. Those developments were later aided "by a stock market that rose to unprecedented heights . . . among the most visible outcomes of these developments was a dramatic rise in donations to universities."[2] The philanthropic capacity of a small number of individuals expanded because of "the rise in the share of wealth owned by the 0.1 percent richest families, from 7 percent in 1978 to 22 percent in 2012."[3] As shown in figure 8.1, this helped to set the stage for a great national expansion of overall philanthropy, reaching $471 billion by 2020.

Aided by a technological revolution, and as the economic boom of the 1980s and 1990s gained momentum, the financial stress in higher education was surging as well. And as the tip of America's wealthiest echelon tripled in size and secured a larger portion of America's growing wealth, several university boards and presidents viewed it as an opportunity to expand their institution's wealth similarly. So, they did.

With the benefit of keen peripheral vision, Stanford University played a tone-setting role in what became an energetic wealth chase. In the early 1980s, several alert colleges and universities began to feel vulnerable and pressured by the federal government's march toward reducing both the indirect cost recovery rate charged on federally sponsored research and the deductibility of charitable contributions.[4] These moves threatened two of their critical revenue streams—research overhead and private gifts. In the face of that pres-

FIGURE 8.1 The rise of American philanthropy by source, 1980–2020

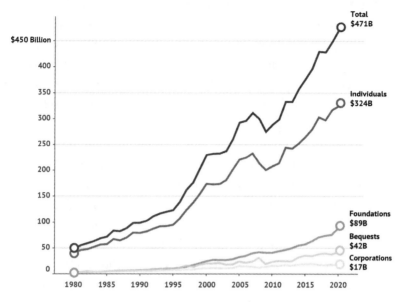

Source: Giving USA 2021: The Annual Report on Philanthropy for the Year 2020 (Chicago: Giving USA Foundation, 2020), 5.

sure, on March 16, 1986, Stanford President Donald Kennedy spoke to a crowd dominated by the university's wealthy alumni in Los Angeles about "the paradox of looking rich, yet feeling poor."[5] Because he thought the actions of the federal government foreshadowed "an authentic financial crisis" for Stanford and others, he delivered an insightful lecture on higher education finances. Kennedy explained that Stanford's "sizable," one-billion-dollar-plus endowment, combined with annual gifts, research overhead, royalties, and other sources, covered only 55 percent of the annual operating expenses. The university remained 45 percent reliant on tuition and was under pressure to slow the rate of tuition growth. As he demystified the real institutional needs behind a mirage of wealth, Kennedy contended that, in fact, his institution required an endowment of $6.5 billion. And with that lecture, he had just set the stage for pursuing it.

Shortly after that seminal exchange, Stanford became the first institution to publicly announce a billion-dollar capital campaign, the stage-setting and quiet phase of which had informally begun in late 1985.[6] In that year,

Harvard's endowment stood at $2.7 billion, Princeton had $1.5 billion, and Yale had $1.3 billion. What happened next was nothing short of a revolutionary surge in college and university wealth. To characterize the growing inequities and inequalities, Charles Clotfelter cited the Biblical phenomenon of the rich getting richer and the poor getting poorer, also known as the "Matthew effect."[7] As the richest colleges and universities were further enriched, the poorer institutions fell farther behind, thereby widening higher education's already stark wealth gaps.

As figure 8.2 shows, in 1985, all philanthropic giving in America totaled $71.69 billion, while voluntary philanthropic support to higher education totaled $6.3 billion. The giving to higher education would then soar, reaching $41 billion from all sources in 2015, the end of Washington's gap-closure century. As HBCUs joined others in the quest for wealth, it made sense to wonder whether the world of negative thinking would continue to render them unworthy, if not invisible. As figure 8.2 also shows, HBCUs indeed fared differently.

The adage "a rising tide lifts all boats" was popularized by President John F. Kennedy, who first used it in a 1963 speech about the broad benefits of a public works project. Given the substantial rise in the philanthropic tide, HBCU boats could easily have been lifted on par with industry leaders, thereby leading to measurable gap closure. Instead, from 1985 (the start of the billion-dollar capital campaign era) to 2015, while all giving increased 5.2 times ($71.7 billion to $376.7 billion), and all higher education fundraising increased 6.4 times ($6.3 billion to $40.3 billion), gifts to HBCUs increased only 3.4 times ($84 million to $288 million). Moreover, only six of the 105 HBCUs had raised over $100 million in a standard capital campaign effort by 2015.[8] Also, by 2015, while Harvard raised over $83 million per month and Stanford raised over $135 million per month, HBCUs collectively raised $24 million per month. Clearly, even if all institutions began at sea level, the risen tide of philanthropy did not lift them all comparably.

In 1988, HBCUs found reason to be hopeful about their philanthropic prospects when Bill and Camille Cosby donated $20 million to Spelman College. Among other things, the investment financed Spelman's first endowed chair in 107 years. At the time, the gift was touted as "by far the largest donation any individual had made to a black college."[9] But by 2015, when princi-

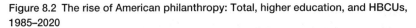

Figure 8.2 The rise of American philanthropy: Total, higher education, and HBCUs, 1985–2020

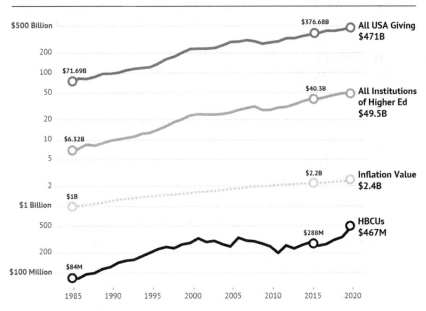

Sources:

All USA giving: *Giving USA 2021: The Annual Report on Philanthropy for the Year 2020* (Chicago: Giving USA Foundation, 2021), 4.

All higher education giving: *2004 Voluntary Support of Education* (New York: RAND Council for Aid to Education, 2004), 4, table 2, https://www.rand.org/content/dam/rand/www/external/news/press.05/03.02.pdf/RAND_VSE_2004.pdf.

HBCU giving: US Department of Education, National Center for Education Statistics, Integrated Postsecondary Education Data System (IPEDS), spring finance component (1990–2021); Digest of Education Statistics table 313.30 (1990–2020), https://nces.ed.gov/programs/digest/d21/tables/dt21_313.30.asp; and IPEDS, finance component final data (1985–89), retrieved from https://nces.ed.gov/ipeds/datacenter.

pal gifts in the hundreds of millions had become the norm for the wealthier institutions, the Cosby gift to Spelman remained the largest modern-era gift by an individual to a single HBCU. In fact, the pattern would persist until late 2020, when MacKenzie Scott donated $560 million to twenty-three separate HBCUs. Remarkably, the Scott investments in HBCUs were neither requested nor restricted. Unfortunately, no inarguable evidence has yet emerged to show that such sizable investments are substantially infectious.

Bill and Camille Cosby said they gave to Spelman because "they love the school," and as "a challenge to other black Americans to support black colleges."[10] MacKenzie Scott said her giving to HBCUs was motivated by the "inequities" that were exposed in the first half of 2020, and to call attention "to organizations and leaders driving change."[11] But what stimulated the largest single investment in a single HBCU in American history over a century ago?

INSTITUTIONAL CONSIDERATION FOR THE RECORD: THE MINDSETS BEHIND A $417 MILLION INVESTMENT IN A SINGLE HBCU

On April 14, 1903, Booker T. Washington delivered a message in New York's Madison Square Garden Concert Hall and attracted what remains the largest endowment investment in an HBCU. Why did a philanthropist provide Tuskegee with a GDP-relative $417 million in 2015 dollars?[12] How did Washington package, market, and sell his institution's value proposition to win multiple transformational investments to thrive, rather than merely transactional gifts to survive? Might any lessons from his fundraising story inform HBCU strategy today?

Washington's Appeal for a Better America

Washington developed two consistent, foundational messages, each designed to motivate two consequential audiences—one white, one Black. He was especially adept at both enchanting and inspiring philanthropists and diverting and sedating racists. On the day when he attracted an unprecedented investment of $600,000, his speech echoed many of the themes he had used with influential white audiences before.

From the start, his message to whites was informed and guided by a theory of progress. His theory was very practical, as he was early in his career when he began working hard to convince Black and white audiences that ignorance was the primary enemy of both races, and education was the only remedy.[13] But he could also be very pragmatic, as he was in the ten minutes he used to deliver his renowned Atlanta Exposition address. He stressed the value of Black lives, saying, "One-third of the population of the South is the Negro race . . . we shall constitute one-third and more of the ignorance and crime of the South, or one-third [of] its intelligence and progress; we shall contribute one-third to the business and industrial prosperity of the South, or we shall prove a veritable body of death, stagnating, depressing, retarding every effort to advance the body politic."[14]

Washington's message was simply to clarify and promote the value proposition of the Black presence in America. He reasoned that Black lives will matter either to the nation's rise or demise depending on whether and how well they are educated to do so. The 1,589-word message worked largely because it signaled racial cooperation with neither social interaction nor premature threats of political agitation. It was widely embraced as a way forward for the country.

By the time he delivered his endowment speech to the wealthiest whites in the world in 1903, he aimed his theory of progress at meriting "a new birth and a new freedom."[15] He repeated the need to use education to conquer the ignorance of Blacks and whites while pursuing racial peace and partnership. He centralized the imperative to redeem "a third of the South." Now more artful than candid about the strategic options for solving "the great race problem," he simply pointed to the folly of colonization, expatriation, amalgamation, and extermination. He favored cooperation, which had not been tried responsibly.[16]

The investment-worthiness of his approach became increasingly clear and compelling as he urged his audience to imagine both the stakes and the outcome. Sharing a vision of a new freedom, Washington spoke of the duty of both races. He said, "Your race has a tremendous responsibility and a rare privilege in connection with the elevation of my people. Unlike other races we did not come among you unbidden; our presence here was forced."[17] He requested that whites be "patient and just" in relation to Blacks. In return, he said, "my duty is to help my race to be patient with itself and just to itself." That meant using education to "prepare all the people to fulfill the duties of citizenship."[18] He invited them to envision a future beyond the current conflicts between races, regions, economies, and definitions of progress. Washington also made brief reference to stronger and weaker races. It was among his controversial devices aimed at neutralizing the concerns of those with "Southern sensibilities"—a device for managing Southern racial terrorism.[19]

Ironically, only briefly did Washington tout the Institute's scaled progress at 2,000 acres, 1,418 students, 22 departments, and 6,000 alumni. So why such a large investment?

Andrew Carnegie was in the crowd and listening with delight. Three days later, he sent a letter committing to an endowment contribution of $600,000, or 5 percent of US Steel Company bonds. His letter was brief but revealing. Comparing him to George Washington, Carnegie admiringly referred to the Tuskegee leader as a "modern Moses, who leads his race and lifts it through education to even better and higher things than a land overflowing with milk and honey."[20] Impressed by Washington's mission, Carnegie wrote, "His work is unique," and "I am satisfied that the serious race question of the South is to be solved wisely, only by following Booker Washington's policy."[21] Washington's plan was to bolster Tuskegee and efforts like it, while winning enough support for the idea of education and racial cooperation as solutions to "the race problem."

With a firm grasp of his audience, Washington thought that the wealthiest whites had the most to lose if they failed to resolve the race problem. Racial hatred and terrorism had the power to destabilize the country again, perhaps provoking yet another war. Thus, he was not "selling" an institution and its needs. Instead, he won investors in the pursuit of a more desirable, supra-racist world that Tuskegee existed to help create. His supporters were financing a tangible way to move to a stabler future. Donating to Tuskegee would help to get them there.

On that journey, Washington and his allies had to endure the South's racial terrorism while constantly appealing to the humanity of "the best class of Southern White people."[22] Washington was well aware that his success hinged on his ability to reach those he called "far seeing" whites. Since he knew they favored education, he had to convince them to finally assert themselves and insist on a Constitution-based, law-abiding America. Unfortunately, he did not live long enough to witness that outcome.

Washington's Appeal for a Black Infrastructure

Largely because Washington never assumed that the "cultured and important class" of whites would ever assert and prevail, his theory of progress pointed Black audiences toward a more tangible outcome. He insisted that they construct "an economic foundation" for the race, once calling it "the secret of civilization."[23] In his first major speech to the Alabama State Teacher's Association in 1882, he urged the educators to learn from "the founders of New England." He said they started by first making "themselves masters of the soil, their sons were schooled and taught trades, then came the small factories and trading houses, then they began to multiply their colleges and professional schools, then followed those in the learned professions and fine arts."[24] He later elaborated, saying, "We shall make our most enduring progress by laying the foundation carefully, patiently, in the ownership of the soil, the exercise of habits of industry and economy, the saving of money and in the securing of the most complete education of hand and head, and the exercise of the Christian virtues."[25] With conviction, he constantly developed and shared this message as incorruptibly true.

Washington emphasized the connection between industrial education, entrepreneurialism, and the generational mandate to lay the coveted foundation. He wanted Black audiences to see their current toil as a necessarily difficult, initial development phase, wherein progress would be measured in terms of securing land, houses, bank accounts, and solid, education-focused family units. With theological flair, he once challenged them, saying, "May we, in laying the foundation for a race, lay it so well that the race can stand securely thereon till it has served the great ends of our Creator."[26] By constantly building schools and businesses, they would enrich their supply of the talent, goods, and services required to earn independence. He literally preached this message to his students.

In 1898, Washington entitled one of his popular campus-based Sunday evening talks "How to Build a Race." He quoted Boston-based Episcopal Bishop Phillips Brooks's charge that "One generation gathers the material and the next builds the palaces." He continued, "Now this is true of all generations . . . and unless the foundation is properly laid—is deeply laid—it is impossible for the succeeding generation to have a very successful career."[27] He eyed his students and called them, "the generation which, in large measure, must gather the material with which to lay the foundation for future success." By commissioning them to be examples of the race's competence, confidence, and wealth, he offered an early version of what Anna Julia Cooper called "enlightened industrialism," or striving to become simultaneously deeply thoughtful and highly useful.[28]

Biographer Louis Harlan called Washington's book *The Future of the American Negro*, "the closest Washington ever came to an inclusive and systematic statement of his social philosophy and racial strategy."[29] With thirty separate references to the need to build a solid foundation, the compilation illuminated his lifelong game plan. It also revealed his constant concern about the threat of Southern barbarism, which is why he stressed the need for equal protection under the law. He cited the race massacres in North and South Carolina in 1898, along with other evidence, to legitimize his concern.[30]

In the last three years of his life, Washington reported to the National Negro Business League (NNBL) the progress made by Blacks in building businesses so that "neither we nor our children will be dependent upon the uncertainties of seeking and holding political office for our success. I repeat we must create positions for ourselves—positions which no man can give us nor take from us."[31] Three months before he died, he offered the NNBL another foundation update, this time contextualizing it with the news that lynching was on the rise. He insisted, "We must have in this country, law administered by the court and not by the mob. Along with the blotting out of lynchings should go that other relic of barbarism. I refer to public hangings. In all of these matters I am pleading not in the interest of the Negro or the White man, but in the interest of a more strong and perfect civilization."[32]

More than any other educational leader, Washington conceived and actualized a clear vision of how to use education to build a race in an environment saturated with the menacing threat and reality of racist terrorism. This foundational focus framed his overall mindset and informed the strategic thinking in his long-term view about the healthiest way for Blacks and America to emerge from grip of slavery. He believed, "If the Vanderbilts, Girards, Peabodys, and Peter Coopers started out poverty-stricken, with untrained minds, in competition with the shrewd and energetic Yankee, and amassed fortunes, what superior opportunities open up before our young men who begin life with a college-trained mind, and in a locality where competition is at its minimum."[33]

Among the obvious reasons why some of Washington's outlook may need to be recovered, here are three: one, the economic foundation he sought to destroy Black poverty and dependency has not yet been built; two, the self-made African American business titans he envisioned to provide the required transformational investments to HBCUs have not yet emerged; and three, the

HBCUs or palaces he sought to educate better citizens are not yet competitively resourced.

INSTITUTIONAL QUESTION FOR THE FUTURE: WHAT IS THE BEST MINDSET ADVICE FOR HBCU LEADERS IN THE PHILANTHROPY-RICH SECOND GILDED AGE?

Only twice has American higher education benefited from a dramatic rise in the tide of transformational philanthropy, both times contextualized by a Gilded Age. With the notable exceptions of Tuskegee and Hampton, HBCUs did not receive transformational funding in the first Gilded Age (1870–1900). Since the start of the second Gilded Age (late 1970s), no HBCU has yet experienced a sustained, measurably fruitful engagement with the philanthropic community, either on par with what Washington generated over a century ago, or, more recently, on pace with the higher-performing institutions.

Unquestionably, the depressed flow of philanthropic support to HBCUs has everything to do with the systemic devaluation of individual and institutional Black life in America. It is difficult to be lifted by the rising tide if your institutional boat is anchored by the philanthropic community's weighty, perhaps jaded, perceptions of HBCUs. Such distortions can effectively stymie advancement prospects, however forceful the rising tide may be. And because they did, the resulting differential flow of philanthropic support has yielded predictable conditions. While many predominantly white institutions in both Gilded Ages have been ushered beyond precarity by multiple alumni and nonalumni benefactors, most HBCUs have barely been fortunate enough to remain alive. And rather than becoming independent and optimized, the very existence of nearly every HBCU can be threatened or terminated by a federal- or state-level policy change.[34] No critical mass of philanthropists has ever concentrated support on a handful of HBCUs sufficient to produce for them a financial profile that removes precarity.[35] Altering that will undoubtedly require new thinking in the philanthropic community consistent with what is highlighted throughout this book. But there are also adjustments that HBCU leaders can make to position their institutions as beneficiaries of that shift.

Two potential mindset shifts among HBCU leaders and advocates may help to drive improved philanthropic returns on the road ahead.

Purging the Moyo "Dead Aid" Mindset

In 2009, Dambisa Moyo published *Dead Aid*, wherein she assessed the impact of $1 trillion in development-related aid from rich Western countries to Africa since the 1960s. Based on her analysis, Western loans and grants "have hampered, stifled and retarded Africa's development."[36] Instead of ending the cycle of poverty, it exacerbated it. Instead of stimulating growth toward independence, it compromised economic growth. She urged those who question the efficacy of the protracted aid to consider that Africa became home to half of the world's poor during that flow. In fact, "Between 1970 and 1998, when aid flows to Africa were at their peak, poverty in Africa rose from 11 percent to a staggering 66 percent. That is roughly 600 million of Africa's billion people trapped in the quagmire of poverty."[37] Based on such outcomes, Moyo disdains what she describes as "the mindset that pervades the West—that aid, whatever its form, is a good thing."[38]

Among the costliest outcomes of the trillion dollars of "relief" has been "a culture of aid-dependency," wherein "African governments view aid as a permanent, reliable, consistent source of income and have no reason to believe that the flows won't continue into the indefinite future. There is no incentive for long-term financial planning, no reason to seek alternatives to fund development, when all you have to do is sit back and bank the cheques."[39] Thus, as the aid exacerbated dependency, it also polluted the thinking of African leaders while stifling agency and entrepreneurism. Africa's worst conditions worsened, resulting in more poverty, more corruption, lower life expectancy rates, a "derelict" educational and physical infrastructure, a hollow tax base, and an "independence dependent on the largesse of their former colonial masters."[40] The mindset that privileged alleviating poverty over promoting growth led Moyo to conclude that the Western aid flow to Africa is "not benign—it's malignant. No longer part of the potential solution, it's part of the problem—in fact aid *is* the problem."[41]

The precipitous deterioration of African mindsets was rooted in the impure motives of the aid bearers. For decades, wealthy Westerners, whether well-meaning individuals or countries, brought a flawed mindset to the challenge of "helping" Africa. Moyo observes that "Deep in every liberal sensibility is a profound sense that in a world of moral uncertainty one idea is sacred, one belief cannot be compromised: the rich should help the poor, and the form of this help should be aid."[42]

Finding a fixed, aid-dominant mindset at the root of Africa's poverty and misery, she calls for a radical rethink of the aid-dependency model. For Moyo, aid itself is a psychology or outlook that yields predictable results. Perhaps unwittingly driven by a crippling dose of pity, the "help poor Africa" mindset was never wired to end poverty, nor to alter the structures that make poverty possible. Instead, the aid is designed to enable the survival of its poor recipients, supplying them with just enough pain relief to cause the providers to feel the pride of having done their part. And the aid provision is most effective when it succeeds in infesting the mindsets of the impoverished, convincing them that their aid-enabled existence is as good as life can and will get.

Moyo's vision of an aid-free, investment-rich solution to the continent's chronic brokenness requires African countries to reduce their toxic dependency on the West. To that end, she recommends that each nation's foreign aid reliance begin to gradually shift from roughly 75 percent of their incoming economic revenue to a healthier 5 percent. She also suggests a shift in the purpose of the incoming revenue to stimulate growth and self-sufficiency, instead of the wonted stagnation and dependency. These more positive outcomes are not even possible when the aid providers and recipients are fixed with an aid-dependent mindset, never mind the minimal accountability about outcomes.

What has all of this to do with HBCUs?

While it is unquestionably far from a perfect analogy to the HBCU situation, Moyo's analysis begs several key questions. How dependent are HBCUs on federal and state funding? To what degree is government funding positioned to facilitate institutional growth versus survival and dependency? Is it possible that a "culture of aid" mindset in the providers and recipients has helped to limit HBCU advancement prospects?

Regarding state aid, there should be little debate about the well-documented crippling effects of the long-standing inequitable state funding to public HBCUs. While the racial disparities were highlighted decades earlier, lawsuits aiming to end and correct the protracted inequities were brought by the leaders of public HBCUs beginning in the 1970s.[43] Not only have these institutions received significantly less funding than their in-state PWI

counterparts, but they have also evolved to "rely on federal, state, and local funding more heavily than their non-HBCU counterparts (54 percent of
overall revenue versus 38 percent)."[44] Relying on a single source far more than
what fitness requires, while receiving far less than what fairness demands, is
a version of the "dead aid" in Africa cited by Moyo. The mindsets that originated these policies and practices were informed and obviously guided by the
racially hostile world of the 1890s, when most public HBCUs were born or
bolstered. Based on the persistent inequities and inequalities, those mindsets
have not yet been fully laid to rest.

One way for today's state officials to change that is to shift from a fixed,
HBCU-unfriendly aid mindset to a growth, HBCU-friendly investment
mindset. That might include new funding initiatives designed to enhance the
HBCU capacity to do a better job of meeting the human resource needs of the
state and nation. Simultaneously, select states should introduce and finance
the concept of an HBCU flagship institution, bringing at least one HBCU
to competitive levels of funding with the state's existing flagship, not one of
which has ever been an HBCU. This is especially appropriate in the six states
(Alabama, Georgia, Louisiana, Maryland, Mississippi, and North Carolina)
that have at least three public HBCUs in their state systems. Creative mergers should be considered, but not in an effort to ensure that the state can save
money. Merging some HBCUs can be a method of adding depth and breadth
to the capacity of an HBCU flagship institution.

Like state funding to HBCUs, federal funding has also been profoundly
inadequate and grossly ill-suited to yield competitive growth. The Department of Education annually routes both individual and institutional aid to
HBCUs. In any given year, that aid is significantly skewed toward individual
grants and loans provided to the students attending HBCUs via the Title IV
program. Since 1964, this program has provided supplemental funding to
help students and institutions. For instance, in 2015, Title IV aid to HBCU
students totaled $3.362 billion. The aid is entirely small-scale and transac-
tional, rather than large-scale and transformational.

Since 1965, there has been a single federal grant program explicitly borne
of a growth mindset and aimed at advancing fundamentally the HBCU capacity to educate, discover, and serve. Title III Part B provides "grants to
eligible institutions to assist them in strengthening their academic, adminis-

trative, and fiscal capabilities."[45] In 2015, $382 million was provided to HB-CUs through that program. This ratio has been consistent. On average, for every nine dollars the federal government annually routes to HBCUs as student aid, it provides one dollar for institutional growth. That amounts to 90 percent transactional and 10 percent transformational. The consequences of that skew are evident in the outcomes, which reveal that it is easier for many students to begin their education at an HBCU, yet more difficult for many to complete it, simply because the institutions are without the endowment wherewithal to facilitate completion.[46]

Since transactional aid has dominated for fifty years, as has the fixed mindset that gave birth to the toxic ratio, what kind of new effort might the federal government launch by viewing HBCUs with a growth mindset? Is there a strategic way to fix the imbalance, one that would also serve both HBCUs and the nation well?

In the interest of one day weaning off all federal institutional support, what if the Title III Part B program were bolstered and then gradually phased out? What if transformational aid was immediately boosted to be on par with transactional aid, and then phased out over the next fifty years? Depending on the quality of governance and campus leadership, HBCUs would then either take advantage and use the funding to become more self-sufficient, or be without it in fifty years, when they would have to survive on their own. With this or similar initiatives, growth mindset ideas can and should set a new tone for the fixed and stale relationship between the federal government and HBCUs.

To those who might question whether it is a federal responsibility to facilitate the institutional growth of HBCUs, the answer is, it is not . . . under normal circumstances. But the federal government has already recognized that HBCU history is no ordinary history. That acknowledgement resides in the original language of the Higher Education Act of 1965, which states a commitment to do at least two things: "to strengthen the educational resources of our colleges and universities and to provide financial assistance for students in postsecondary and higher education."[47] The language points to both institutional and individual assistance. Title IV has been a relatively robust way to keep the commitment to provide individual assistance (pursuant to the individual value proposition discussed in chapter 6). By comparison, Title III Part B has been consistently anemic (cited, in the same chapter, as the institutional value proposition). A new growth mindset approach is simply a way to finally get the institutional commitment right. Moreover, the reason to correctly execute on a previously acknowledged commitment is not to position the government to help correct the past; it is to position HBCUs to help create the future.

Adopting the Mount Rushmore Mindset

What about the private sector? No matter what adjustments are made in the HBCU relationship with state and federal governments, the private sector has always been, and will remain, the primary source of support for HBCUs. With recent annual philanthropic giving to higher education likely to remain above $50 billion per year, what kind of mindsets in the HBCU community might create different outcomes for HBCUs?

If the long-standing fixed mindsets among public officials have indeed helped to keep most HBCUs frozen in a relatively transactional, hand-to-mouth existence, it is worth considering whether it has also helped to fix some of the mindsets in the HBCU community. That is, are some HBCU leaders too focused on the flow of public sector aid, which has invariably been limited relative to the scale of private philanthropic resources, which may be more accessible based on the power of persuasion? And could those public aid–focused mindsets within HBCU leadership be partly responsible for their relative lack of fruitful engagements with the private sector?

Between 1985 and 2015, seventy-two different colleges and universities successfully completed a capital campaign for at least one billion dollars.[48] Could new mindsets help to finally move an HBCU or historically minority-serving institution toward that list?

Rather than further speculate about the existing mindsets of private philanthropists or HBCU campus leaders, it might be more instructive to advise on what constitutes an optimal growth mindset for both sides to now adopt.

There are many ways to categorize the motivations and mindsets of both donors and fundraisers. Several studies have segmented philanthropy, suggesting that it has seven faces, or twenty-two motivations, or sixteen identifiable interaction patterns.[49] But regarding the scope and scale of capital campaign results, two modes tend to prevail in the interplay between fundraisers and philanthropists. The two modes can be contrasted by their likely outcomes, wherein one yields smaller, less ambitious campaigns, and the other yields far larger campaigns, akin to those since the start of the billion-dollar capital campaigning era. In fact, one mindset might be symbolized by an image of the American Red Cross, which is effective at quickly raising money to be responsive to the various crises around the world. The other mindset is indicative of Mount Rushmore, a Depression-era venture that attracted small and large investments from donors motivated to establish a very stable and permanent site and symbol of national pride and confidence.[50] With higher education in mind, the approaches to the fundraising for each can generally be further distinguished as follows:

- One is more an appeal to the conscience of the philanthropist, as if encouraging them to donate and be a part of something good, while the other is more an appeal to their ego, as if intriguing them to endow and be a part of something great.
- One tries to tap into the missionary or savior mindset of potential prospects, while the other targets those with a pioneer or explorer mindset.
- One resembles disaster relief philanthropy, as contrasted with venture philanthropy.
- One is more likely to attract a save-the-day gift, and the other a create tomorrow investment.
- In the narrative of one appeal, an observer might imagine hearing violins in the background, evoking sadness and pity, but as the other appeal evolves, one might hear trumpets, evoking greatness and posterity.

Based on outcomes alone, the relationship between America's philanthropic community and the HBCU community has tended toward the Red Cross aid-dominant mindset, rather than the Mount Rushmore investment-dominant mindset. A reversal of this trend is essential to enhancing the ability of select HBCUs to shape better citizens.

Finally, in 1946, not long after lamenting the absence of "rich Negroes," and nearing the midpoint between the two Gilded Ages, Du Bois told a Knoxville College gathering, "Today the private institutions are facing the fact that unless they receive increased contributions, not now in sight, and these funds reach large figures, they must either close or become fully state schools."[51] Even if by 2015 a handful of African Americans had become wealthy enough to make a transformational difference at select HBCUs, systemic racial disparities and basic African American needs have remained vast. And it is folly for HBCU leaders to be duped by the mythologizing around annual Black buying power exceeding $1 trillion.[52]

In 2019, the median wealth of Black families ($24,100) trailed that of white families ($188,200), as did their respective mean wealth levels ($142,500 and $983,400).[53] And with only seven of America's 614 billionaires being African American, it is not optimal for the most aspiring HBCUs to focus on Black wealth alone.[54]

Since the start of the billion-dollar capital campaign era, only one major campaign to bolster a Black institution has magnetized significant philanthropy from the Black community—a scaled effort to raise at least half a billion dollars to establish the first and only National Museum of African American History and Culture. In that quest, with his ability to attract transformational support specifically from the Black community, Dr. Lonnie Bunch is described as having "raised the bar for Black philanthropy."[55] In a campaign to raise $540 million, African Americans dominated the group of individuals who gave $1 million or more. In addition, African American organizations provided 28 percent of institutional support, and were well represented among those who gave smaller-scale gifts. That campaign was indubitably reflective of the investment-intensive growth mindset approach to advancement. The HBCU community should examine the nature of the museum's successful appeal, just as those in the philanthropic community should examine why select HBCUs are similarly worthy of scaled, transformational investments.

FOR THE MINDSET

The campus leaders who can generate bold, investment worthy ideas will make their campuses more attractive to philanthropists who can provide the transformational capital necessary to finally remove the stifling bandwidth tax of financial stress.[56]

The Fluttering Veil
over HBCUs

HBCUs have yet to become the very best versions of themselves, largely due to the general absence of three key things—an elevated value proposition, iceberg governance, and transformational investments. They may have moved African Americans up from slavery, poverty, and marginality, but they are long overdue in moving themselves up from precarity. The next quarter-century will determine whether the veil is lifting or lowering over their potential optimization. Yet a larger veil now flutters, too, over our democracy and the planet. Because HBCUs have always focused their education on the habitability of the world around them, they would abandon their calling to ignore it now, even in its broadest terms. Accordingly, a re-architecture imperative stares at a higher education industry that has typically been both blind to the best practices within the HBCU tradition and far more captivated by capital and stature than by character and relevance. The stars are now aligned for all of that to change.

This perspective is indispensable because a growth mindset about the fluttering veil over HBCUs can reveal new ways to close the gap between what the campuses teach best and what the world needs most.

CHAPTER NINE

The Re-architecture Ultimatum

Overview of Transformation Four:
Up from Uncertainty, 2015 and Ongoing

Civilization, we have said, is fellowship. As men rise out of barbarism they "have regard" for one another. Their interests are pooled. They have agreements of common purpose and, hence, of mutual understanding. It is these agreements which provide content for education.

Alexander Meiklejohn, *Education Between Two Worlds*, 1942

The ending of all unnatural rifts is healing work. When different groups within what should be a natural community clash against each other, that also is disease. That is why healers say that our people, the way we are now divided into petty nations, are suffering from a terrible disease.

Ayi Kwei Armah, *The Healers*

An iconic bronze statue of Booker T. Washington was unveiled on April 5, 1922, and now sits just inside Tuskegee University's main entrance. Washington's longtime adviser and secretary, Emmett Jay Scott, led a special effort to ensure that the $25,000 required to finance it came from African American donors alone. Over one hundred thousand responded favorably.[1] Known as "Lifting the Veil of Ignorance," the statue became the symbol of Washington's role as the most consequential, results-driven leader of the African American emergence from enslavement.

Among those who amplified the ambiguous message of the monument was novelist Ralph Ellison, who attended Tuskegee from 1933 to 1936. To Ellison's chagrin, Tuskegee was better at preparing budding blacksmiths than budding Black writers, so it was unsurprising when he later wrote about it so unflatteringly.[2] In his award-winning *Invisible Man*, Ellison's nameless protagonist stands before the frozen image, observes the fluttering veil, and confesses that he is "unable to decide whether the veil is really being lifted, or lowered more firmly into place." He wonders whether he is "witnessing a revelation or a more efficient blinding."[3]

A similar airborne veil flutters, metaphorically, over both Washington's reputation and the future of HBCUs. More consequentially, it hovers threateningly, too, over both the democracy and the planet.

INSTITUTIONAL CONSIDERATION FOR THE RECORD: THE GAP-WIDENING CENTURY, THE CHANGE IMPERATIVE, AND FIXING MORE THAN INEQUALITY

Together with other imagined observances to honor the long-awaited blossoming of American democracy, there was supposed to be an HBCU equity celebration by now. The key shapers of the Black educational infrastructure envisioned a century-long gap-closure agenda that should have been realized by 2015. W. E. B. Du Bois saw HBCU graduates helping to impart a distinctively African gift to humanity, Booker T. Washington saw his entrepreneurial graduates building the economic foundation required to elevate a truly disadvantaged people, and Mordecai W. Johnson saw a concurrent quest to correct both Black marginality and HBCU precarity. All three leaders envisioned many Black colleges surging to competitive levels of institutional strength, productivity, and prominence, minimally on par with the best in the higher education industry. But because this kind of gap closure remains unrealized, most HBCUs are now without the competitively optimized institutional profiles suitable for shaping the very best citizens.

The most recent ideal climate for aggressive gap closure began roughly six decades after the last of the three agendas was articulated by Johnson in 1928. The individual wealth surges late in the twentieth century represented an opportunity-rich climate for institutional wealth surges. But there were lingering climate toxicities, too. As described earlier in this book, when a plurality of American mindsets defined success largely (if not exclusively) in terms of racial integration or inclusion, the neglect of the HBCU infrastructure agenda was foreseeable. The timing was especially unfortunate. Since the vision to end HBCU precarity had been progressively blurred by the desegregation haze of the 1970s, the campuses were already becoming invisible at the start of the billion-dollar capital campaign era of 1980s. Thus, just as the overall climate for gap closure appeared to improve, the forecast for gap closure worsened.

Du Bois, Washington, and Johnson consistently concerned themselves with HBCUs relative to Ivy League institutions, the widely perceived pace-setters of institutional strength in the higher education enterprise. Mindful of their aspirations and expectations, a snapshot of the current state of gap closure between HBCUs and their wealthiest competition is provided below.

THE INCLUSION AGENDA SUMMARIZED

Although "prior to 1954, over 90 percent of black students were educated in HBCUs,"[4] figure 9.1, below, reveals how the vast majority of African American students in higher education shifted from HBCUs to non-HBCUs between 1954 and 2015.

That is the top-line message about Johnson's inclusion agenda. In fact, by 2015, almost half of the 3.8 million African American college students were enrolled in either community colleges or in the for-profit sector, as figure 9.2 shows.

HBCUs AND THE AMERICAN PHILANTHROPY SURGE

The second Gilded Age, which featured a dramatic increase in all giving, included an impressive increase in giving to American higher education, as shown in figure 9.3.

Since the giving to HBCUs was minuscule by comparison, the gap widened over the very century wherein the goal was to narrow it.

HBCUs AND THE PURSUIT OF ENDOWMENT STRENGTH

Tuskegee's Booker T. Washington and Harvard's Charles Eliot placed an emphasis on endowment back in 1906, during the first Gilded Age. When the second Gilded Age stimulated billion-dollar capital campaigning in the 1980s, the emphasis on endowment was revived with only a handful of institutions prospering. But unlike in the first era, no HBCU has yet prospered sustainably and competitively.

FIGURE 9.1 The inclusion agenda: African American enrollment, HBCU vs. non-HBCU, 1954–2015

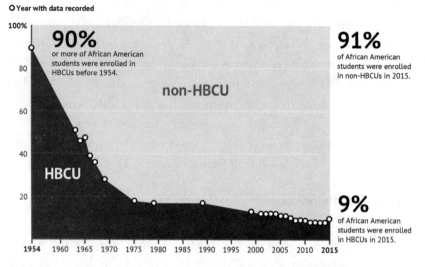

Sources: Nampeo D. McKenney, Virginia H. Williams, and Sylvia. Small, *The social and economic status of Negroes in the United States, 1970.* (Washington, DC: U.S. Department of Commerce, Bureau of the Census (BLS Report No. 394, Series P-23, No. 38), (1971), https://www2.census.gov/library/publications/1971/demographics/p23-038.pdf.; US Department of Education, National Center for Education Statistics, Integrated Postsecondary Education Data System (IPEDS) Fall Enrollment component final data (1980-2020), https://nces.ed.gov/ipeds/datacenter/.

Washington, Du Bois, and other contemporary leaders envisioned HB-CUs amassing large endowments, even while orienting the education of African Americans to yield more humane outcomes. Again, as a way to honor their infrastructural dreams for HBCUs, it is appropriate to consider their progress from the start of the billion-dollar capital campaign period to the end of the Washington gap closure century (1985–2015). How has the financial strength of the top ten private HBCUs changed relative to that of both the "Ivy-plus" institutions and the top ten liberal arts institutions?[5] And has more or less progress been made by the top ten public HBCUs relative to the top public non-HBCUs?

Figures 9.4 and 9.5 reveal conditions according to the two key metrics that best capture the widened gaps—endowment and the endowment-expense ratio (EER). (A list of all the institutions compared in these figures can be found in appendix A.)

Again, the early African American educational vision was not merely about HBCU growth, but about closing the gap between HBCUs and the

FIGURE 9.2 The inclusion agenda: Percentages of African American students
enrolled by institution type in 2015

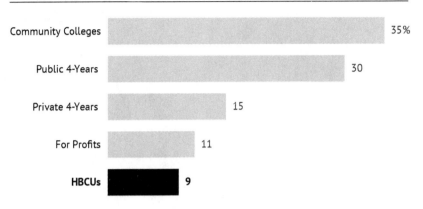

Source: US Department of Education, National Center for Education Statistics, Integrated Postsecondary Education Data System, fall enrollment component final data (2015).
Files generated using NCES Trend Generator, https://nces.ed.gov/ipeds/TrendGenerator.

institutions built and bolstered by African American enslavement, a goal that has proven to be largely elusive. In 1985, the average of the top ten HBCU endowments was a mere 2.2 percent of that of the Ivy-plus institutions and 14 percent that of the top ten liberal arts institutions. Yet with giving to higher education surging from $6.3 billion to $40.3 billion (see figure 9.3) over the next three decades, the gap only widened between private HBCU endowments and the wealthiest private institutions in their industry. By 2015, the average of the top ten HBCU endowments had shifted from 2.2 percent of the average Ivy-plus endowments to 1.1 percent. Similarly, the 2015 average of the top ten HBCU endowments relative to the average of the top ten private liberal arts institutions shifted from 14 percent in 1985 to 11 percent in 2015. The relative status of public HBCUs revealed even greater gaps than those between the private HBCUs and their wealthy counterparts.

As figure 9.5 reveals, the endowment-expense ratio (EER) tells a similar story, especially for the private institutions, where the EER is most relevant as a measure of strength.

In 1985, the average EER gap between HBCUs and the Ivy-plus group was less than a point and a half, but by 2015 it had grown to more than four points. Similarly, the HBCU–liberal arts college gap grew from almost four points in 1985 to over eight points by 2015.

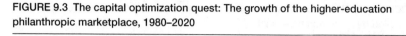

FIGURE 9.3 The capital optimization quest: The growth of the higher-education philanthropic marketplace, 1980–2020

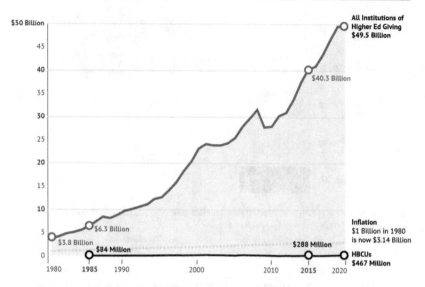

Sources: All higher education giving: 2004 Voluntary Support of Education (New York: RAND Council for Aid to Education, 2004), 4, table 2, https://www.rand.org/content/dam/rand/www/external/news/press.05/03.02.pdf /RAND_VSE_2004.pdf; *HBCU giving:* US Department of Education, National Center for Education Statistics, Integrated Postsecondary Education Data System (IPEDS), spring finance component (1990–2021); *Digest of Education Statistics,* table 313.30 (1990–2020), https://nces.ed.gov/programs/digest/d21/tables/dt21_313.30.asp; and IPEDS, finance component final data (1985–89), retrieved from https://nces.ed.gov/ipeds/datacenter.

While many other gaps could be listed, it is most telling that, by 2015, at least fifteen HBCUs had not yet amassed an endowment as large as that which Washington secured for Tuskegee by 1915. Moreover, in constant dollars, Washington's $2 million in 1915 would be a GDP-relative $932 million in 2015, an endowment level that no HBCU has amassed, even by 2020.[6] That may make a profound statement about the governance and leadership patterns in HBCUs, the traditionally skewed preferences of America's philanthropic community, or both. Yet no matter the causes, when institutions are underendowed and tuition dependent while enrolling a traditionally under-resourced, academically needy target population, their instability and uncertainty tend to be more acute.

Without question, the closure of the institutional wealth gap would finally set some HBCUs on a pathway to capital and character optimization. And this would lift, rather than lower, their familiar veil of precarity. But since a

FIGURE 9.4 The capital optimization quest: Average HBCU endowments, relative to the wealthiest institutions

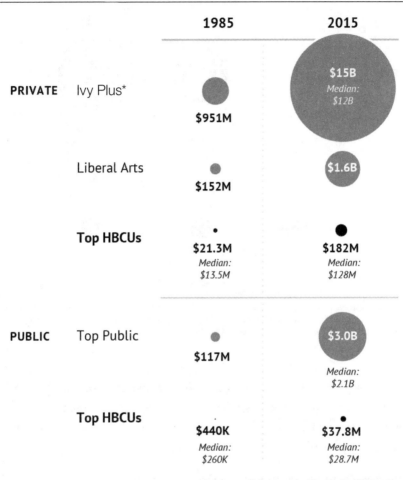

	1985	2015
PRIVATE Ivy Plus*	$951M	$15B Median: $12B
Liberal Arts	$152M	$1.6B
Top HBCUs	$21.3M Median: $13.5M	$182M Median: $128M
PUBLIC Top Public	$117M	$3.0B Median: $2.1B
Top HBCUs	$440K Median: $260K	$37.8M Median: $28.7M

Medians are shown when there's a 30% or more change between the average and the median. This suggests the presence of outliers in the spread of data points.

Sources: US Department of Education, Higher Education General Information Survey (1970) and Integrated Post-secondary Education Data System (IPEDS) (1985–2015). All HBCU endowment data from: National Center for Education Statistics, IPEDS, spring finance component (1990–2021); Digest of Education Statistics, table 313.30 (1990–2020), https://nces.ed.gov/programs/digest/d21/tables/dt21_313.30.asp; and IPEDS, finance component final data (1985–89), retrieved from https://nces.ed.gov/ipeds/datacenter.

*Ivy League plus Stanford and MIT.

FIGURE 9.5 The capital optimization quest: HBCU endowment-expense ratios relative to the wealthiest institutions

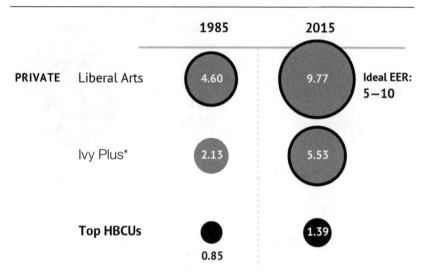

Sources: US Department of Education, Higher Education General Information Survey (1970) and Integrated Postsecondary Education Data System (IPEDS) (1985–2015). All HBCU endowment data from: National Center for Education Statistics, IPEDS, spring finance component (1990–2021); Digest of Education Statistics, table 313.30 (1990–2020), https://nces.ed.gov/programs/digest/d21/tables/dt21_313.30.asp; and IPEDS, finance component final data (1985–89), retrieved from https://nces.ed.gov/ipeds/datacenter.
*Ivy League plus Stanford and MIT.

scaled push for gap closure will depend on the emergence of a much stronger appetite for cooperative change than America has ever witnessed or required, it is worth considering the prospects for such a seismic shift in the mindsets of some very powerful people.

THE CHANGE IMPERATIVE AND FIXING MORE THAN MERE INSTITUTIONAL INEQUALITY

Ultimately, this call for investment-driven structural change is aimed at two communities—higher education and philanthropy—that have been strikingly change-averse. Both have been stubbornly beholden to an American status quo with longstanding inequities. Worse yet, their joint resistance to reform is rooted in their similar mindsets and motives, hardened during their centuries-long, intertwined evolution. Major players in both sectors could have had much more to do with the perfection of American democracy than either group has ever attempted. But the lack of a meaningful democracy push by colleges and universities is particularly negligent.

Throughout the history of American higher education, many have called on its institutions to do more to meet the pressing needs of the country. Of particular note, president Harry S. Truman appointed a Commission on Higher Education, which generated a comprehensive six-volume report beginning in 1947. It called for significant change in the industry. Describing America as being in "a time of crisis," the Commission underscored the need to reshape "education for a fuller realization of democracy in every phase of living."[7] The first of its kind, this document set the tone for other similar reports, commissioned by subsequent US presidents, each calling for meaningful change in higher education. In 2006, secretary of education Margaret Spelling's Commission on the Future of Higher Education issued its report urging systemic reform throughout the education pipeline.[8] At the time, it added volume to a roar of other studies, reports, books, and articles, each with recommendations about how higher education must be transformed. Noting the likely futility of these blaring calls for reform, Robert M. Diamond, as president of the National Academy for Academic Leadership, analyzed higher education's persistent stubbornness and concluded, "Significant change will never occur in any institution until the forces for change are greater in combination than the forces preserving the status quo. And in colleges and universities, the forces for resisting change are extremely powerful."[9] Much of this inflexibility developed as American higher education grew and became standardized and normalized in American life.

In his authoritative history of the development of higher education, published in 1965, Laurence Veysey aptly described its tangled roots of uniformity and rigidity. Veysey argued that there have been few deviations from the innovative patterns and the stable structure set in American higher education by 1910. Offering unique and sustainable innovations, Harvard's Eliot was key in redefining the nature of undergraduate education, and Hopkins's Daniel Gilman led in the effort to innovate at the graduate level. Referred to as an "academic boom," the advances between 1890 and 1910 included deanships, academic departments with a recognized chairman, a calculated scale of faculty rank, administrative growth, an emphasis on public relations, and "bold schemes of institutional advancement."[10]

The era also included the emergence of uniform college entrance requirements and a movement to accredit all institutions that met minimal standards. Veysey argued that in and just beyond the 1890s, the development of higher education was hardened in its most critical and lasting respects. Then, with confidence, he asserted that once institutions adopted the changes of that era, "thereafter the main task becomes one of maintenance, or at most of continued construction along duplicatory lines. *An architect is then no longer required, only a contractor.*"[11] (Emphasis added.)

Veysey's obvious celebration of the seminal influence of Eliot and Gilman also functions as a biting critique of higher education leadership ever since. By implication, the presidents of America's colleges and universities since Eliot and Gilman, with only rare exceptions, have operated as "contractors," ostensibly hired to manage institutions in thematically similar ways with little variation.

If Veysey's interpretation was accurate in 1965, presidential tenures and legacies have generally hardened even more in their bureaucratic and character sameness since then. Several major "design developments" have clearly emerged since his pronouncement, including the rise of community colleges, for-profit institutions, online learning, and open curricula.[12] But few of the changes indicate a fundamental redesign of the organizations or their values. Instead, there is a more intense leadership emphasis on keeping pace with evolving curricular and credentialization patterns, enhancing campus living and learning environments, and attracting sizable philanthropic investments. Nor is there much variation in the basic mindsets of those the institutions have graduated. Strikingly few American campuses have made a recognizably serious and scaled attempt to shape higher-character, democracy-minded citizens akin to the HBCU vision and tradition. The resulting decades-long reproduction of largely fixed mindsets is rooted in the fact that the crystallization of the structure and presidency of the American university are not the only patterns that hardened over time.

Again, the protracted story of higher education's development and spread of knowledge matters. Beyond the crystallization of university architecture and stewardship, the higher education curriculum also took centuries to harden, even as it expanded. From the start, increased resources created more degrees of freedom for leaders imagining how to stabilize their institutional identity and footing. And as Craig Wilder revealed, "The expansion of the

northern and southern academies in the decades before the Civil War accelerated the politicization of science and the institutionalization of race."[13] As the
slave economy grew, the curricular justification for racism was financed to
expand from a theological basis to a scientific and sociological basis. And for
an academy already incentivized to find harmony with the allegiant sources of
its multigenerational wealth, there was no controversy as it gradually broadened the intellectual rationale for the exploitative slave economy. The grantors
and grantees enjoyed a mutually beneficial relationship. As selected universities became more prosperous and powerful, their slaveholding benefactors
received a most coveted vindication accompanied by unparalleled prestige.
Wilder assessed the pattern and asserted, "As Atlantic slavery underwrote the
production of knowledge, it distorted the knowable."[14]

The broad and long-range consequences of this process must not be un-
derestimated. A comfortable and well-wrought inequity-tolerant world was
normalized, expanded, and abided with the aid of higher education's stamp
of approval. And, ironically, even though theology was the axis around which
the original American higher education curricula turned, it does not appear to
have ever produced enough graduates with the conviction to disrupt and correct the stark, protracted realities of human bondage, injustice, and extreme
inequity. After centuries, the abolitionist mindset may have finally helped to
provoke the battle that ended slavery, but the supremacist mindsets that favored such inhumanity remained resilient in their focus on a much larger war
against a Constitution-based multicultural democracy. The supremacists may
have been wounded by losing the Civil War, but they were never defeated.

It is tragic, yet understandable, that this mindset conditioning would have
such a long shadow in American life. To this day, large numbers of Americans have neither been taught nor expected to help facilitate the country's full
emergence from her nonegalitarian past. As a consequence of this negligence,
the evidence of widespread, higher education–instilled moral outrage about
injustice and inequality remains thin. But that is understandable, too.

In a sense, this is the flip side of the adjustment the young Booker T.
Washington made to the "weather-like" barbarism shaping his world and
worldview. For well over three centuries, the curricular menu available to millions of American college students evolved to preserve the innocence and be-
neficence of those who authored and prospered from sustained wrongdoing.

And as generations of white students consumed this curriculum, inequity and supremacy discreetly became normalized, and the students' capacity to respond with outrage was on a par with their capacity to be outraged about a rainy day. Largely unnoticed, it was simply accepted as occasionally inconvenient.

Meanwhile, it became increasingly unlikely that any significant number of college presidents would do anything to alter these trends. Most had too much to lose. Their contractor mindsets predictably inclined them toward indifference to such societal conditions, precisely because so many of them prioritized garnering favor and funding from the wealthy. And it had always been bad form for presidents to question or be bothered by how the privileged class of real and potential donors became so privileged. Tellingly, Yale, Princeton, Columbia, Georgetown, and scores of other institutions have only recently begun removing from buildings and schools the names of donors whose wealth was derived from human enslavement. It matters that such moves seemed to be triggered less by presidential surges in moral conscience than by their acquiescence to external pressures.

Simply put, it is disturbingly clear that contractor-led institutions, whether in higher education or philanthropy, will only yield the same narrow and flawed outcomes that preserve or worsen our normalized inequities. And the only way to correct for that is to begin countering it by finding leaders who will prioritize the re-architecture of both sectors, ideally in a joint, aggressive venture to shape more and better citizens.

The following two essential imperatives of the re-architecture agenda are offered as a mindset advisory for those in the higher education and philanthropic communities.

INSTITUTIONAL QUESTION FOR THE FUTURE: HOW CAN A RE-ARCHITECTURE STRATEGY HELP TO SAVE THE DEMOCRACY AND THE PLANET?

In the initial quarter of the twenty-first century, humanity faces a convergence of crises. A worldwide health crisis is worsened by multiple leadership and economic crises. Moral and ethical crises are framed by global issues of racial injustice and extreme inequality. These troubles have emerged with significant help from a higher education tradition of producing people who are inclined to abide and exploit an inequity-authored status quo, rather than disrupt and humanize it. And because the proliferating crises are unsustainable and worsening, the world now deserves and requires better leaders and citizens.

Thus, in addition to the inequity veil now fluttering over many HBCUs, other veils, some as thick as winding sheets, may be more consequential. And if they are lowering, catastrophic outcomes could ensue, nationally and globally. Some may recognize it as an imperative to lift such veils, but the stakes seem high enough to regard the task as an ultimatum.

Can American higher education lead an effort to produce better citizens with the veil-lifting capacity to shape a better world? Can all colleges and universities now serve as the epicenter for aligning human talent with humanity's direst needs, drawing heavily and benefitting greatly from the HBCU example? Pursuant to the optimization theme herein, it makes sense to utilize character and capital as frames for the re-architecture undertaking.

RE-ARCHITECTING CHARACTER

If the American undergraduate experience is to finally yield more recognizably humane outcomes, the most relevant history from which it can and should draw is the HBCU tradition. There is a clear need for all higher education institutions to replicate the Fisk- or HBCU-based "officer corps" idea.[15] Similar to many HBCUs, the Fisk faculty and campus culture prepared students with mindsets designed to shape a new world by doing battle against those with mindsets designed to defend an old one. American higher education today must prepare students for different—but related—battles in the same mindset war. Minimally, future college graduates must enter society with new, high-character mindsets equipped to win on two key fronts: the battle to save the democracy, and the battle to save the planet. Each requires some elaboration before looking ahead.

Character and the Battle to Save the Democracy

The flaws compromising America's quest to become a more perfect union derive from an identity crisis evident at the nation's conception. At its only Constitutional convention in 1787, "of the fifty-five delegates nearly half, including a number of northerners, possessed slaves."[16] The eventual first president, George Washington, did not arrive at the Philadelphia-based meeting

with three of his more than two hundred enslaved human beings to offer
the antislavery argument of the debate. There was no debate. While the lofty
language of equality infused the founding documents, there was no great controversy about who, beyond privileged white men, was included in the circle
of equality drawn by the phrase "we the people." However stark and brutal,
the issue of racial abuse was not as central to America's identity struggle at its
first founding as it would become at its second.[17] By the time of the second
founding, stimulated by a Civil War and Reconstruction, America's identity
debate featured sharp divisions. The differences boiled down to very different
directions or destinations after the nation's rebirth. And one question became
more important than all others, even if it was ignored by those without the
courage to ask or answer it: would "we the people" finally mean all American
citizens, or just the descendants of those who had shaped the world based on
unassailable class privilege, male dominance, and racial conceit?

Frederick Douglass asked a version of that question when he compellingly
pointed to the persistent destination choice facing America in his 1869 speech
"Our Composite Nationality."[18] In the midst of America's rebirth, midwifed
by the equality-enhancing Thirteenth, Fourteenth, and Fifteenth Constitutional Amendments, Douglass saw the Reconstruction pivot as the nation's
long-awaited emergence "from the darkness and chaos of unbridled barbarism."[19] He believed "we are at the beginning of our ascent," and "we are destined to grow and flourish," because that is what Reconstruction's pivot was
encouragingly signaling. As he welcomed the fundamental shift as "both a
sign and a result of civilization," he stood to address the question that necessi-
tated both the Civil War and the aforementioned Constitutional amendments:
is America "better or worse for being composed of different races of men?"[20]

The quest to become a "more perfect union," thereby fully realizing the
vision set forth in the US Constitution, cannot be completed in the absence
of a robust, humane, and widely shared answer to Douglass's question. More
than any other educational objective in America, finding such clarity and
meaningful common ground must be prioritized. What if American higher
education now led the way in generating and democratizing a firm answer to
that question, while devising plans to inform and enrich the nation's entire
education pipeline accordingly? There is little debate that the quality of de-

mocracy nationwide, if not worldwide, may rely upon the successful execution of that and similar initiatives.

Douglass thought so. He simply could not have conveyed a clearer message about how much he valued America's diversity. He said, "Our greatness and grandeur will be found in the faithful application of the principle of perfect civil equality to the people of all races and creeds."[21] With profound sympathy and empathy for the Chinese immigrants being persecuted at the time, Douglass offered them a full-throated welcome. He saw strength in our expanding diversity, affirming that "a smile or a tear has no nationality."[22] Douglass forcefully affirmed the beauty of America's uniqueness as "the most conspicuous example of composite nationality in the world," and he saw harvesting that growing diversity as the foundation for America's eventual exceptionalism.[23] He argued that a diversity-based pursuit of equality and pluralism would make America the first-ever "perfect national illustration of the unity and dignity of the human family."[24] That was Douglass's idea of a more perfect union. Nor did he see progress as a move backward in the direction of superior and inferior races, genders, classes, religions, or nationalities. Instead, it was movement forward in the direction of human equality and democracy. Not white supremacy, but pluralism was the pathway to America's true destiny and humanity's true calling. But Douglass easily recognized in 1869 that America was only barely aspiring to actualize pluralism.

More than 150 years since Douglass's destiny advisory, America has progressed slowly, and often with great reluctance and uncertainty. Valuing and harvesting diversity have typically been demanded from, not by, most of America's higher education and elected leadership. And, inarguably, the most impressive, sustained surge toward pluralism in response to demand came out of the HBCU tradition. These institutions authored a course-corrective rebuke of the disjuncture between American conduct and American ideals. Their work culminated with the public phase of the civil rights movement of the 1950s and 1960s. The Civil Rights Act of 1964 and the Voting Rights Act of 1965 were major, tangible outcomes, but the changes went far beyond legislation. More than any other effort before it, the movement triggered a broad, pluralist awakening in the American citizenry. It motivated many to join African Americans in the quest for true equality, including women, Native

Americans, Asian Americans, Latine Americans, multiracial Americans, and the lesbian, gay, bisexual, transgender, and queer communities.

The first quarter of the twenty-first century has steadily intensified a more complex version of the destiny dissonance illuminated by Douglass in 1869. For a variety of reasons, the stakes seem higher and the threat to democracy now appears to be at least as great as it was just prior to the second founding. Many Americans who have had the benefit of a college education still reject the composite nationality vision set forth in the Constitution and thereafter articulated by Douglass and so many others. The mindset divide over the country's direction has made the fragility of American democracy seem more apparent than its strength. As one political scientist assessed in January 2021, "There is no advanced industrial democracy in the world more politically divided, or politically dysfunctional than the United States today."[25] These extreme conditions may warrant a far more energized version of what the HBCU tradition yielded.

But some may conclude that democracy is insufficiently imperiled to justify a quest to re-architect all of higher education. It may be premature to push for a scaled return to the HBCU tradition of enriching student mindsets and character to pursue the common good. But there is another reason why an HBCU-style re-architecture ultimatum now deserves humanity's undivided attention.

Character and the Battle to Save the Planet

Beyond serving as a model for repairing the democracy, what if the HBCU experience served as an apt analogue for remedying the world's climate crisis? How?

The aphorism "some people change when they see the light, others when they feel the heat" is commonly attributed to Caroline Schoeder.[26] While it is often used in a business context, the saying is truest, by far, in the context of the global climate crisis that continues to actively warm the planet. The light regarding carbon dioxide's growing threat to human existence has glared since the 1980s, even if the specter of it was sensed for decades before that.

In 1979, MIT's Jule Charney, widely regarded as the father of modern meteorology, convened the nation's leading climate experts to determine whether humanity would face an irreversible climate catastrophe. Charney and his group reported the "incontrovertible evidence" of rising atmospheric concentrations of carbon dioxide linked to human conduct, including the burning of fossil fuels and the removal of the earth's trees. They warned, "A wait-and-see policy may mean waiting until it is too late."[27] In hindsight, the ensuing ten-year period from 1979 to 1989 represented "an excellent opportunity to solve the climate crisis."[28] But because the observed light of science was relatively "heat free," there has been minimal change.

As a result of this negligence, "More carbon has been released into the atmosphere since . . . 1989, than in the entire history of civilization preceding it."[29] In other words, instead of taking appropriate action after seeing the light, as the scientists had warned, most of the politicians were unpersuaded when the experts announced, in air-conditioned rooms, the probable arrival of unbearable heat. Simply put, they ignored the light because they had yet to personally feel the heat.

In the absence of radical changes, today's college students will literally feel the heat that was long ago and repeatedly signaled by the sharpening light of science and more recently underscored by the accumulation of stark evidence.[30] It is difficult to imagine that there have ever been clearer indications of a re-architecture ultimatum facing the leaders of educational, philanthropic, political, and socioeconomic networks and systems worldwide.

Analogously speaking, the global climate crisis facing America and the world today is not unlike the sociopolitical climate crisis confronted by HBCUs throughout so much of their history. It is not difficult to see a number of African American HBCU presidents as the Jule Charneys who constantly warned America of the incontrovertible evidence about democracy's brokenness. Nor is it difficult to see the parallels between what HBCUs had to do to help detoxify the sociopolitical environment in order to heal the country, and what American higher education must now do to help detoxify the physical environment in order to heal the planet. A closer look at the HBCU experience may reveal that America is where African Americans and HBCUs were in their darkest days.

HBCU advocates, leaders, and graduates pointed to serious threats to the sociopolitical climate, and their constant warnings were ignored long before America's politicians began denying Charney's warnings in 1979. Democracy's climate for African Americans had always been toxic. During their enslavement, the air was thick with barbaric hate. Following the Civil War,

Reconstruction arrived with the same optimism and promise as the 2015 Paris Agreement, which was viewed as a long-awaited cooperative attempt to bring physical climate relief. Unfortunately, defying decency, sanity, and longevity, hopes were dashed in both cases.[31] During the post-Reconstruction period, the noxious environment worsened and made life for most African Americans the equivalent of a daily "I can't breathe" lament. The fumes of Southern hate caused many to flee north seeking better air. But they found a familiar pollution there, too. Everywhere they went was uninhabitable, or soon became so.

Thus, from the start, HBCU leaders knew they had to shape a different kind of citizen of America and the world. Why? Their sociopolitical climate conditions demanded it. Based on that toxicity alone, HBCU leaders could never presume that their graduates would experience the luxury of living like other American citizens in such a polluted republic. They could not. The lingering winds of barbarism and hypocrisy still whirled fear and hopelessness. The scent of possible relief was utterly undetectable.

America is now where African Americans and HBCUs have typically been.

Even the political environments were similarly feckless. A variety of elected state and federal officials who could have halted the deterioration in both the sociopolitical and physical climates were typically without the courage or will to act. What to do was never mysterious. Regarding both climates, politicians had multiple opportunities to set a new, healthier direction, thereby avoiding a catastrophe.[32] Yet, in the face of well-known threats to human life, their fealty to privilege and political power rendered them impotent. In each case, the politicians spent decades calculating the cost to themselves. They refused to solve the problem even as signs of an imperiled quality of life worsened. Partisan and regional divides and constant disinformation extended the paralysis. And as the evidence of the unsustainability of it all grew starker, it became clear that only a scaled demand would leave the powerbrokers with no choice.

To be sure, HBCU leadership had sensed the gravity of their climate problem long ago. They knew the entire educational infrastructure for African Americans had to emphasize much more than mere literacy. They had to educate and shape extraordinary citizens with enough insight, character, and poise to withstand the gale force winds of hate and brutality. They had to shape citizens to be ready to live in a world perpetually at risk of disruption, chaos, and a ubiquitous existential threat. So they did.

And now, American higher education is where HBCUs were.

America's colleges and universities are now challenged to consider, more thoughtfully than ever before, how to shape a future in the face of extreme dangers. And the relevance of the HBCU experience is rich and should be purposefully mined.

More specifically, many should find it instructive that HBCUs led the effort to cleanse their environment of hate by steadily graduating citizens equipped with the mindsets and skill sets required to bring relief. They did not succeed in totally eliminating the menace. Of necessity, they played a long game, and effectively reduced the threat. And this happened all because their work to shape better citizens turned into a movement that demanded and realized measurable and demonstrable change. They shaped citizens who would keep in mind the high road and the big picture, and who would seek justice without revenge. In short, they shaped citizens who were different from those typically produced elsewhere in American higher education. In particular, America's non-HBCUs were seemingly content to blithely produce a silent majority, largely indifferent to how America had enslaved, oppressed, subjugated, othered, and embittered so many people of color and limited means throughout its quest to for sustainable world leadership.

More generally, HBCU learning communities have also demonstrated that, when facing existential threats, colleges and universities can educate warrior citizens fit for the battle to reduce the peril. In fact, not only have they proven that on-campus environments can be re-architected and enriched to yield profoundly different outcomes, they have also already confronted the stupefying negligence of those with the power to make a difference. And in the face of that negligence, HBCU graduates worked to steadily reduce the sociopolitical heat, while setting the stage for longer-term sociopolitical climate repair.

In essence, HBCUs have already demonstrated how an appropriately scaled educational effort can diminish an unsurprisingly scaled existential crisis. If addressing the threats to democracy was regarded by HBCU leaders as a matter of urgency then, there is ample reason to regard democracy's repair as an *emergency* now. And that is precisely what is required of American higher education at this time—a widely shared emergency response that will effectively remove the ominous veils now fluttering over the nation and world that HBCUs were born to remake.

RE-ARCHITECTING CAPITAL

A broken democracy cannot heal a broken planet. Therefore, to have any hope of healing both, today's philanthropic community must play a consequential role. An obvious option is to use grantmaking to incentivize profound change in higher education by establishing effective crisis-mitigation programming and more humane campus cultures. For that to happen, a critical mass of philanthropists must decide to alter their long-standing patterns of thinking and investing.

In *Stamped from the Beginning*, Ibram Kendi offered an interesting perspective on the mindsets of those who ignited US charitable giving. Of America's wealthy founders, who championed "freedom" as an inalienable right at a time when many of them enslaved other Americans, he said, "For these rich men, freedom was not the power to make choices; freedom was the power to create choices. . . . Power came before freedom. Indeed, power creates freedom, not the other way around—as the powerless are taught."[33]

From the start, America's philanthropists have used sizable, transformational investments to grant the leaders of its colleges and universities the freedom to make the best choices they could imagine, pursuant to the best educational experiences they could conceive. Those philanthropic choices and the educational experiences they have funded reveal a thematic consistency, perhaps discouraging enough to warrant a kind of "philanthro-pessimism."

America's charitable community has held an unambiguous viewpoint about which institutions deserve such freedoms and which do not. Over time, they have had much to do with higher education's indifference in the face of burgeoning inequity and inequality. In and between two Gilded Ages, they enabled the emergence of higher education's upper tier, or gated communities for the privileged. Unfortunately, the exploding scale of American wealth has not altered the excessive skew of American giving. As figure 9.6 helps to illuminate, no critical mass of philanthropists has yet converged to dramatically break American philanthropy's worn and costly patterns. The usual institutions thrive, while most others fight to survive. From the start of the billion-

FIGURE 9.6 The capital optimization quest: HBCU fundraising relative to the top 20 fundraising institutions: 1985–2015–2020

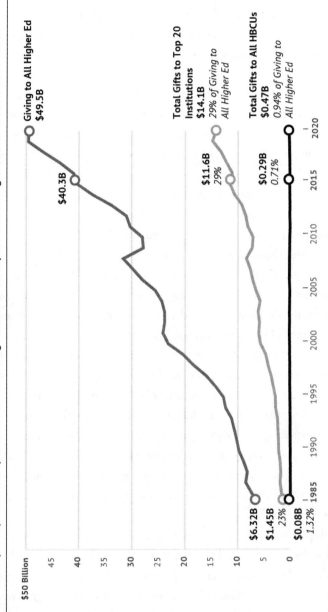

Sources: All higher education giving: 2004 Voluntary Support of Education (New York: RAND Council for Aid to Education), 4, table 2, https://www.rand.org/content/dam/rand/www/external /news/press.05/03.02.pdf/RAND_VSE_2004.pdf; top twenty fundraisers: Data provided in the context of personal interviews with officials at the Voluntary Support of Education, RAND Council for Aid to Education; HBCU giving: US Department of Education, National Center for Education Statistics, Integrated Postsecondary Education Data System (IPEDS), spring finance component (1990–2021); Digest of Education Statistics, table 313.30 (1990–2020), https://nces.ed.gov/programs/digest/d21/tables/dt21_313.30.asp; and IPEDS finance component final data (1985–89), retrieved from https://nces.ed.gov/ipeds/datacenter.

dollar capital campaign era in 1985 to the end of the gap-closure century in 2015, the top gatherers of wealth, overall, have consistently continued to dwarf all other campuses, but especially HBCUs. No Black college has ever pierced the top twenty, nor have HBCUs ever collectively done so in a single year. This is especially ironic because HBCUs authored the higher education paradigm most useful for meeting many of today's unique, high-stakes challenges.

The persistence of these inequitable patterns can lead reasonable observers to wonder whether both the educational and philanthropic communities can now somehow deftly pivot to generate radically different outcomes? Again, the HBCU tradition provides a model for that kind of pivot in higher education. But a more sizable, HBCU-like progressive movement is now required. And the only force that can provoke scaled change in higher education is a different aspect of the re-architecture ultimatum—that is, a transformation of the incentive structure that has always been a dominant driver of change on America's campuses. And there is a model for that kind of philanthropic pivot, too.

The titans of the slave economy incentivized and bent American higher education to their will, ultimately exerting extraordinary control over the curricula and the mindsets, ambitions, and agendas of generations of graduates. Similarly, the titans of today's innovation economy can now incentivize and bend American higher education toward more humane outcomes, while delivering a long overdue and firm rebuke to the inhumane patterns set by their predecessors in both philanthropy and higher education. For instance, progressive philanthropists might start by channeling meaningful investments toward those institutions willing to take seriously the need to proactively resolve the nation's democracy crisis and the world's climate crisis. This kind of change requires a fundamental, perhaps Copernican mindset shift in the way philanthropists think about which institutions are investment worthy and, therefore, freedom worthy.

If enough philanthropists experience such a mindset shift, a new set of colleges and universities can embrace the task of fitting their campus culture to democratic, environmentalist, and pluralist ideals. The process itself would inject new evaluative metrics into philanthropic scrutiny and change conversations regarding what and who deserves transformational support. America's philanthropic tradition of distributing higher education resources based on an elitist definition of greatness would finally begin to shift to targeting them based on a curative definition of goodness.

While there are a few isolated models for this kind of agenda pivot in American philanthropy, three relatively scaled efforts deserve special mention. First, it is too soon to predict the sustainable impact of MacKenzie Scott's mindset-altering benevolence. By investing over four billion dollars in 384 unconventional recipients (including $560 million to twenty-three HBCUs) beginning in the winter of 2020, she created a seismic shift in American philanthropy.[34] Departing from many of the norms of nationally scaled giving, her unorthodox mindset led her to select grantees "with special attention to those operating in communities facing high projected food insecurity, high measures of racial inequity, high local poverty rates, and low access to philanthropic capital."[35] Scott joined other billionaires as a signatory to the "giving pledge," created by Warren Buffett, Melinda French Gates, and Bill Gates in 2010. Their collective goal is to "shift the norms of philanthropy," by giving in a manner similar to several of their innovative predecessors, especially John D. Rockefeller and Andrew Carnegie.[36] Scott has already echoed the breadth of America's early era benefactors by giving to so many atypical targets. It remains to be seen whether she and other modern era philanthropists will provide deep, transformational investments in selected uncommon recipients, as did Rockefeller and Carnegie.[37]

Second, Jamie Merisotis was appointed president and chief executive officer of the Lumina Foundation in 2008. Informed by a career-long focus on realizing a quality education for all Americans, especially first-generation and low-income students, Merisotis immediately prioritized an equity agenda. He took the helm of Lumina with a growth mindset and the redesign aims of an architect, rather than a fixed mindset wired for contractor-style sameness. Driven also by a keen sense of our shared humanity, he saw immigration as an asset rather than a threat to America. And he positioned the foundation's grantmaking and messaging to make Lumina a greater force for democratizing and thereby diversifying the nation's talent base.[38] Merisotis has led with an unambiguously egalitarian perspective. He said at one point, "Our workforce and our democracy are enhanced as a result of these more diverse populations actually being educated. This is about our collective well-being. . . . We need to be thinking about 'them' as 'us.' It's our future, not their future."[39]

Finally, when Darren Walker interviewed for the opportunity to lead the Ford Foundation in 2013, he, too, brought the growth mindset of an architect, scaled appropriately to suit his larger stage. With the opportunity to distribute well over a half billion dollars per year, he was asked to clarify how he would approach the foundation's presidency. He said, "I would want to use the platform of being president of the Ford Foundation to really deeply interrogate the structures and systems and cultural practices in our country that increase the likelihood of more inequality in our society and of more exclusion and marginalization of people, particularly low-income people, people of color."[40] Based on unconventional grantmaking, Walker is now successfully executing that strategy, thus aligning Ford with the pursuit of pluralist and equitable ideals like few others.[41]

Following these three examples, the philanthropic community might want to avoid being defined by two ironies that literally span what may be the lifetime of America. In her assessment of how capitalism's greed-inspired climate denialism "broke the planet," Kate Aranoff determined that, "bringing down emissions means declaring trillions of dollars worth of fossil fuel assets—all those reserves that can't be safely burned—worthless. If carried out, this would represent the single largest evaporation of private wealth since the Emancipation Proclamation."[42]

It is a bleak enough irony that the capitalism that drove America's sunrise ran on the control of dark bodies, while the capitalism now driving the planet's sunset runs on the control of dark fossil fuels. Yet, there is a bleaker irony. At the nation's birth, it was clear that many power-hungry people in and beyond America were willing to preserve a wealth-generating exploitative system, even if it killed others. But as the nation and planet now totter, it is becoming clear that many power-hungry people in and beyond America are willing to preserve a wealth-generating exploitative system even if it kills us all.

FOR THE MINDSET

The way philanthropists decide to invest in higher education's best re-architecture strategies can determine whether the veil over a new future for humanity is lifting or lowering.

Perspective Five

The Messianic Promise of HBCUs

From the start, African American HBCU leaders knew that shaping a better world would require them to shape better citizens. They provided concept proof with their three "up from" transformations, culminating in a democracy-advancing civil rights movement. American higher education must now use an HBCU approach to successfully re-architect campus life and outcomes. Nothing short of a scaled cooperative effort to shape string shooters will position humankind to realize what Du Bois envisioned as a "great united humanity."

This perspective is decisive because a growth mindset about the messianic promise of HBCUs can motivate the most consequential philanthropists to recognize the untapped power they have to ensure that we shape the better people the world now desperately needs.

CHAPTER TEN

The String Shooters

There is no such thing as a neutral educational process. Education either functions as an instrument which is used to facilitate integration of the younger generation into the logic of the present system and bring about conformity or it becomes the practice of freedom, the means by which men and women deal critically and creatively with reality and discover how to participate in the transformation of their world.

Paulo Freire/Richard Shaull,
Pedagogy of the Oppressed, 1970

When I discover who I am, I'll be free.

Ralph Ellison, *Invisible Man*, 1952

Education is where we begin. We begin after we are called. We are called and that is when and how we all begin. There is a calling. We are called upon to be. We can only be by becoming. What we become depends upon the calling we choose to follow.

Anthony P. Farley, *Perfecting Slavery*, 2005

A healer needs to see beyond the present and tomorrow . . . to see years and decades ahead. Because healers work for results so firm that they may not be wholly visible till centuries have flowed into millennia.

Ayi Kwei Armah, *The Healers*

A merican higher education must be re-architected to meet the challenge of shaping better citizens. The task will remain especially arduous if we do not aggressively stimulate a widely shared sense of urgency about it. But that is where America finds itself in the first quarter of the twenty-first century. There are reasons to be skeptical and confident.

Like the colleges and universities they attend, throngs of students represent a Western culture that has traditionally privileged capital over character, competition over cooperation, and exclusion over belonging. In particular, both individuals and institutions seem spellbound by the same wealth chase. Also enchanted are many faculty, especially those with expertise of relevance to wealth creation and expansion. As campuses have become more affluent, countless graduates have emerged far more driven to live comfortably in today's inequitable system than to question, oppose, or transform it for the betterment of humanity. And too few graduates evidence a capacity to be outraged or disturbed by a global economy that generates thousands of winners and billions of losers.

How did American higher education shift from being a wresting place for the inquisitive to a breeding place for the acquisitive?[1] It was a decades-long journey. In a turn toward vocationalism, "between the two world wars, for the first time in American history, a college education became an essential part of the success strategy of those who sought fortune or prestige in the United States . . . college after college modified its curriculum, admissions standards, and student life to accommodate the practical and status-minded perspectives of its new students and benefactors."[2] By the 1940s, a college education became widely perceived as the best admissions ticket to the middle class. Ironically, as most of the HBCUs were quietly preparing to challenge America to become democratic, many of the nation's white campuses became incubators for those aspiring to become aristocratic.

In fact, the wealth-quest mindset has saturated American culture. It helped to drive the billion-dollar capital campaign era that exacerbated inequality in higher education. It also drove the more recent capital surge of the top 1 percent of Americans in the early twenty-first century.[3] How stark is inequality? Not only have eight billionaires amassed as much wealth as the poorest 3.6 billion people on the planet, with six of the eight being Americans, but 84 percent of the world's population, or more than 6.2 billion people, live on less than $20 per day.[4]

In the hierarchy of challenges to our shared values, rethinking the distorted wealth chase should be a matter of urgency. However, beyond stimulating more relevant philanthropic behavior, it cannot be prioritized when the world is facing a clear emergency. As highlighted in the previous chapter, two related existential threats warrant immediate attention: America's imperiled democracy, and the world's imperiled planet.

John Dewey said of democracy, "It has to be born anew every generation and education is its midwife."[5] At this point, American higher education, as midwife, must deliver a constitutional democracy that is more pluralistic and egalitarian than ever before, while simultaneously shaping and galvanizing the kind of citizens who can save the planet. Admittedly, that is a tall order.

In fact, the script is now flipped on American higher education. Whereas HBCUs spent their first fifty years performing a basic literacy miracle, all of the nation's colleges and universities must now perform an unprecedented civic literacy miracle. They must develop robust warriors for the common good, or citizens with new mindsets infused with humanitarian values.

And that is why higher education leadership matters most. Success will first require a fundamentally different form of campus leadership. Again, contractor-style presidents with mindsets fixed on what Veysey called "maintenance" and "continued construction along duplicatory lines," will, in all likelihood, be disinclined and ill-equipped to meet the larger challenges.[6] Conversely, presidents and boards with growth mindsets wired for re-architecture are uniquely well-suited to alter life in a largely calcified postsecondary sector.

But is it possible to reimagine the same educational system that failed to adjust itself as today's major crises gradually and menacingly emerged? And can it be re-architected in time to shape new, corrective mindsets before it is too late? In a sense, it does not matter. America must lead because no other educational system in today's world is nearly as well-equipped to meet the challenge.

INSTITUTIONAL CONSIDERATION FOR THE RECORD: RE-ARCHITECTURE AS ACTIVATED BY MAYS AND BROADENED BY CLARK

It is unfortunate that Veysey focused so minimally on the architectural heft of Alexander Meiklejohn, who presided over Amherst College from 1912 to 1923. In a sense, his entire tenure was devoted to redesigning a campus culture and curriculum so that it would provide a robust answer to a question he posed at Amherst's centennial celebration on June 22, 1921. Deeply concerned about the need to shape people capable of guiding an uncertain America, Meiklejohn asked, "Which shall it be—an Anglo-Saxon aristocracy . . . or a Democracy?"[7] Unfortunately, under great pressure from Amherst trustees and faculty, he resigned within two years of posing that question. Yet the choice embedded in his question, an echo of what Frederick Douglass assessed, still reverberates in and beyond America a century later.[8]

Not long after Meiklejohn's efforts were cut short, an HBCU president, Dr. Benjamin Elijah Mays, began designing his own democracy-centered approach to higher education. And on the heels of his success, an HBCU-educated scholar, Dr. Kenneth Clark, sounded an alarm and called into question all of American higher education. Both leaders evidenced profoundly important architectural instincts, focusing far more on the direction of American society than on merely insisting that African Americans have equal access to a comfortable lifestyle somewhere therein.

CAMPUS-BASED RE-ARCHITECTURE AS ACTIVATED BY MAYS

Aided by a selfless peripheral vision, Mays agreed to lead a relatively unknown Morehouse College in 1940. Over nearly three decades, he became one of the most distinguished presidents in the history of American higher education. Because the college rarely exceeded a graduating class of one hundred, fewer than twenty-five hundred men graduated on Mays's twenty-seven-year watch. Yet a disproportionately high number of them became distinguished leaders in religion, education, civil rights, politics, law, medicine, and the arts. Those outcomes were possible because he focused as much on the design and duty of the individual as on the design and health of the institution.

Two years into his presidency, Mays published a set of prescriptive ideas for how American higher education should change.[9] He conveyed both a global perspective on the problems facing people of color and a seasoned, philosophical perspective urging HBCUs to play a far more progressive role. He began by defining the problem: America was "a semi-democratic and a semi-Christian nation."[10] In light of that observation, in his view, shaping a better undergraduate experience was a key to shaping a better nation and world. And rather than target "Negro colleges" alone, he insisted that his prescriptive advice was "not wholly unrelated to the role of higher education generally."[11] He simply wanted Black liberal arts colleges to model new outcomes worthy to be emulated by all of higher education.

Mays's proposed blueprint for a dynamic campus culture focused on developing the internal characteristics of the liberal arts graduate. His plan featured four priorities for campuses seeking to equip students to graduate with mindsets and skill sets geared to shape a new and better world. First, Mays thought all campuses "should be experiment stations in democratic living."[12] He disdained the authoritative leadership styles of many college presidents, and instead favored student and faculty empowerment. By enabling student experimentation with democratic practices on campus, they would value, pursue, and demand it beyond graduation in the larger society.

Second, Mays wanted campuses to be "community-minded," by tying student brainpower and faculty expertise to the needs of the citizens in the surrounding communities. Their outreach would include tutoring youths, offering money management advice to parents, and teaching Sunday school. He saw it as a way to cultivate selflessness while avoiding elitism.

Third, by promoting solid citizenship, especially via voter registration and participation, the campuses could "contribute their share to the saving and developing of democracy in this country."[13] He thought America could become a model of true democracy for the world if colleges would "accept their responsibility to make their faculties and students citizenship-minded."[14]

Fourth, Mays was well aware of how white scholars had spent more than two centuries distorting knowledge to legitimize and accommodate racial oppression. He insisted that HBCUs assume leadership by nurturing and hosting a new kind of scholarship, free of prejudice and bias in the sciences, art, religion, and the humanities. They would be "scholars of the first magnitude."[15]

To pursue these goals, Mays mastered what educators would later refer to as "the hidden curriculum." Beyond the formal curriculum and the semiformal extracurriculum, the informal hidden curriculum consists of the student values, postures, and behavioral norms associated with doing well.[16] The general Morehouse campus culture featured broad communications to encourage an embrace of these values and ambitions. Mays sought to redefine, redesign, and individualize a new brand of character development, contextualized by the promotion of democratic practices, community service, good citizenship, and sound scholarship. Beyond producing intellectually sharp students, he wanted them to be "good people" as well. More than superior scholars, he wanted faculty with high integrity to prioritize graduating "honest men who can be trusted both in public and private life—men who are sensible to the wrongs, sufferings, and injustices of society and who are willing to accept responsibility for correcting the ills."[17] By emphasizing selected historical narratives (including those of African Americans, Jews, and the Greek and Roman classics), Mays wanted his students to have a more grounded, well-rounded view of life.[18] Similarly, by promoting a brand of Christian spirituality and an activism more aligned with justice than injustice, he would help ensure that students received a measure of poise, stability, strength, and courage sufficient "to carry on in the midst of chaos and insecurity."[19]

Mays motivated his graduates to battle injustice aggressively, yet compassionately. His improvement of the undergraduate experience was pursuant to societal transformation. He focused on shaping citizens for a "true democracy." Thus, his most meaningful legacy would be measured off campus in the conduct of his alumni. As he phrased it in a speech ten years later, the ultimate goal is to "improve the human product."[20]

While many men benefited from his consequential philosophy, Mays proved the concept most with his extended mentoring of Martin Luther King, Jr., a 1948 Morehouse graduate. King entered college reading at an eighth-grade level, having been deliberately underserved by the Atlanta public school system. Yet he graduated fully prepared for his journey toward a Boston University doctorate and, subsequently, a Nobel Peace Prize, a national holiday, and a granite memorial on the National Mall. With a single graduate, Mays validated the importance of the hidden curriculum as minimally on par with all other curricula in enhancing student development. The influence of Mays was detectable both in King's expectations and his critiques of America.

Among the reasons why the Mays presidency uniquely departed from national norms was his emphasis on involving faculty and stressing democracy. Faculty played an indispensable role in refining the new campus culture, especially in their constant messaging to students. Mays joined his faculty in an elevated interpretation of how real democracy looks and feels, in contrast to what they observed as democracy malpractice in America.

But there were other faculty-focused and democracy-centric leaders on whose shoulders Mays stood. In his 1927 inaugural address at Howard University, Mordecai Johnson described his as a quest for an America where all are free, intelligent, and "contributors to the common good," and he then lamented, "that country has not yet been attained."[21] In 1938, as she sought to stabilize Frelinghuysen University, Anna Julia Cooper said she needed leaders and teachers who could help to "work and pray for a better, nobler, truer America."[22] In 1939, Mary McLeod Bethune asked of America, "Is it to be a Democracy of the lynching mob and flaunted law . . . or . . . of law and order, of the 14th Amendment?"[23] Three years later, she insisted, "We are Americans who cherish in our hearts a desire for one practical democracy for all."[24]

The HBCU community's more visible emphasis on democracy was framed as a kind of appeal to America's better angels. This was the case with the United Negro College Fund's numerous fundraising ads, wherein they explicitly connected "UNCF colleges and themes of freedom and democracy."[25] However, particularly within the confines of the campus, many in the HBCU community were more direct.

Kenneth Clark once touted the "Athenian greatness" of Howard's faculty during the 1930s and 1940s. He said, "They protested, they infected their students with an unquenchable spirit of rebellion and protest. They made clear to us the essential perversion and destruction of human values inherent in American racism. They dissected the hypocrisy of the verbal promises of democracy and the perpetuation and intensification of racism in American society."[26] Howard's location in the nation's capital may have afforded its faculty more pedagogical freedom than those faculty based in HBCUs in the deep South, who had to be careful to not trigger lethal responses from racist Southerners.[27] To be sure, many in these campus communities chose not to embrace the protest agenda. In fact, a number of HBCU trustees, staff, and faculty members discouraged activism and sometimes served as informants for state agents and their allies.[28] Yet in and beyond the classrooms, and with varying degrees of caution and openness, many HBCU faculty served as the high priests of campus cultures oriented less to secure lush lifestyles for individuals and more to encourage engagement with the work of actively altering the direction of their world.

By comparison, the original managers of American higher education during the early nineteenth century established a tradition of silence in the face of the atrocities in the world around them. Again, their silence when the slave trade dominated the world economy was as deafening as it was tone-setting. Mays was conspicuously different. He was especially effective in redesigning the Morehouse undergraduate experience to sharpen student sensibilities to societal injustice. Silence was not an option for him and those he helped to educate. He added texture, definition, and focus to the campus culture, making the experience more purpose driven. In doing so, Mays effectively shifted the axis around which the value proposition of higher education turned from a private good toward a public good. Equipping mindsets to enhance the democracy's tangibility became at least as valuable as enhancing skill sets to enrich the individual's employability.

BROAD-BASED RE-ARCHITECTURE AS PRESCRIBED BY CLARK

As Mays neared the end of his Morehouse presidency in the spring of 1967, two Harvard scholars, Christopher Jencks and David Riesman, offered an analysis of HBCUs in the *Harvard Educational Review.*[29] Like a high-voltage lightning strike, their reference to HBCUs as "academic disaster areas" was the most oft-quoted charge in the storm of controversy that followed. In many ways, their article was thematically consistent with the conclusions drawn in a long list of reports and assessments about HBCUs, largely by white federal officials, scholars, and media outlets.[30] But this controversy was different.

Without questioning the authority, research methods, or accuracy of the Harvard scholars, *Time* magazine offered a compendium of the most negative assertions, generally referring to the assessment as a "soberly scathing judgment."[31] But since most Black leaders and scholars saw nothing sober in the charges against them, their responses were strident and immediate. In their respective letters to the editor of the *Harvard Educational Review*, Fisk University's Stephen J. Wright said the Jencks-Riesman article had "a shattering effect upon Negro educators and those who support the colleges"; Hugh Gloster of Hampton University called the research "racial vanity," and pointed to the "disaster area" that is American sociological scholarship, if this is "an example of meritorious work in the field"; and Dillard University president

Albert Dent called it the stereotyping of Negro colleges "based on 'impressions,' hearsay, and 'anecdotes.'"[32]

Ironically, Howard University had already planned an extended celebration of its centennial that year. The series of events included an April 16–18, 1967, conference focused on the theme "The Higher Education of Negro Americans: Prospects and Programs." The Jencks-Riesman controversy was at its peak, and several of the speakers predictably offered robust defenses of HBCUs against the sweeping charge of inferiority. Drs. Kenneth and Mamie Clark, both Howard graduates and developmental psychologists, were celebrity intellectuals who conducted the research at the foundation of the *Brown v. Board of Education* decision.[33] Kenneth Clark served as the keynote speaker for the Howard conference and was expected to offer the strongest rebuke of Jencks and Riesman. Yet, instead of punishing the two Harvard scholars by delivering a definitive litany of HBCU virtues, he completely changed the tone and texture of both the conference and the controversy.[34]

Clark startled many by literally embracing the controversial conclusion drawn by Jencks and Riesman, saying "Negro colleges and universities are academically inferior."[35] As he emphasized the contextual dynamics of HBCU development, he said these institutions still "reflect the cumulative inferiority of segregated education and the inevitable pathology of a racist-segregated society which inflicts upon lower-status human beings a debilitating, humanly-destructive form of public education, both in the South and the North."[36] Their lack of funding and morale were obvious contributors, as was the "self-hatred" constantly prescribed and instilled by American society. Clark took issue with the popular presumption that white higher education should be a model for HBCUs. He called HBCUs "mockeries," to the extent that "they reflected the contamination and moral erosion and emptiness of White colleges and universities in an America that presented itself before the world as a democratic society."[37] He advised that HBCUs stop "imitating" and "aping" white colleges and universities, because they are "the source of inferiority in American education."[38]

Clark then pivoted toward his expected task, but with a decided twist. He broadened his analysis by essentially holding up a large mirror to white institutions, describing them as inferior because "they are contaminated with the pervasive disease of racism."[39] He said, "Harvard, Yale, Princeton, Columbia, the University of California, have failed the American people more desperately, and insidiously than . . . Negro colleges." Clark's list of white higher education's failures boiled down to two critical flaws. First, they were wayward in that they had become "ruthlessly competitive and anxiety-producing," and overly focused on "content retention" for test scores. Second, they were guilty of negligence, inasmuch as they had "remained detached and non-relevant" to the "major domestic issues of our times."[40]

Clark joined the chorus of disagreement with Jencks and Riesman not because he thought their conclusion about HBCUs was wrong. He simply found their argument to be self-servingly incomplete. And while much of his indictment of white higher education was drawn from a recent critique he had prepared for a scholarly journal that summer, his speech at Howard struck a more aggressive tone.[41] He highlighted the negligence of white institutions, saying,

> Our great academically revered American universities and colleges have remained *eloquently silent* on obvious and elementary issues of social and racial justice in America and have contributed significantly to the development of armaments or scientific techniques for the manipulation of man, for the destruction of man, but I repeat, have remained eloquently silent while the burden of sowing the seeds of torment and rebellion against injustice had to be borne by Negro colleges. It became almost a hallmark of a prestigious institution of higher education—that their faculty or students *not be contaminated with the unfinished business of American democracy.*[42] (Emphasis added)

Clark concluded that white higher education had not "fulfilled their responsibility and obligation to develop and train human beings with a morally relevant and socially responsible intelligence."[43] As a result, they had become "major bastions of a subtle and persistent form of white supremacy."[44] Clark demystified the Ivy League narrative of preeminence, and essentially cautioned his Howard audience that presuming superiority is just as problematic as presuming inferiority.

While it barely resembled the speech this pro-HBCU crowd expected, Clark ended it by pointing to "an irony," which may have been the highest HBCU praise cited throughout the entire controversy. He said, "It may very well become the task of the inferior, predominantly Negro school to save the soul of society."[45] With this suggestion, he echoed a number of leaders before him, especially Du Bois, who "saw the black people of the nation as critical transformers and redeemers of the destiny of the world."[46] Clark would later tie the nation's fate to the destiny of African Americans, calling it "the 'nuclear' irony of American history."[47]

Clark was remarkably prescient about America's fate. Given the recent indications of a troubled destination for both the democracy and the planet, it is worth asking how long and at what cost will the eloquent silence of American higher education persist?

The best answer to that question may depend on the emergence of new, investment-worthy ideas from higher education's leaders. And those ideas must invariably center on the re-architecture of institutions so that more of them will be fully equipped to shape better citizens.

INSTITUTIONAL QUESTION FOR THE FUTURE: WHAT KIND OF PEOPLE SHOULD BE INTENTIONALLY SHAPED BY THE MOST INVESTMENT-WORTHY INSTITUTIONS?

This overall narrative offers a way to see HBCUs differently. See them confront the unique challenge of being born and immediately facing the headwinds of American barbarism and hypocrisy. See the deeply humane way in which their original leaders, Black and white, developed not a pedagogy of revenge, but a hostility-free embrace of the American ideal. See the steadfast commitment of African American educators to actualize a more perfect union for all, including the descendants of those who had authored their protracted abuse. Take the long view and see their transformation of a once-shackled people up from enslavement, illiteracy, poverty, and marginality. But see also the current, veil-lifting challenge of a fourth transformation—up from precarity—which may be the most difficult yet.

Ironically, it is an ideal time to revive, bolster, and proselytize the HBCU tradition of producing citizens who, rather than being eloquently silent and detached in the face of lethal societal ills, became eloquently equipped and inclined to measurably remedy them.

How can all of American higher education now pivot toward an updated version of that HBCU tradition? What kind of individuals should the new campus cultures seek to incubate?

SHAPING BETTER CITIZENS

It is for good reason that this book has had a mantra-like reliance on the phrase "shaping better citizens." The concept is grounded in the HBCU tradition of privileging distinctively humane outcomes. The civil rights movement for the benefit of American democracy was intentional. How can all of American higher education lead an effort to meet today's challenges more intentionally?

There are multiple ways to frame the mindset competencies required to preserve both the democracy and the planet. This book is not a prescription for what all institutions must do, but a guide to the kinds of strategic conversations all institutions must have. Each campus should lean on the best practices and discover its own unique frame. Below are three suggestions, all evident in the HBCU tradition. They constitute a final advisory statement, offered as a ladder or guide to thinking about the mindsets of the better citizens for whom a deeply troubled world yearns.

Shaping "Destination Citizens"

First, the arrival of new mindsets may minimally require a scaled perspective shift, not unlike the individual awakening Du Bois shared in his second autobiography. At the age of seventy-two, he critiqued his lifelong aspiration as misguided, lamenting:

> At first my criticism was confined to the relation of my people to the world movement. I was not questioning the world movement in itself. What the white world was doing, its goals and ideals, I had not doubted were quite right. What was wrong was that I and people like me and thousands of others who might have my ability and aspiration, were refused permission to be a part of this world. It was as though moving on a rushing express, my main thought was as to my relations with the other passengers on that express, and not to its rate of speed or its destination.[48]

With this insight, Du Bois recognizes that he had presumed the humanity and sanity of those responsible for the general idea and flow of progress. By narrowly recognizing racism as the key obstruction, he defined the challenge of the century as that of a color line, across which he and others would find the coveted inclusion and belonging. Success would arrive when Blacks were finally welcomed as part of "we the people." Late in life, Du Bois regretted his blindness to the trouble signs flashing across the sky of his evolving career.

The implications of Du Bois's awakening are key. He recognized the foolishness of focusing on seat selection while "ignoring the train's destination and speed." His outlook had been impaired. Where the flow of Western civilization was concerned, he had neglected or minimized the constant, clear, and compelling signs of substantial trouble on the approaching horizon. This was Du Bois's mindset that eventually led him to conclude in 1961, at the age of ninety-three, "Capitalism cannot reform itself; it is doomed to self-destruction."[49]

Thus, by exchanging his customary microscope for a telescope to inform his daily outlook, Du Bois was motivated to reshape his perspective on what constitutes a meaningfully relevant life. In particular, the long view forced him to confront the futility of vying for preferred placement, perhaps a first-class seat on a train possibly bound for calamity. By fully prioritizing the common good over personal gain, Du Bois pivoted from a "seat mindset" to a "destination mindset." In so doing, he became a "destination man."

One way to understand the challenge of shaping better citizens is to highlight the wisdom and current relevance of Du Bois's pivot. In a sense, the dominant producers and consumers of American higher education have shared the same seat mindset from which Du Bois pivoted. Especially as the drivers of the world economy evolved from information to technology, knowledge, and innovation, colleges and universities have only matured in meeting the demands of students who, like Du Bois, have been engrossed in a seat competition. And, like Du Bois, they have pursued a well-appointed lifestyle, while remaining minimally inclined to question where the train called Western civilization is going, or how fast.

Given the dire need to target the health of the democracy, including the unfinished justice agenda, and the health of the planet, perhaps shaping destination citizens ought to be prioritized. But note that the destination mindset is supplemental, rather than entirely substitutional for the seat mindset. Campuses must seek to equip students with both a skill set relevant to seat selection, and a mindset relevant to the train's direction. Like doing well and good, both are critical.

If newly designed campus cultures can help to shape citizens who are less seat focused and more destination focused, thereby backgrounding selfishness and foregrounding selflessness, then the repair movement can accelerate. The civil rights movement happened because relatively large numbers of destination citizens were shaped at and by HBCUs for the precise purpose of making it happen.

Shaping "Second-Day Citizens"

The Mays example offers a second, next-tier way to frame the goal of the new campus cultures. Ironically, Mays made the decision to attend Bates College (1917–20) to help disprove the myth of Black inferiority. He was enriched in the process of doing so, saying, "Bates College did not emancipate me; it did the far greater service of making it possible for me to emancipate myself, to accept with dignity my own worth as a free man."[50] Like several of the Black men of his era—Charles Hamilton Houston, 1915 (NAACP strategist behind the *Brown* decision); William Hastie, 1925 (first Black federal judge); and Charles R. Drew, 1926 (inventor of large-scale blood banks and innovator of blood transfusions)—all of whom attended or graduated from Amherst College on the watch of Alexander Meiklejohn, Mays was sufficiently welcomed and developed at Bates to find his voice in life. Thus, in a sense, he felt commissioned to ensure that Morehouse would do at least as much for its students as Bates had done for him.

With that mindset and agenda, he had advantages at Morehouse. As an African American man leading a campus of African American men, his biography mattered. Because he had already withstood the headwinds of racism, he brought an authentic voice of authority to his encouraging and challenging campus messages. He had credibility when he challenged his students to "understand every item in the Constitution of the United States," and to have "a complete knowledge of every decision the United States Supreme Court had handed down in behalf of minorities since the founding of this country."[51] But, beyond their intellect, his advisories also targeted their psychology and theology. He frequently urged students to discover their own voice in life, or to wake up and embrace what God had assigned them to do as a service to the world. In one among many similar campus speeches, he insisted, "I will serve you and I will serve this institution as if God almighty sent me into the world for the specific purpose of being the Sixth President of Morehouse College."[52] Mays was living what he was advising. His core belief that each and every student had to discover his unique calling was behind one of his most popular quotes: "Whatever you do, strive to do it so well that no man living and no man dead and no man yet to be born could do it any better!"[53] Mays thought every human being was here for a reason, and thus was obligated to discover what they were born to do. On his watch as president, many graduates emerged fully confident, willing, and prepared to be forces for good in the world.

In both his leadership style and his redesign of the campus culture, the Mays presidency was unique. His persona and impact were textured illustrations of a quote popularly attributed to Mark Twain: "The two most important days in your life are the day you are born and the day you find out why."[54] This is a deeper sense in which Mays carried himself as a man who was living the call-answered life he urged his students to live. And beyond explicitly declaring that his service in the role as the sixth president was a matter of destiny, he conducted himself that way.[55] He consistently exuded the confidence of a person who had experienced his second day.

For a person to have a second day, like Mays, means experiencing a "why I was born day." Mays arrived at such a clarity of purpose that he found the boundless energy, drive, and confidence to do the work he felt convinced he was uniquely born to do. Thus, instead of following the desires of their parents, peers, or some other external force, second-day people are guided by their own soul, heart, and spirit. Billions of human beings have had their first day, but it is not a stretch to surmise that very few have had their second; that is, only a tiny fraction of human beings have been fortunate enough to experience a profoundly clear sense of being especially called to a specific role that offers the world a unique gift. It is a powerful, spiritual experience, and the fruit of it tends to be universally recognizable as "good." That was Mays. He was a consequential, second-day man who shaped Morehouse College into a consequential, second-day campus.

Even people who are not aware of the second day concept can have a sense of it. Bronnie Ware, a palliative caregiver, spent eight years providing comfort and a listening ear while sitting by the bedsides of people in the process of dying. She eventually summarized their life-changing lessons, regrets, and insights into five major themes. The top regret was, "I wish I'd had the courage to live a life true to myself, not the life others expected of me."[56] In other words, most people either wished they had experienced their second day, or wished they had heeded the call after having a sense of their true purpose. This implies that having your second day and ignoring it may be worse than never having your second day at all.

The reason why that is so relevant now is because second-day citizens, like mission-driven, destination citizens, tend to lead more consequential lives. In the first half of the twenty-first century, it is already clear that living a truly consequential life means working with others to measurably remediate the imperiled democracy, planet, or both. And, as with the progressive change that resulted from the civil rights movement, measurable progress will be more apparent as more campuses engage in the work of shaping better citizens. Ideally, institutions that excel at shaping second-day citizens will eventually deserve to be referred to as second-day institutions, a title of honor to classify those campus communities that have reached their highest stage of development. And, based on the logic herein, the journey to that outcome will likely be facilitated by a compelling capital and character optimization strategy that is wisely executed by campus leadership.

Shaping "String Shooters"

If one of the highest stages of institutional maturity and optimization is to be measurably adept at annually positioning a critical mass of students to experience their second day or to become destination literate, what might be the best way to express the highest stage of individual development? Again, consider the context.

The first half of the twenty-first century has already featured significant climate, health, moral, ethical, economic, and leadership challenges, all of which have exacerbated many of the world's humanitarian emergencies.[57] If it is true that the world may now need America to do something unprecedented, it is also true that America may now need US higher education to provide something it has never before provided—a scaled, cooperation-inducing educational effort to neutralize a scaled, competition-induced existential threat. Indifference and inaction could be lethal. America and the world may pay the ultimate price for failing to react sooner to higher education's protracted factory-style proliferation of first-day competitors for seats. But more than destination-oriented, second-day citizens, perhaps the highest stage of the mindset competency required to effectively address today's multiple crises is to task colleges and universities with shaping more "string shooters."

What is a string shooter?

The concept is drawn from the novel *The Healers*, first published by Ayi Kwei Armah in 1979.[58] The story is set in late nineteenth-century Ghana, just before the gradual British takeover of the kingdom of Asante. In most cases, the entry of non-Africans into Africa was for exploitative purposes, featuring a soft preamble, often by Christian missionaries.[59] In this case, the colonists arrived slowly, methodically seducing and manipulating Asante's leaders with money, alcohol, and power. The insidious creep of the disruption served as its veil. Dizzied and weakened by the flux, tribal conflicts grew, and African values were gradually abandoned. With perfect timing, the British would exert superior military force, enabling them to, at will, control and exploit African lives and land. It was a recurring theme.

Yet well before the full invasion, Densu, the story's main protagonist, entered his twentieth year aspiring to be "a different kind of man." In recent years, life in his hometown of Esuano was gradually dimmed by the shadow of conflicting ideals. Few sensed an existential threat lurking behind all the signs of change. The hawkish Brits hovered like a toxic stratospheric mist, poised to descend, choke, and kill those unaccustomed to, or intolerant of, a life without freedom. As if fearful of looking up, most tried to preserve their daily routines, despite the omens. But a new normal was clearly afoot.

For instance, as the festival season arrived, the climate surrounding the events had also been slowly, yet conspicuously shifting. The season's ceremonial games, which once symbolized the vigor of youth in a show of group wholeness, had morphed into a clash of individuals in a pursuit of personal greatness. Matches that had once elicited a cooperative mindset now sparked a fiercely competitive one. The contests featured a mix of mental and physical challenges, including solving riddles, wrestling, swimming, and running. Relative to the other entrants, Densu possessed exceptional intelligence, speed, strength, accuracy, confidence, and overall fitness. But because his mindset was incompatible with the cutthroat nature of the contests—the cunning appeal to the killer instinct—he was a reluctant participant.

As the weeklong games reached the final stages, Densu was tied for the lead with Appia, the crown prince of Esuano. The winner would be declared based on a culminating contest of marksmanship. Each was challenged to shoot a tethered pigeon out of the sky as it neared its highest point in flight. Appia brought down his bird on the second life-destroying blast of his gun. Going last, if Densu could kill his bird with one shot, he would be the champion.

But Densu had an idea. He quietly found a way to express his persistent, heartfelt discomfort with the toxic values driving the games and increasingly contaminating the entire culture. As he took aim, he fired a single shot, heard across space and time as it represented a firm rebuke of the deceptive and manipulative mindsets.

> The judge looked down astonished at the string which had so recently held the liberated bird. . . .
> "What happened, Densu?"
> "You saw what happened," Densu answered. "I missed the bird."
> "Deliberately," the judge persisted. "You shot to hit the string, not the pigeon."
> "I missed the bird," Densu said again. He did not stay to hear what else the judge would say. Turning away from the scene of competition, he walked toward the river.[60]

Instead of shooting the bird, Densu deliberately shot the string that freed the bird. He possessed sharp, state-of-the-art skills, but he refused to use them in accordance with prevailing expectations. Faced with a choice, instead of preserving control, he released it. Instead of taking a life, he liberated one. And instead of profiting personally by staying where the championship crown would be served to him, he walked toward a life where profiting collectively is all that matters—a life where the champions are those who serve.

His act was both a poignant presentation of the kind of person he had become and a persuasive illustration of the kind of people he felt they all should become. His action beckoned the contestants to another mindset and a different way of life. He urged them to embrace an effective way to make of their old world, a new world.

It was a deliberate choice. Given his talent, Densu had the option to excel in the system that had transfixed everyone around him, but he chose to follow neither the crowd nor the culture of those who masterfully manipulated the crowd. He chose to be a string shooter. In so doing, he changed the system itself, using his expertise for a higher purpose. And after making a profound statement, he "walked toward the river," determined to help usher in a more humane way of life.

The lessons are timeless. As a second-day citizen, Densu responded to the growing crises in his world with neither an eloquent nor an inarticulate silence. His choice to shoot the string symbolized his clear intention to spend the rest of his life as an engaged force for good. In his world, that meant joining "the healers," a small, magnetic community of those with growth mindsets, steadfastly devoting themselves to the eventual wholeness of a broken humanity. By definition, they were destination-minded string shooters.

In today's world, the corrective efforts may be different, but the mindsets driving them are consistent. Among the Asante in the 1860s, as with HBCUs a century later, the aim was to shape people who would heal an imperiled world. Each believed that such work would enable the long-awaited arrival of societal conditions barely detectable since the rise of the West—a radically humane, belonging-intensive, egalitarian society. Not only did the healers aspire to realize a world resembling that which HBCU communities targeted, but their goal was also akin to what the US Constitution referred to as "a more perfect union," what Douglass called "our composite nationality," and what King popularized as "the beloved community."[61] Collectively, the vision is that of a better world wherein a balanced state of equality and justice are a way of life. And no matter the era in human history, shaping better citizens has consistently been the key to shaping that better world.

FOR THE MINDSET

Shaping world-class string shooters should now be the urgent quest of every college campus in and beyond America.

Epilogue

"You are saying our time is not now?" Nyaneba asked.
"I am saying this is seed time, far from harvest time," Damfo said.

Ayi Kwei Armah, *The Healers*

Nearly every major point outlined in this book lived within me when I assumed the presidency of Morehouse College in January 2013. Convinced that it was "our harvest time," we sought to actualize these and similar ideas and set a new trajectory for HBCUs and others. We planned to converge a faculty and administrative team capable of optimizing both character and capital for the first time ever. But in truth, those aspirational seeds were planted back when I was a Morehouse student in the late 1970s. The Mays effect on the campus culture remained palpable when I first arrived, eight years after his retirement. In my sophomore year, following a one-on-one encounter with Dr. Mays, my heart was set on becoming an educator and leading an effort to truly transform a campus. Undoubtedly, I had experienced my "second day."

The character optimization ideas for both my presidency and this book were born then and there. So was my belief in the need to shape better citizens. My thinking and sense of destiny only deepened over time, even amid many changes and shifts in the higher education landscape.

My fuller appreciation of capital optimization was sparked when I headed north for graduate school at Harvard University. Similar to Du Bois's transition from Fisk to Harvard years ago, I was astounded by the resource gap between the two campuses. I immediately saw evidence of what happens when leadership emphasizes capital (Harvard) versus character (Morehouse). I wondered and asked, why not optimize both on a single campus, simultaneously?

That question infused my mindset as I completed graduate study at Harvard in 1985. Soon thereafter, I visited with my grandmother Ida Anita Nix, who never attended college but ensured that all five of her children did. She immediately insisted that I seek the presidency of an HBCU. When I asked her why she was so passionate about it, she said, "They need you, and that's the kind of work that'll get you into heaven!" I was encouraged by both her vocational and theological advice, and I kept it in heart and mind as I prepared to shift from the classroom to the office.

My understanding of capital optimization was fortified once I launched my career at the Massachusetts Institute of Technology. Providentially, my arrival there in 1985 coincided with the fertilization of the billion-dollar capital campaign era. By spending nearly all of my sixteen years at MIT in institutional advancement, I eventually played a key role in keeping the Institute competitively strong. I also sharpened my strategic mindset about how selected HBCUs might finally conquer precarity. And on the MIT campus, I began incubating ideas for a reframed relationship between HBCUs and the philanthropic community.

The move to an executive deanship at George Washington University, followed by the unique experience of directing the White House Initiative on HBCUs in the Obama administration, refined my perspectives on the dire need for true optimization. While at the White House, I drew on those ideas and began to publicly tout the "cathedral vision," echoing the 1898 trustee-enabled quest to make the Tuskegee Institute a "cathedral in the Black Belt."[1]

By the time I stood up to be inaugurated at Morehouse College on February 14, 2014, I framed my address as a nod to Du Bois, entitling it, "The World of Our Dreams." I described the optimization vision, referring to it then as "capital and character preeminence," a Mount Everest–style challenge, for which my team and I were the Sherpas. Every major concept in that inaugural address is in this book, including Ellison's fluttering veil, which enabled me to highlight another ambiguous image, even more suitable to that occasion.

I directed the audience's attention to the college logo, the top half of which is a bright shining sun, with the bottom half a band of thick, billowing clouds. Just below the clouds are the Latin words, "Et Facta Est Lux," or "and light was made." The implied mandate is to make the glow of one's life bright enough to disperse, rather than attract the copious clouds of discord and doubt. Thus, human agency can literally bring the light of a new day. I was convinced then and now that the world's better citizens can dictate whether life's veils are lifting instead of lowering, and whether life's clouds are burning off, rather than rolling in. That was our unclouded vision for Morehouse. But because my stay there was briefer than what true optimization required, I have planted those ideas in this book, as seedlings to be harvested one day, in the fullness of time, by others.

Two final thoughts on our aborted quest. First, very few writers have enriched me with their every publication, as has my friend Ayi Kwei Armah. In my view he is, by far, the wisest man alive. Among so many other things, he fascinated me with his keen awareness of a world not defined by and transfixed with hierarchical, supremacist, and elitist values. Using Africa's most ancient documents, he looked beyond the age of western domination, military rulers, pharaohs, dynasties, emperors, and dictators. There, he located Africa's social memory about which we know too little. Ayi Kwei convinced me to shift from "preeminence," as a north star. I embraced "optimization," because it is less vulnerable to the hierarchical and hypercompetitive impulses emphasized in the western world.

I annually handed Ayi Kwei's books to my freshmen, with emphasis on *The Healers*, from which I have drawn the "string shooters" theme and the quotes to open each chapter. He insisted that, unlike deceivers and manipulators, string shooters are liberators and healers. They enable truth, light, and life. And string shooters are now the perfect vaccine for a world that, perhaps largely unwittingly, suffers from a pandemic of greed, selfishness, fear, and hate.

Finally and relatedly, as the light began to dim on my presidential tenure, Eddie "Blue" Weaver, a thirty-four-year veteran of the Morehouse physical plant division, led a group of his coworkers into my conference room. Blue wanted me to know that he and the crew fully embraced our capital and character preeminence vision, and they committed themselves to doing everything in their power to make it a reality. At his urging, and with great passion, they each firmly asserted their determination to bring a light to the campus as powerful as any brought by our most important benefactors.

Sadly, Blue unexpectedly passed away within a few weeks of that momentous meeting. Over the course of decades, I successfully convinced some of the world's wealthiest, most significant influencers to embrace the idea of shaping better citizens through campus optimization. But since the moment that vision sparked inside of me as a Morehouse sophomore, no endorsement of our lofty quest was more authentically majestic, fruitful, and pure than Blue's. He was a courageous force for good. He was a string shooter! His light will forever glow among the best people who have ever devoted themselves to making a better world.

Comparison Institutions for Figures 9.4 and 9.5

Ivy+

Brown University
Columbia University
Cornell University
Dartmouth College
Harvard University
Massachusetts Institute of
Technology
Princeton University
Stanford University
University of Pennsylvania
Yale University

Top Liberal Arts Institutions

Amherst College
Bowdoin College
Carleton College
Claremont McKenna College
Grinnell College
Middlebury College
Pomona College
Smith College
Swarthmore College
Wellesley College
Williams College

Top Private HBCUs

Claflin University
Clark Atlanta University
Dillard University
Fisk University
Hampton University

Howard University
Morehouse College
Spelman College
Tuskegee University
Xavier University of Louisiana

Top Public Institutions

College of William and Mary

Georgia Institute of Technology
  (main campus)

University of California-Berkeley

University of California-Irvine

University of California-Los
  Angeles

University of California-San Diego

University of Michigan-Ann Arbor

University of North Carolina at
  Chapel Hill

University of Virginia (main
  campus)

University of Wisconsin-Madison

Top Public HBCUs

Delaware State University

Florida A&M University

Jackson State University

Morgan State University

North Carolina A&T State
  University

North Carolina Central University

Prairie View A&M University

Southern University and A&M
  College

Tennessee State University

University of Maryland Eastern Shore

Institutions Referenced
in Figure 9.6

Universities with the Most Appearances in the Annual Top 20 in Year-end
Fundraising Results, 1985–2020

Institution	Year founded	Number of times in the Top 20, 1985–2020
1. Harvard University	1636	36
2. Yale University	1701	36
3. University of Pennsylvania	1740	36
4. Columbia University	1754	36
5. Duke University	1838	36
6. University of Washington	1861	36
7. Cornell University	1865	36
8. University of Southern California	1880	36
9. Stanford University	1885	36
10. Johns Hopkins University	1876	34
11. Massachusetts Institute of Technology	1861	33
12. University of California-Los Angeles	1919	31
13. University of Michigan	1817	30
14. University of California-Berkeley	1868	29
15. University of Wisconsin-Madison	1848	27

Institution	Year founded	Number of times in the Top 20, 1985–2020
16. New York University	1831	26
17. Indiana University	1820	25
18. University of Minnesota	1851	25
19. University of California-San Francisco	1864	23

Source: All higher education giving: *2004 Voluntary Support of Education*, RAND Council for Aid to Education, 4, table 2, https://www.rand.org/content/dam/rand/www/external/news/press.05/03.02.pdf/RAND_VSE_2004.pdf;

Top Twenty Fundraisers: *Voluntary Support of Education*, RAND Council for Aid to Education.

Notes

Prologue

1. Henry G. Badger, "Colleges That Did Not Survive," *Journal of Negro Education* 35, no. 4 (Autumn 1966): 306. Badger added this caveat: "The present estimate of [losing] 200 or more could easily be too low."
2. Badger, 311.
3. Higher Education Act of 1965, Pub. L. 89-329, Sec. 322 (2), approved November 8, 1965, https://www.govinfo.gov/content/pkg/COMPS-765/pdf/COMPS-765.pdf.
4. Ayi Kwei Armah, *The Healers* (Senegal: Per Ankh edition, 2016), 52–55. Used with permission.

Introduction

1. Jeffrey M. Jones, "Confidence in Higher Education Down Since 2015," Gallup Blog, October 9, 2018, https://news.gallup.com/opinion/gallup/242441/confidence-higher -education-down-2015.aspx; Scott Jaschik, "Falling Confidence in Higher Ed," Inside Higher Ed, October 9, 2018, https://www.insidehighered.com/news/2018/10/09/gallup -survey-finds-falling-confidence-higher-education; Brandon Busteed, "Wake Up Higher Education. The Degree Is on the Decline," *Forbes*, September 25, 2020, https://www .forbes.com/sites/brandonbusteed/2020/09/25/wake-up-higher-education-the-degree -is-on-the-decline; Doug Lederman, "The Incredible Shrinking Higher Ed Industry," Inside Higher Ed, October 14, 2019, https://www.insidehighered.com/news/2019/10/14 /higher-ed-shrinks-number-colleges-falls-lowest-point-two-decades.
2. Charles T. Clotfelter, *Unequal Colleges in the Age of Disparity* (Cambridge, MA: Harvard University Press, 2017), 75.
3. Dominic J. Brewer, Susan M. Gates, and Charles A. Goldman, *In Pursuit of Prestige: Strategy and Competition in U.S. Higher Education* (New Brunswick, NJ: Transaction Publishers, 2004).
4. Clotfelter, *Unequal Colleges*, 36. Clotfelter notes specific measures of institutional competitiveness where HBCUs fall behind: tuition dependency, 161; lack of unique marketing, 186; brain drain, 224; and class drain, 238–39.
5. US Department of Education, National Center for Education Statistics, Digest of Education Statistics, "Fall Enrollment of U.S. Residents in Degree-Granting Postsecondary Institutions, by Race/Ethnicity: Selected Years, 1976 through 2029," table 306.30, https://nces.ed.gov/programs/digest/d19/tables/dt19_306.30.asp, and "Fall Enrollment in Degree-Granting Historically Black Colleges and Universities, by Sex of Student and Level and Control of Institution: Selected Years, 1976 through 2020," table 313.20, https://nces.ed.gov/programs/digest/d21/tables/dt21_313.20.asp.

6. Nina Mjagkij, *Light in the Darkness: African Americans and the YMCA, 1852–1946* (Lexington: University Press of Kentucky, 1994), 114.

7. Various aspects of the resulting generational tension are summarized by both Mjagkij, *Light in the Darkness*, 101, and Randal M. Jelks, *Benjamin Elijah Mays: Schoolmaster of the Movement* (Chapel Hill: University of North Carolina Press, 2014), 74–79.

8. Subject files, Student Work Department, undated and 1927–1932 (Box 11, Folder 5), letter 1, p. 2, National Council of the Young Men's Christian Associations of the United States of America, Colored Work Department (University of Minnesota Libraries, Kautz Family YMCA Archives, 1927–1932).

9. Subject files, Student Work Department, "Report of the Commission Appointed by the Home Division Committee to Study the Future of the Colored Student Work, Especially in Relation to the New Student Division," 6–7.

10. Subject files, "Report of the Commission," 7.

11. Subject files, letter from R. H. King.

12. Richard I. McKinney, *Mordecai, the Man and His Message: The Story of Mordecai Wyatt Johnson* (Washington, DC: Howard University Press, 1997), 263.

13. Edwin R. Embree, *13 Against the Odds* (New York: Viking Press, 1945), 186.

14. The fuller story behind Tuskegee's endowment growth is told in chapters 6 and 7 of this book.

15. Commonly cited HBCU challenges include:
    Governance: See Charles Nelms and Alvin J. Schexnider, "Strengthening Governance at Historically Black Colleges and Universities," *Diverse: Issues in Higher Education*, April 5, 2020, https://diverseeducation.com/article/172253;
    Deferred maintenance: See *Historic Preservation: Cost to Restore Historic Properties at Historically Black Colleges and Universities*, US General Accounting Office (Washington, DC: February 1998), https://www.gao.gov/assets/rced-98-51.pdf;
    Financial stress: See Gregory N. Price, "1 in 10 HBCUs Were Financially Fragile Before COVID-19 Endangered All Colleges and Universities," The Conversation, June 24, 2020, https://theconversation.com/1-in-10-hbcus-were-financially-fragile-before-covid-19-endangered-all-colleges-and-universities-140528; and Krystal L. Williams and BreAnna L. Davis, *Public and Private Investments and Divestments in Historically Black Colleges and Universities*, Minority-Serving Institutions Series (Washington, DC: American Council on Education, January 2019), https://www.acenet.edu/Documents/Public-and-Private-Investments-and-Divestments-in-HBCUs.pdf;
    Stiffening competition for talent: See Richard F. America, "Can HBCUs Compete?," *The Journal of Blacks in Higher Education*, October 24, 2012, https://www.jbhe.com/2012/10/can-hbcus-compete; and "Historically Black Colleges Struggle as More Students Pursue 'Mainstream' Educations," Debtwire, January 3, 2019, https://www.debtwire.com/info/historically-black-colleges-struggle-more-students-pursue-mainstream-educations;
    Widespread perception of HBCUs as troubled: See Wadzanai Mhute, "'Your Heritage Is Taken Away': The Closing of 3 Historically Black Colleges," *New York Times*, June 28, 2019, https://www.nytimes.com/2019/06/28/us/hbcu-closed-graduates.html.

16. James D. Anderson, *The Education of Blacks in the South, 1860–1935* (Chapel Hill: University of North Carolina Press, 1988), 8.</NLIST>

17. Heather Andrea Williams, "We Are Striving to Do Business on Our Own Hook: Organizing Schools on the Ground," in *Self-Taught: African American Education in Slavery and Freedom* (Chapel Hill: University of North Carolina Press, 2005), 80–95.

18. Carol S. Dweck, *Mindset: The New Psychology of Success* (New York: Ballantine Books, 2006).

19. Dweck, *Mindset*, 142–46.

20. Joe M. Richardson, "Edgar B. Stern: A White New Orleans Philanthropist Helps Build a Black University," *The Journal of Negro History* 82, no. 3 (Summer 1997): 328, doi: 10.2307/2717676.

21. For example, the United Negro College Fund sponsored an institutional capacity-building initiative for years. While it had tepid involvement from member institutions when I consulted with them in the 1990s, all 37 UNCF member institutions are actively engaged in capacity-building activities as of fall 2022, with primary support provided by the Gates Foundation and Blue Meridian Partners.

22. The Afropessimist would look at this table and note that the change in these progressions barely warrants the use of the word "up." In the Afropessimist view, emancipation and the civil rights movement are little more than "point[s] of transition between modes of servitude and racial subjection," as noted by Saidiya V. Hartman, *Scenes of Subjection: Terror, Slavery, and Self-Making in Nineteenth-Century America* (New York: Oxford University Press, 1997), 6.

Chapter 1

1. On Washington's sellout reputation, see Robert J. Norrell, *Up from History* (Cambridge, MA: Harvard University Press, 2009); on Du Bois's elitist reputation: Kyle Beckham and Shirin Vossoughi, "From the Poverty of Culture to the Power of Politics: The Evolution of W. E. B. Du Bois," *Diaspora, Indigenous, and Minority Education* 14, no. 2 (2020): 75–86, doi: 10.1080/15595692.2020.1733958.

2. Crisply and clearly summarized by Norrell, *Up from History*, 438.

3. The insistence on a more contextualized assessment of Washington is not a new idea. Aside from Norrell's *Up from History*, other reassessments include Donald J. Calista, "Booker T. Washington: Another Look," *The Journal of Negro History* 49, no. 4 (October 1964): 240–55, doi: 10.2307/2716459; Louis R. Harlan, "The Secret Life of Booker T. Washington," *The Journal of Southern History* 37, no. 3 (August 1971): 393–416, https://www.jstor.org/stable/i312294; Lawrence J. Friedman, "Life 'in the Lion's Mouth': Another Look at Booker T. Washington," *The Journal of Negro History* 59, no. 4 (October 1974): 337–51, doi: 10.2307/2717315; John P. Flynn, "Booker T. Washington: Uncle Tom or Wooden Horse," *The Journal of Negro History* 54, no. 3 (July 1969): 262–74, doi: 10.2307/2716669; and several essays in Rebecca Carroll, *Uncle Tom or New Negro?* (New York: Broadway Books, 2006).

4. Louis R. Harlan, Raymond W. Smock, and Geraldine McTighe, eds., *The Booker T. Washington Papers* (Urbana: University of Illinois Press, 1972–89), 1:12.

5. Harlan, Smock, and McTighe, *Booker T. Washington Papers*, 2:58.

6. Eric Foner, *Freedom's Lawmakers*, revised ed. (Baton Rouge, LA: LSU Press, 1996), xi.

7. Rayford W. Logan, *The Negro in American Life and Thought: The Nadir, 1877–1901* (New York: Dial Press, 1954).

8. United States Congress, *Testimony Taken by the Joint Select Committee Appointed to Inquire into the Condition of Affairs in the Late Insurrectionary States, Alabama* (Washington, DC: Government Printing Office, 1872), vols. 8–10.

9. *Testimony Taken*, 8:61–73.

10. *Testimony Taken*, 9:1019; Norrell, *Up from History*, 45–47, summarizes only some of Alston's experiences.

11. Stewart E. Tolnay and E. M. Beck, *A Festival of Violence: An Analysis of Southern Lynchings, 1882–1930* (Urbana: University of Illinois Press, 1995), 47.

12. Harlan, Smock, and McTighe, *Booker T. Washington Papers*, 8:395.

13. Edwin T. Arnold, *What Virtue There Is in Fire* (Athens: University of Georgia Press, 2009), 68.

14. To preserve the memory of the 6,500 lives lost to lynching in America, the Equal Justice Initiative keeps an online calendar of such crimes featuring daily reminders. The reminder for April 27, 1899, tells this story of Mitchell Daniel, "lynched by his white neighbors" for "talking too much" about the Hose lynching; see "White Georgia Mob Lynches Man for 'Talking Too Much' About Another Lynching," Equal Justice Initiative, https://calendar.eji.org/racial-injustice/apr/27.

15. Emma Thornbrough, "Booker T. Washington as Seen by His White Contemporaries," *The Journal of Negro History* 53, no. 2 (April 1968): 169, doi: 10.2307/2716490.

16. Daniel Goldstone, *Inherently Unequal: The Betrayal of Equal Rights by the Supreme Court, 1865–1903* (New York: Walker & Company, 2011), 179.

17. Douglas A. Blackmon, *Slavery by Another Name* (New York: Doubleday, 2008), 196.

18. Norrell, *Up from History*, 308–09.

19. Campbell Gibson and Kay Jung, "Historical Census Statistics on Population Totals by Race, 1790 to 1990, and by Hispanic Origin, 1970 to 1990, for the United States, Regions, Divisions, and States" (Population Division working paper 56, US Census Bureau, Washington, DC, September 2002), https://www.census.gov/content/dam/Census/library/working-papers/2002/demo/POP-twps0056.pdf.

20. Mary Frances Berry and John W. Blassingame, *Long Memory: The Black Experience in America* (New York: Oxford University Press, 1982), 265.

21. Ray Stannard Baker, *Following the Color Line: An Account of Negro Citizenship in the American Democracy* (New York: Doubleday, Page & Co., 1908), 242. Baker does not cite the date of this quote, but Hoke Smith served as Georgia governor from 1911 to 1921.

22. William F. Holmes, *The White Chief: James Kimble Vardaman* (Baton Rouge: Louisiana State University Press, 1970), 36.

23. Harlan, Smock, and McTighe, *Booker T. Washington Papers*, 8:662–63; Thornbrough, "Booker T. Washington," 174.

24. Harlan, Smock, and McTighe, 11:483. This was casually reported in the press release covering Washington's Florida tour, including his visit to Lake City.

25. Norrell, *Up from History*, 307.

26. David Zucchino, *Wilmington's Lie: The Murderous Coup of 1898 and the Rise of White Supremacy* (New York: Atlantic Monthly Press, 2020), 65–76.

27. Tolnay and Beck, *Festival of Violence*, 17.

28. Harlan, Smock, and McTighe, *Booker T. Washington Papers*, 3:29. Note that Ida B. Wells Barnett offered a similar estimate of 10,000 lynchings since the Civil War. See Philip Dray, *At the Hands of Persons Unknown: The Lynching of Black America* (New York: Modern Library, 2003), xi.

29. Norrell, *Up from History*, 108.

30. Ibram X. Kendi, *Stamped from the Beginning* (New York: Bold Type Books, 2017), 70.

31. Ishmael Reed, foreword to *Up from Slavery*, by Booker T. Washington (New York: Signet Classics, 2010), xi.

32. W. E. B. Du Bois, "Jefferson Davis as a Representative of Civilization," in *W. E. B. Du Bois: A Reader*, ed. David Levering Lewis (New York: Henry Holt, 1995), 17.

33. W. E. B. Du Bois, "A Final Word," in *The Philadelphia Negro: A Social Study* (The Oxford W. E. B. Du Bois), ed. Henry Louis Gates, Jr. (New York: Oxford University Press, 2014), 413, Kindle.

34. David Levering Lewis, *W. E. B. Du Bois: Biography of a Race, 1868–1919* (New York: Henry Holt, 1993), 277.

35. Review of *The Souls of Black Folk*, by W. E. B. Du Bois, *New York Times*, April 25, 1903, https://archive.nytimes.com/www.nytimes.com/books/99/04/25/specials/dubois-souls .html.

36. Henry Louis Gates, Jr., "The Black Letters on the Sign: W. E. B. Du Bois and the Canon," series introduction to W. E. B. Du Bois, *Black Reconstruction in America* (The Oxford W. E. B. Du Bois), ed. Henry Louis Gates, Jr. (New York: Oxford University Press, 2014), xiv.

37. Du Bois insists in *Black Reconstruction* that "the overthrow of Reconstruction was in essence a revolution inspired by property, and not a race war" (p. 510). For a critique, see John N. Robinson III, "W. E. B. Du Bois and the Racial Economics of Inclusive Capitalism," Social Science Research Council, January 22, 2019, https://items.ssrc.org /race-capitalism/w-e-b-du-bois-and-the-racial-economics-of-inclusive-capitalism.

38. Reiland Rabaka, *Against Epistemic Apartheid* (New York: Lexington Books, 2010), 223.

39. W. E. B. Du Bois, "The Color Line and the Church," in *W. E. B. Du Bois: A Reader*, ed. Meyer Weinberg (New York: Harper & Row, 1970), 217.

40. W. E. B. Du Bois, editorial, *Crisis*, November 1910, 10.

41. W. E. B. Du Bois, "Woman Suffrage," *Crisis*, April 1915, 285.

42. Du Bois, "Final Word," 414.

43. Lewis, *Du Bois: Biography of a Race*, 111.

44. W. E. B. Du Bois, "The Negro College," *Crisis*, August 1933, 177.

45. W. E. B. Du Bois, "The Talented Tenth: Memorial Address," in Lewis, *Du Bois: A Reader*, 347.

46. Lisa D. Cook, "Violence and Economic Activity: Evidence from African American Patents, 1870–1940," *Journal of Economic Growth* 19, no. 2 (2014): 221–57.

47. Cook, 234–35.

Chapter 2

1. Eric Anderson and Alfred A. Moss, Jr., *Dangerous Donations: Northern Philanthropy and Southern Black Education, 1902–1930* (Columbia: University of Missouri Press, 1999); James D. Anderson, *The Education of Blacks in the South, 1860–1935* (Chapel Hill: University of North Carolina Press, 1988).

2. John Michael Lee, Jr., and Samaad Wes Keys, *Land-Grant but Unequal: State One-to-One Match Funding for 1890 Land-Grant Universities*, Office for Access and Success Policy Brief (Washington, DC: Association of Public and Land-Grant Universities, September 2013), https://www.aplu.org/library/land-grant-but-unequal-state-one-to -one-match-funding-for-1890-land-grant-universities/file.

3. Eric Foner, *Reconstruction: America's Unfinished Revolution, 1863–1877*, updated ed. (New York: Harper Perennial, 2014), 96.

4. Foner, *Reconstruction*, 199–201.

5. Donald G. Tewksbury, *The Founding of American Colleges and Universities Before the Civil War* (New York: Teachers College, Columbia University, 1932), 28.

6. Henry G. Badger, "Colleges That Did Not Survive," *Journal of Negro Education* 35, no. 4 (Autumn 1966): 306, doi: 10.2307/2294130; Walter Crosby Eells, "Surveys of Higher

Education for Negroes," *Journal of Negro Education* 5, no. 2 (April 1936): 245–51, doi: 10.2307/2292161. Eells derives this total from 61 surveys of higher education conducted before 1935. The earliest survey was for the year 1915, published in 1916.

7. William Preston Vaughn, *Schools for All: The Blacks and Public Education in the South, 1865–1877* (Lexington: University Press of Kentucky, 1974), 19.

8. For more on the sheer brutality of southern White supremacists see: Foner, *Reconstruction*, 19–123; Leon F. Litwack, "Hellhounds," in *Trouble in Mind: Black Southerners in the Age of Jim Crow* (New York: Vintage Books, 1998), 280–325; and everything written by and about Rust College graduate Ida B. Wells, especially Wells's book, *A Red Record. Tabulated Statistics and Alleged Causes of Lynchings in the United States, 1892-1893-1894* (Chicago: Donohue & Henneberry, 1894).

9. James D. Anderson, "Philanthropic Control over Private Black Higher Education," in *Philanthropy and Cultural Imperialism*, ed. Robert F. Arnove (Bloomington: Indiana University Press, 1982), 147–77.

10. Heather Andrea Williams, *Self-Taught: African American Education in Slavery and Freedom* (Chapel Hill: University of North Carolina Press, 2005), 5.

11. This pattern is summarized by Thomas Webber, *Deep Like the Rivers* (New York: W. W. Norton, 1978); Vincent Harding, *There Is a River: The Black Struggle for Freedom in America* (New York: Harcourt Brace, 1981); and Anderson, *Education of Blacks*.

12. Anderson, *Education of Blacks*, 15.

13. Williams, *Self-Taught*, 77.

14. Anderson, *Education of Blacks*, 6.

15. Monroe N. Work discusses the percentage of Negro illiterates in 1910 in *Negro Year Book and Annual Encyclopedia of the Negro* (Tuskegee, AL: Negro Year Book Company, Tuskegee Institute, 1913), 146, https://ia800204.us.archive.org/14/items/negroyearbook00resegoog/negroyearbook00resegoog.pdf; Loretta Funke discusses Negro illiteracy in 1910 relative to other countries in "The Negro in Education," *Journal of Negro History* 5, no. 1 (January 1920): 19, doi: 10.2307/2713498; Nampeo D. R. McKenney, *The Social and Economic Status of the Black Population in the United States: An Historical View, 1790–1978*, Current Population Reports, Special Series P-23, no. 80 (Washington, DC: US Department of Commerce, Bureau of the Census, 1979), 91, table 68, https://www2.census.gov/library/publications/1979/demographics/p23-080.pdf; Thomas D. Snyder, ed., *120 Years of American Education: A Statistical Portrait* (Washington, DC: US Department of Education, National Center for Education Statistics, January 1993), 21, table 6, https://nces.ed.gov/pubs93/93442.pdf.

16. McKenney, *Social and Economic Status*, 91, table 68.

17. Funke, "The Negro in Education," 19. Note that Funke's 70 percent literacy rate by 1910 differs from McKenney, who puts the rate at 67 percent at that time.

18. Snyder, *120 Years of American Education*, 21.

19. Eric Foner, *Freedom's Lawmakers*, revised ed. (Baton Rouge, LA: LSU Press, 1996), xi.

20. Foner, *Freedom's Lawmakers*, xxiv.

21. Foner, xiii.

22. Jed H. Shugerman, "The Creation of the Department of Justice: Professionalization Without Civil Rights or Civil Service," *Stanford Law Review* 66, no. 121 (January 2014): 121–72, http://www.stanfordlawreview.org/wp-content/uploads/sites/3/2014/01/66_Stan._L._Rev._121_Shugerman.pdf.

23. For the literacy data, see McKenney, *Social and Economic Status*, 91, table 68; for the voter registration data, see Lawrence Goldstone, *On Account of Race* (Berkeley, CA: Counterpoint, 2020), 234.

24. Colleen Walsh, "A Renewed Focus on Slavery," *Harvard Gazette,* November 22, 2019, https://news.harvard.edu/ gazette/story/2019/11/harvard-initiative-to-deepen-study-of -its-historical-ties-to-slavery.

25. Radcliffe Institute for Advanced Study, *Report of the Presidential Committee on Harvard and the Legacy of Slavery* (Cambridge, MA: President and Fellows of Harvard College, 2022), 5, https://legacyofslavery.harvard.edu.

26. *Harvard and the Legacy of Slavery*, 7, 15.

27. Noah Remnick, "Yale Defies Calls to Rename Calhoun College," *New York Times*, April 27, 2016, https://www.nytimes.com/2016/04/28/nyregion/yale-defies-calls-to-rename -calhoun-college.html.

28. Jennifer Schuessler, "Princeton Digs Deep into Its Fraught Racial History," *New York Times*, November 6, 2017, https://www.nytimes.com/2017/11/06/arts/princeton-digs -deep-into-its-fraught-racial-history.html; Paige Gross, "A Slave Auction, Slave-Owning Presidents: Princeton U. Unveils a Dark Past," NJ.com, November 8, 2017, https://www .nj.com/mercer/2017/11/princeton_u_addresses_history_of_slavery_with_proj.html.

29. Krystal Knapp, "Princeton University to Remove Woodrow Wilson's Name from International Affairs School, Residential College," Planet Princeton, June 27, 2020, https:// planetprinceton.com/2020/06/27/princeton-university-to-remove-woodrow-wilsons -name-from-international-affairs-school-residential-college.

30. Marisa J. Fuentes and Deborah Gray White, eds., *Scarlet and Black: Slavery and Dispossession in Rutgers History*, vol. 1 (Newark, NJ: Rutgers University Press, 2016).

31. "Georgetown Reflects on Slavery, Memory, and Reconciliation,".Georgetown University, https://slavery.georgetown.edu/wp-content/uploads/2016/08/GU-WGSMR-Report-Web .pdf; Saahil Desai, "The First Reparations Attempt at an American College Campus Comes from Its Students," *The Atlantic*, April 18, 2019, https://www.theatlantic.com /education/archive/2019/04/why-are-georgetown-students-paying-reparations/587443.

32. Chris Kenning, "Confederate Monument's Removal OK'd by Judge," *Courier Journal* (Louisville, KY), June 20, 2016, https://www.courier-journal.com/story/news/local /2016/06/20/judge-mayor-can-remove-confederate-monument/86131244.

33. Craig S. Wilder, *Ebony and Ivy: Race, Slavery, and the Troubled History of America's Universities* (New York: Bloomsbury, 2013).

34. Wilder, *Ebony and Ivy*, 11.

35. Tewksbury, *Founding of American Colleges*, 28.

36. Wilder, *Ebony and Ivy*, 1.

37. Wilder, 114.

38. Senator Jefferson Davis, April 12, 1860, 37th Cong., 1st sess., *Congressional Globe* 106, 1682, https://memory.loc.gov/ll/llcg/052/0700/07401682.tif.

39. Claudia Goldin and Lawrence F. Katz, *The Race Between Education and Technology* (Cambridge, MA: Harvard University Press, 2008).

40. W. E. B. Du Bois, *The Souls of Black Folk* (New York: Barnes & Noble Classics, 2003), 10. First published 1903 by A. C. McClurg & Co. (Chicago).

41. Manning Marable, *How Capitalism Underdeveloped Black America* (Chicago: Haymarket Books, 2015), 56, Kindle.

42. David Brion Davis, *Inhuman Bondage* (Oxford: Oxford University Press, 2006), 298. Note that this is one of the more far-reaching conclusions to be considered at the foundation of any responsible discussion of reparations.

43. Two key books that discuss the importance of Black enslavement to the American economy: Walter Johnson, *River of Dark Dreams: Slavery and Empire in the Cotton Kingdom* (Cambridge, MA: Harvard University Press, 2013); and Edward E. Baptist, *The Half Has Never Been Told: Slavery and the Making of American Capitalism* (New York: Basic Books, 2014).

44. Baptist, *Half Has Never Been Told*, xxv.

45. Samuel H. Williamson and Louis P. Cain, "Measuring Slavery in 2020 Dollars," MeasuringWorth, 2022, www.measuringworth.com/slavery.php; Baptist, in *Half Has Never Been Told*, notes that the slave economy generated "almost 2 billion pounds of [cotton] in 1860."

46. Tewksbury, *Founding of American Colleges*, 16.

47. Wilder, *Ebony and Ivy*, 212.

48. See Wilder, *Ebony and Ivy*, part 2 (chaps. 5–8), for numerous illustrations of how the development of knowledge in the American academy helped to justify racism and sustain inequity.

49. The documented African American objection to this tradition of white supremacy dates to at least the late eighteenth century. See Dorothy B. Porter, "The Organized Educational Activities of Negro Literary Societies, 1828–1846," *Journal of Negro Education* 5, no. 4 (October 1936): 555–76, https://www.jstor.org/stable/2292029.

50. Silvio Bedini, *The Life of Benjamin Banneker*, second ed. (Baltimore: Maryland Historical Society, 1999), 158.

51. Bedini, *Life of Benjamin Banneker*, 162.

52. "The Nation's Problem: A Speech Delivered by Hon. Frederick Douglass, Before the Bethel Literary and Historical Society in Washington, DC, April 16, 1889," in *Negro Social and Political Thought 1850–1920*, ed. Howard Brotz (New York: Basic Books, 1966), 312.

53. See also Ibram X. Kendi, *Stamped from the Beginning* (New York: Bold Type Books, 2017), for a compelling treatment of this history.

54. W. E. B. Du Bois, "A Negro Student at Harvard at the End of the Nineteenth Century," in *W. E. B. Du Bois: A Reader*, ed. David Levering Lewis (New York: Henry Holt, 1995), 274. In 2020, multiple universities were trying to enhance the undergraduate experiences of groups they previously excluded. For more on this, see *Advancing Diversity and Inclusion in Higher Education*, Office of Planning, Evaluation and Policy Development, Office of the Under Secretary (Washington, DC: US Department of Education, November 2016), https://www2.ed.gov/rschstat/research/pubs/advancing-diversity-inclusion.pdf.

55. Charles J. Ogletree, Jr., "Litigating the Legacy of Slavery," *New York Times*, March 31, 2002, https://www.nytimes.com/2002/03/31/opinion/ litigating-the-legacy-of-slavery.html; Dr. Ruth J. Simmons, conversation with the author, December 15, 2020.

56. *Slavery and Justice: Report of the Brown University Steering Committee on Slavery and Justice* (Providence, RI: Brown University, 2006), https://slaveryandjustice.brown.edu/sites/default/files/reports/SlaveryAndJustice2006.pdf.

57. *Slavery and Justice*.

58. *President's Commission on Slavery and the University: Report to President Teresa A. Sullivan* (Charlottesville: University of Virginia, 2018), 15, https://slavery.virginia.edu/wp-content/uploads/2021/03/PCSU-Report-FINAL_July-2018.pdf.

59. "Universities Studying Slavery," https://slavery.virginia.edu/universities-studying-slavery

60. Wilder, *Ebony and Ivy*, 289.

Chapter 3

1. Thomas D. Snyder, ed., *120 Years of American Education: A Statistical Portrait* (Washington, DC: US Department of Education, National Center for Education Statistics, January 1993), https://nces.ed.gov/pubs93/93442.pdf.

2. Claudia Goldin and Lawrence F. Katz, *The Race Between Education and Technology* (Cambridge, MA: Harvard University Press, 2008), chap. 1.

3. For an effective summary of this period, see Merle Curti and Roderick Nash, *Philanthropy in the Shaping of American Higher Education* (New Brunswick, NJ: Rutgers University Press, 1965), chap. 6.

4. Daniel Coit Gilman, *The Launching of a University* (New York: Dodd, Mead & Company, 1906), 4.

5. Gilman, *Launching of a University*, 145–58. Gilman delivered a speech, "Remembrances; Looking Backwards Over Fifty Years," at the 1904 semi-centennial of the University of Wisconsin, in which he touts the progress of university education in America.

6. Henry James, *Charles W. Eliot*, volume II (Boston: Houghton Mifflin, 1930), chap. 11.

7. As a relative share of the GDP, this would be the same as a university receiving a gift of nearly $919 million in 2019; see Samuel H. Williamson, "Seven Ways to Compute the Relative Value of a U.S. Dollar Amount: 1790 to Present," MeasuringWorth, 2022, https://www.measuringworth.com/calculators/uscompare/index.php.

8. Thomas Wakefield Goodspeed, *A History of the University of Chicago: The First Quarter Century* (Chicago: University of Chicago Press, 1916), chap. 10.

9. Curti and Nash, "Great Gifts for New Universities," in *Philanthropy*, chap. 6.

10. Norman E. Tutorow, *The Governor: The Life and Legacy of Leland Stanford* (Spokane, WA: Arthur H. Clark, 2004), 714.

11. Orrin Leslie Elliott, *Stanford University: The First Twenty-Five Years 1891–1925* (Stanford, CA: Stanford University Press, 1937), 571.

12. Wilson openly defended the KKK, called Negroes an "ignorant and inferior race," resegregated the federal government, and lauded D. W. Griffith's 1915 film *Birth of a Nation* (orig., *The Clansman*) after screening it at the White House. See Dylan Matthews, "Woodrow Wilson Was Extremely Racist—Even by the Standards of His Time," Vox, November 20, 2015, https://www.vox.com/policy-and-politics/2015/11/20/9766896/woodrow-wilson-racist.

13. James Axtell, *The Making of Princeton University* (Princeton, NJ: Princeton University Press, 2006), chap. 1.

14. Ray Stannard Baker, *Woodrow Wilson, Life and Letters, Princeton 1890–1910* (New York: Doubleday, Page & Co., 1927).

15. "Funds and Balances (Balance as of July 31, 1902)," in *Annual Reports of the President and the Treasurer of Harvard College, 1901–02*, 54.

16. Baker, *Woodrow Wilson*, 148.

17. Williamson, "Seven Ways to Compute."

18. Baker, *Woodrow Wilson,* 149.

19. Axtell, *Making of Princeton,* 4.

20. Michael Rosenthal, *Nicholas Miraculous: The Amazing Career of the Redoubtable Dr. Nicholas Murray Butler* (New York: Farrar, Straus and Giroux, 2006), 395.

21. Rosenthal, *Nicholas Miraculous,* 140.

22. Rosenthal, 398.

23. Rosenthal, 410.

24. Rosenthal, 398.

25. "President Eliot's Inaugural Address, October 19, 1869," in *The Development of Harvard University Since the Inauguration of President Eliot, 1869–1929,* ed. Samuel Eliot Morison (Cambridge, MA: Harvard University Press, 1930), lix–lxxviii. While Eliot said he favored the intellectual emancipation of women (lxxi), he might have more accurately urged the intellectual emancipation of men, given their confining, suffocating attitudes toward women. While his affirmation was progressive at that time, his caution was also detectable.

26. Eliot's significance in transforming Harvard is summarized in Bernard Bailyn et al., *Glimpses of the Harvard Past* (Cambridge, MA: Harvard University Press, 1986), chaps. 3–6.

27. John T. Bethell, *Harvard Observed: An Illustrated History of the University in the Twentieth Century* (Cambridge, MA: Harvard University Press, 1998), 16–22.

28. Bethell, *Harvard Observed,* 22, for all data and details from the 1904 campaign.

29. Bethell, 22.

30. Harry R. Lewis, *Excellence Without a Soul* (New York: Public Affairs Books, 2006), 34.

31. Lewis, *Excellence Without a Soul.*

32. Bethell, *Harvard Observed,* 46.

33. Robert A. McCaughey, *Stand, Columbia: A History of Columbia University in the City of New York, 1754–2004* (New York: Columbia University Press, 2003), 133. It would be intriguing to examine these 28 donors in order to determine how many of them profited from the enslavement of African Americans, since that industry was the primary wealth creator at the time.

34. James, *Charles W. Eliot,* 350.

35. Louis R. Harlan, Raymond W. Smock, and Geraldine McTighe, eds., *The Booker T. Washington Papers* (Urbana: University of Illinois Press, 1972–89), 4:472.

36. Harlan, Smock, and McTighe, *Booker T. Washington Papers,* 1:165 and 7:118.

37. Harlan, Smock, and McTighe, 3:391.

38. Harlan, Smock, and McTighe, 7:22.

39. Harlan, Smock, and McTighe, 8:131.

40. Harlan, Smock, and McTighe, 4:435.

41. Harlan, Smock, and McTighe, 9:72.

42. Emmett J. Scott and Lyman Beecher Stowe, *Booker T. Washington: Builder of a Civilization* (Garden City, NY: Doubleday, Page & Co., 1916), 248.

43. Tom Wheeler, *Who Makes the Rules in the New Gilded Age?* (Washington, DC: Brookings Institution, December 12, 2018), https://www.brookings.edu/research/who-makes-the-rules-in-the-new-gilded-age; David Remnick, *The New Gilded Age: The New Yorker Looks at the Culture of Affluence* (New York: Random House, 2000).

44. Richard White, *The Republic for Which It Stands* (New York, Oxford University Press, 2017), 3.

45. Curti and Nash, *Philanthropy,* 111.

46. Curti and Nash, 111.
47. See Edward T. O'Donnell, "Are We Living in the Gilded Age 2.0?," History.com, January 31, 2019, https://www.history.com/news/second-gilded-age-income-inequality. For a fuller treatment, see the book on which O'Donnell's article is based: Edward T. O'Donnell, *Henry George and The Crisis of Inequality* (New York: Columbia University Press, 2017).
48. Curti and Nash, *Philanthropy*, 111.
49. Arthur M. Cohen and Carrie B. Kisker, *The Shaping of American Higher Education: Emergence and Growth of the Contemporary System*, 2nd ed. (San Francisco: Jossey-Bass, 2010), chap. 3.
50. Thomas Piketty, *Capital in the Twenty-First Century* (Cambridge, MA: Harvard University Press, 2017), chap. 7.
51. David Huyssen, "We Won't Get Out of the Second Gilded Age the Way We Got Out of the First," Vox, April 1, 2019, https://www.vox.com/first-person/2019/4/1/18286084 /gilded-age-income-inequality-robber-baron.
52. Robert J. Samuelson, "The $100 Trillion Question: What to Do About Wealth?," *Washington Post*, May 5, 2019, https://www.washingtonpost.com/opinions/the-100 -trillion-question-what-to-do-about-wealth/2019/05/05/d7c174d4-6dd8-11e9-be3a -33217240a539_story.html. Samuelson's findings are based on the report by Michael Batty et al., *Introducing the Distributional Financial Accounts of the United States*, Finance and Economics Discussion Series 2019-017 (Washington, DC: Board of Governors of the Federal Reserve System, 2019), doi: 10.17016/FEDS.2019.017.
53. Bob Lord, "America 2018: Even More Gilded Than America 1918," Inequality.org, September 28, 2018, https://inequality.org/great-divide/america-2018-more-gilded -america-1918.
54. Carnegie awarded Tuskegee a gift of $600,000 in 1903. See Harlan, Smock, and McTighe, *Booker T. Washington Papers*, 7:120. An analysis of the speech Washington delivered to provoke the transformational investment from Carnegie appears in chapter 8.
55. Harlan, Smock, and McTighe, *Booker T. Washington Papers*, 10:284–91, 5:612–25; Booker T. Washington, *My Larger Education* (New York: Humanity Books, 2004), 243. Reprint; citation refers to the Humanity edition.

Chapter 4

1. Craig S. Wilder, *Ebony and Ivy: Race, Slavery, and the Troubled History of America's Universities* (New York: Bloomsbury, 2013), 225–27.
2. Paula J. Giddings, *Ida: A Sword Among Lions* (New York: HarperCollins, 2008), 216.
3. For Lester Ward as father of American sociology, see "Lester Ward," American Sociological Association, https://www.asanet.org/about/governance-and-leadership/council /presidents/lester-ward.
4. Thomas F. Gossett, *Race: The History of an Idea in America*, new ed. (New York: Oxford University Press, 1997), 166; Giddings, *Sword Among Lions*, 216. There is no apparent evidence that Ward opined about what drove the aspirations of the many white men who habitually raped Black women.
5. Louis Menand, *The Metaphysical Club: A Story of Ideas in America* (New York: Farrar, Straus and Giroux, 2001); Louis Menand, "Morton, Agassiz, and the Origins of Scientific Racism in the United States," *Journal of Blacks in Higher Education* no. 34 (Winter 2001–02): 110–13, doi: 10.2307/3134139.

6. Menand, *Metaphysical Club,* 109.

7. W. E. B. Du Bois, *Dusk of Dawn* (New Brunswick, NJ: Transaction Publishers, 2009), 58. Reprint, citations refer to the Transaction edition.

8. W. E. B. Du Bois, "The Talented Tenth: Memorial Address," in *W. E. B. Du Bois: A Reader,* ed. David Levering Lewis (New York: Henry Holt, 1995), 350.

9. W. E. B. Du Bois, *The Education of Black People: Ten Critiques, 1906–1960,* ed. Herbert Aptheker (New York: Monthly Review Press, 1973), xii.

10. W. E. B. Du Bois, "The Conservation of Races," in *Negro Social and Political Thought: Representative Texts, 1850–1920,* ed. Howard Brotz (New York: Basic Books, 1966), 483–92.

11. Du Bois, "Conservation," 486.

12. Du Bois, "Conservation," 489.

13. W. E. B. Du Bois, "Strivings of the Negro People," *The Atlantic,* August 1897.

14. Du Bois, "Conservation," 489.

15. Du Bois, "Conservation," 490.

16. Du Bois, "Conservation," 489.

17. David Levering Lewis, *W. E. B. Du Bois: The Fight for Equality and the American Century 1919–1963* (New York: Henry Holt, 2000), 311.

18. Raymond Wolters, *The New Negro on Campus: Black College Rebellions of the 1920s* (Princeton, NJ: Princeton University Press, 1975), 3–28.

19. W. E. B. Du Bois, *The World and Africa: An Inquiry into the Part Which Africa Has Played in World History* (New York: International Publishers, tenth printing, 1978); W. E. B. Du Bois, "The Future of Wilberforce University," *Journal of Negro Education* 9, no. 4 (October 1940): 553–70, doi: 10.2307/2292801.

20. "The Tradition of White Presidents at Black Colleges," *Journal of Blacks in Higher Education* 16 (Summer 1997): 95, doi: 10.2307/2962918.

21. The HBCU campuses where Du Bois delivered twelve major speeches: Fisk University 1898, 1908, 1924, 1933, 1938; Hampton Institute 1906; Howard University 1930; Wilberforce University 1940; Lincoln University 1941; Talladega College 1944; Knoxville College 1946; Johnson C. Smith University 1960. For the text of most of these speeches, see Aptheker, *Education of Black People.*

22. Du Bois, *Education of Black People,* 61, 67, 73, 66.

23. Du Bois, *Education of Black People* , 26.

24. Du Bois, *Education of Black People,* 92.

25. Meyer Weinberg, *A Chance to Learn: A History of Race and Education in the United States* (Cambridge: Cambridge University Press, 1977), 279.

26. Du Bois, *Education of Black People,* 138.

27. David Levering Lewis, *W. E. B. Du Bois:The Fight for Equality and the American Century 1919–1963* (New York: Henry Holt, 2000), 475.

28. Du Bois, *Education of Black People,* 179.

29. Du Bois, *Education of Black People,* 179.

30. Du Bois, *Education of Black People,* 185.

31. Du Bois, "Talented Tenth," 347–53.

32. Richard V. Reeves, "The New Politics of Character," *National Affairs* 20 (Summer 2014), https://www.nationalaffairs.com/publications/detail/the-new-politics-of-character.

33. W. E. B. Du Bois, "A Negro Student at Harvard at the End of the Nineteenth Century," in Lewis, *Du Bois: A Reader,* 271–86.

34. Richard I. McKinney, *Mordecai, the Man and His Message: The Story of Mordecai Wyatt Johnson* (Washington, DC: Howard University Press, 1997), 265–66.
35. Du Bois, "Conservation," 490.
36. Du Bois, "Conservation," 487.
37. Du Bois's sensibility about HBCUs and race development was modeled for him while he studied at Fisk University. See David Levering Lewis, *W. E. B. Du Bois: Biography of a Race, 1868–1919* (New York: Henry Holt, 1993), 73.
38. Du Bois, *Education of Black People*, 26.
39. W. E. B. Du Bois, "Does the Negro Need Separate Schools?," *Journal of Negro Education* 4, no. 3 (July 1935): 335, doi: 10.2307/2291871.
40. W. E. B. Du Bois, "The Negro College," *Crisis*, August 1933, 177.
41. W. E. B. Du Bois, "The Future and Function of the Private Negro College," *Crisis*, August 1946, 254.
42. Vincent Harding, "W. E. B. Du Bois and the Black Messianic Vision," in *Black Titan: W. E. B. Du Bois*, ed. John Henrik Clarke et al. (Boston: Beacon Press, 1970), 54.
43. Harding, "Du Bois and the Black Messianic Vision," 53.
44. Du Bois, *Education of Black People*, 129.
45. Stephanie Saul, "Historically Black Colleges Finally Get the Spotlight," *New York Times*, July 18, 2021, https://www.nytimes.com/2021/07/18/us/hbcu-colleges-universities.html.
46. Du Bois, "Future of Wilberforce University."
47. W. E. B. Du Bois, "The Laboratory in Sociology at Atlanta University," in Lewis, *Du Bois: A Reader*, 167. Du Bois laments his precarious conditions, saying, "We lack proper appliances for statistical work and proper clerical aid."
48. Zachery R. Williams, *In Search of the Talented Tenth: Howard University Public Intellectuals and the Dilemmas of Race, 1926–1970* (Columbia: University of Missouri Press, 2009), 21–22.
49. W. E. B. Du Bois, *The Souls of Black Folk* (New York: Barnes & Noble Classics, 2003), 16. First published 1903 by A. C. McClurg & Co. (Chicago).
50. Other examples of academic initiatives based at HBCUs with significant steeple potential: the Wiley College debate team, the physics program at Hampton University, the pre-med program at Xavier University, and the Howard University Fine Arts division.
51. For a comprehensive snapshot of racial inequities as of 2022, see *Under Siege: The Plot to Destroy Democracy*, State of Black America (New York: National Urban League, 2022), https://soba.iamempowered.com/sites/soba.iamempowered.com/files/NUL-SOBA-2022 -ExecSummary-web.pdf.

Chapter 5

1. W. E. B. Du Bois, "The Conservation of Races," in *Negro Social and Political Thought: Representative Texts, 1850–1920*, ed. Howard Brotz (New York: Basic Books, 1966), 489.
2. Louis R. Harlan, Raymond W. Smock, and Geraldine McTighe, eds., *The Booker T. Washington Papers* (Urbana: University of Illinois Press, 1972–89), 14:410.
3. Harlan, Smock, and McTighe, *Booker T. Washington Papers*, 414.
4. Nina Mjagkij, *Light in the Darkness: African Americans and the YMCA, 1852–1946* (Lexington: University Press of Kentucky, 1994), 111.
5. Raymond Wolters, *The New Negro on Campus: Black College Rebellions of the 1920s* (Princeton, NJ: Princeton University Press, 1975), 341.
6. Langston Hughes, "Cowards from the Colleges," *Crisis*, August 1934, 226–28.

7. Theodore Kornweibel, Jr., "An Economic Profile of Black Life in the Twenties," *Journal of Black Studies* 6, no. 4 (June 1976): 312, https://www.jstor.org/stable/2783764; Meyer Weinberg, *A Chance to Learn: A History of Race and Education in the United States* (Cambridge: Cambridge University Press, 1977), 278.

8. Wolters, *New Negro on Campus*, 17.

9. Weinberg, *Chance to Learn*, 280–81.

10. Stephan Thernstrom and Abigail Thernstrom, *America in Black and White: One Nation, Indivisible* (New York: Simon & Schuster, 1997), chap. 9.

11. Marybeth Gasman, *Envisioning Black Colleges: A History of the United Negro College Fund* (Baltimore: Johns Hopkins University Press, 2007), 171.

12. Two examples of HBCU advocates touting HBCU productivity without substantiating the data are: Jason Patel, "8 Incredible Stats You Didn't Know About HBCUs," NICHE Resources, February 16, 2021, https://s.niche.com/unknown-facts-about-hbcus; and Dana L. Merck, "20 Amazing Facts About HBCUs," March 10, 2016, https://www.linkedin.com/pulse/20-amazing-facts-hbcus-dana-l-merck-mpa.

13. W. E. B. Du Bois, *The Souls of Black Folk* (New York: Barnes & Noble Classics, 2003), 16. First published 1903 by A. C. McClurg & Co. (Chicago).

14. E. Franklin Frazier, "Durham: Capital of the Black Middle Class," in *The New Negro*, ed. Alain Locke (New York: Arno Press, 1975).

15. E. Franklin Frazier, *The Black Bourgeoisie* (New York: Simon & Schuster, 1957).

16. Frazier, *Black Bourgeoisie*, 234.

17. David O. Levine, *The American College and the Culture of Aspiration, 1915–1940* (Ithaca, NY: Cornell University Press, 1986).

18. For further reading on King's late-life mindset shifts, see Peniel Joseph, *The Sword and the Shield: The Revolutionary Lives of Malcolm X and Martin Luther King Jr.* (New York: Basic Books, 2020); and Tavis Smiley, *Death of a King: The Real Story of Dr. Martin Luther King Jr.'s Final Year* (New York: Little, Brown, 2014).

19. Clayborne Carson and Kris Shepard, eds., *A Call to Conscience: The Landmark Speeches of Dr. Martin Luther King, Jr.* (New York: Hachette Book Group, 2001), 71. Kindle.

20. Martin Luther King, Jr., "Beyond Vietnam" in *A Call to Conscience: The Landmark Speeches of Dr. Martin Luther King, Jr.*, ed. Clayborne Carson (New York: Warner Books, 2001), 157–58.

21. Smiley, *Death of a King*.

22. David Karen, "The Politics of Class, Race, and Gender: Access to Higher Education in the United States, 1960–1986," *American Journal of Education* 99, no. 2 (February 1991): 214, doi: 10.1086/443979.

23. William G. Bowen and Derek Bok, *The Shape of the River: Long-Term Consequences of Considering Race in College and University Admissions* (Princeton, NJ: Princeton University Press, 1998), 7; Karen, "Politics of Class," 214.

24. On athletes, see William C. Rhoden, *Forty Million Dollar Slaves: The Rise, Fall and Redemption of the Black Athlete* (New York: Three Rivers Press, 2006), chap. 5; on faculty, see Zachery R. Williams, *In Search of the Talented Tenth: Howard University Public Intellectuals and the Dilemmas of Race, 1926–1970* (Columbia: University of Missouri Press, 2009), 189–200.

25. Lawrence Ross, *Blackballed: The Black and White Politics of Race on America's Campuses* (New York: St. Martin's Press, 2015), 138. Ross's entire fifth chapter offers a detailed account of campus-based racism from the Reagan years (1980s) to the Obama years (through 2016).

26. Howard J. Ehrlich, *Campus Ethnoviolence and Policy Options*, Institute Report No. 4 (Baltimore: National Institute Against Prejudice and Violence, 1990):

27. Stephen Wessler and Margaret Moss, *Hate Crimes on Campus: The Problem and Efforts to Confront It* (Washington, DC: Office of Justice Programs, US Department of Justice, 2001), https://www.ojp.gov/pdffiles1/bja/187249.pdf.

28. W. E. B. Du Bois, *The Education of Black People: Ten Critiques, 1906–1960*, ed. Herbert Aptheker (New York: Monthly Review Press, 1973), 196.

29. Du Bois, *Education of Black People*, 203.

30. Of unknown origin, this faculty-to-student advisory, "a change in perspective is worth 100 points of IQ," permeated the MIT campus culture, where I lived as a housemaster and worked as a fundraiser for sixteen years, from 1985 to 2001.

31. Olivia Beavers, "Condoleezza Rice Says America Was Born with a Birth Defect: Slavery," *The Hill*, May 7, 2017, https://thehill.com/homenews/news/332307-condoleezza-rice -says-america-was-born-with-a-birth-defect-slavery.

32. Juliana Menasce Horowitz, Anna Brown, and Kiana Cox, *Race in America 2019* (Washington, DC: Pew Research Center, 2019), 4, https://www.pewresearch.org/social -trends/2019/04/09/race-in-america-2019/#terminology.

33. Craig S. Wilder, *Ebony and Ivy: Race, Slavery, and the Troubled History of America's Universities* (New York: Bloomsbury, 2013), 77.

34. Doug Lederman, "In Giving to Colleges, the One Percenters Gain," Inside Higher Ed, January 27, 2016, https://www.insidehighered.com/news/2016/01/27/giving-colleges -hits-another-record-high-wealthy-institutions-get-most.

35. Quoted in Gasman, *Envisioning Black Colleges*, 96.

36. Quoted in Gasman, 96.

37. Gasman, 138.

38. Quoted in Gasman, 141.

39. Marybeth Gasman and Nelson Bowman III, "How to Paint a Better Portrait of HBCUs," *Academe* 97, no. 3 (May–June 2011): 25, https://www.aaup.org/article/how -paint-better-portrait-hbcus.

40. Claude M. Steele, "A Threat in the Air: How Stereotypes Shape Intellectual Identity and Performance," *American Psychologist* 52, no. 6 (June 1997): 613–29, doi: 10.1037//0003 -066x.52.6.613; Margaret Shih, Todd L. Pittinsky, and Nalini Ambady, "Stereotype Susceptibility: Identity Salience and Shifts in Quantitative Performance," *Psychological Science* 10, no. 1 (1999): 80–83, doi: 10.1111/1467-9280.00111. These are two of many articles that discuss how stereotype threats can influence thinking well beyond the immediate targets or subjects of the negativity.

41. "Thurgood Marshall College Fund Partnering with Apple to Inspire the Next Generation of Talent," press release, Thurgood Marshall College Fund, March 10, 2015, https://www.tmcf.org/events-media/tmcf-in-the-media/thurgood-marshall-college-fund -partnering-with-apple-to-inspire-the-next-generation-of-talent.

Chapter 6

1. W. E. B. Du Bois, "The Conservation of Races," in *Negro Social and Political Thought: Representative Texts, 1850–1920*, ed. Howard Brotz (New York: Basic Books, 1966), 490.

2. W. E. B. Du Bois, "Does the Negro Need Separate Schools?," *Journal of Negro Education* 4, no. 3 (July 1935): 335, doi: 10.2307/2291871.

3. Neil Lanctot, *Negro League Baseball: The Rise and Ruin of a Black Institution* (Philadelphia: University of Pennsylvania Press, 2004), chaps. 4 and 5.

4. Jackie Robinson, "What's Wrong with Negro Baseball?," *Ebony*, June 1948, 16–24.

5. Lawrence D. Hogan, *Shades of Glory: The Negro Leagues and the Story of African-American Baseball* (Washington, DC: National Geographic Society, 2006), 352.

6. The idea of two leagues coexisting, or somehow merging, appeared to be at the heart of a perceived contradiction, even if only because it ran counter to the conventional ideas of profitability. Branch Rickey and other MLB decision makers were genuinely concerned that desegregation would sacrifice team or league marketability, including and especially regarding fans and sponsors. Another factor was the expected racist reaction of MLB's white players, a third of whom were from the south. A thoughtful analysis of the challenges of integration is offered by Leslie A. Heaphy, "Moving Toward Integration," chap. 12 in *The Negro Leagues 1869–1960* (Jefferson, NC: McFarland, 2003), 180–97.

7. Donn Rogosin, *Invisible Men: Life in Baseball's Negro Leagues* (Lincoln: University of Nebraska Press, 2020): 183.

8. Hogan, *Shades of Glory*, 182.

9. William C. Rhoden, *Forty Million Dollar Slaves: The Rise, Fall and Redemption of the Black Athlete* (New York: Three Rivers Press, 2006), 100, 102.

10. Rhoden, *Forty Million Dollar Slaves*, 102.

11. Rhoden, 123.

12. The short list of exceptions might include institutions like Oberlin (1833), Berea (1855), Antioch (1850), and others led by those with the courage to educate and shape graduates to challenge society's values, rather than merely consume and reflect them.

13. Craig S. Wilder, *Ebony and Ivy: Race, Slavery, and the Troubled History of America's Universities* (New York: Bloomsbury, 2013), chap. 7.

14. Louis R. Harlan, Raymond W. Smock, and Geraldine McTighe, eds., *The Booker T. Washington Papers* (Urbana: University of Illinois Press, 1972–89), 2:66.

15. David Levering Lewis, *W. E. B. Du Bois: Biography of a Race, 1868–1919* (New York: Henry Holt, 1993), 73.

16. Benson R. Snyder, *The Hidden Curriculum* (New York: Alfred A. Knopf, 1971).

17. Jelani M. Favors, *Shelter in a Time of Storm: How Black Colleges Fostered Generations of Leadership and Activism* (Chapel Hill: University of North Carolina Press, 2019), 3.

18. Langston Hughes, "Cowards from the Colleges," *Crisis*, August 1934, 226–28.

19. Hughes, "Cowards," 226.

20. Hughes, 228.

21. Notable among the critics of HBCU campus life were St. Clair Drake, who was fired from the faculty of Dillard University for supporting students in a Jim Crow protest on a city bus, and H. Rap Brown, who was expelled from Southern University for participating in sit-ins. See St. Clair Drake, "The Black University and the American Social Order," *Daedalus* 100, no. 3 (1971): 833–97; and H. Rap Brown, *Die Nigger Die!* (Chicago: Lawrence Hill Books, 1969), 58. For an effective summary of the history of the HBCU repression of faculty and student protest, see Matthew Quest, "A Concise History of the Repression of Black Protest at HBCUs," Black Agenda Report, September 19, 2018, https://www.blackagendareport.com/concise-history-repression-black-protest-hbcus.

22. Daniel C. Thompson, *Private Black Colleges at the Crossroads* (Westport, CT: Greenwood Press, 1973), 16.

23. Favors, *Shelter in a Time of Storm*, 2.

24. Rhoden, *Forty Million Dollar Slaves*, 106–7.

25. Nick Anderson and Lauren Lumpkin, "The Historic MacKenzie Scott Gifts to Historically Black Colleges and Others: Which Schools Got How Much," *Washington Post*,

January 5, 2021, https://www.washingtonpost.com/education/2020/12/18/mackenzie
-scott-college-donation-list-hbcus.

26. MacKenzie Scott, "116 Organizations Driving Change," Medium.com, July 28, 2020,
https://mackenzie-scott.medium.com/116-organizations-driving-change-67354c6d
733d.

27. Jack Trout and Steve Rivkin, *Differentiate or Die: Survival in Our Era of Killer Competition* (New York: John Wiley & Sons, 2000); W. Chan Kim and Renée Mauborgne, *Blue Ocean Strategy: How to Create Uncontested Market Space and Make the Competition Irrelevant* (Boston: Harvard Business School Press, 2005).

28. Rowena Patton, *Find Your Unique Value Proposition, in Principle and Practice, to Dominate Your Real Estate Market* (Asheville, NC: AllStarPowerhouse, 2017), chap. 1, 20–52.

29. Michael L. Lomax, "Six Reasons HBCUs Are More Important Than Ever," UNCF. org, https://uncf.org/the-latest/6-reasons-hbcus-are-more-important-than-ever. Lomax, CEO and President of the United Negro College Fund, originally posted this piece on Medium.com, December 14, 2015, https://medium.com/@DrMichaelLomax/6-reasons -hbcus-are-more-important-than-ever-6572fc27c715.

30. Marybeth Gasman and Nelson Bowman III, "How to Paint a Better Portrait of HBCUs," *Academe* 97, no. 3 (May–June 2011): 25, https://www.aaup.org/article/how -paint-better-portrait-hbcus.

31. One version of this can be found on the YouTube video of Jesse Jackson's *Saturday Night Live* monologue (*SNL* season 10, aired October 20, 1984, on NBC) at 3:40, https:// www.youtube.com/watch?v=BKLZ4cTYy3E.

Chapter 7

1. Walter Kimbrough, "HBCU Presidency Trends Demand Attention," *Florida Courier*, July 14, 2017, https://www.flcourier.com/commentaries/hbcu-presidency-trends -demand-attention/article_3ade573c-e33e-57e4-a525-4ab0b71cac8c.html.

2. The first five presidents of Tuskegee: Booker T. Washington, 1881–1915; Robert Russa Moton, 1915–35; Frederick D. Patterson, 1935–53; Luther H. Foster, 1953–81; Benjamin F. Payton, 1981–2010. The Tuskegee trustees then made the following decisions about who would serve in the office of president: Charlotte P. Morris, interim, 2010; Gilbert L. Rochon, 2010–13; Matthew Jenkins, acting, 2013–14; Brian L. Johnson, 2014–17; Charlotte P. Morris, interim, 2017–18; Lily D. McNair, 2018–20; Charlotte P. Morris, interim, 2020–21; Charlotte P. Morris, 2021–present, as of this publication.

3. For a summary of governance culpability in the *Titanic* tragedy, see Chris Berg, "The Real Reason for the Tragedy of the Titanic," *Wall Street Journal*, April 12, 2012, https:// www.wsj.com/articles/SB10001424052702304444604577337923643095442.

4. Samuel M. Nabrit and Julius S. Scott, Jr., *Inventory of Academic Leadership: An Analysis of the Boards of Trustees of Fifty Predominantly Negro Institutions* (Atlanta: Southern Fellowships Fund, 1968), https://eric.ed.gov/?id=ED040664.

5. Nabrit and Scott, *Inventory of Academic Leadership, 12.*

6. Nabrit and Scott, 17–22.

7. Nabrit and Scott, 17–22.

8. Association of Governing Boards of Universities and Colleges, *The Urgency of Now: HBCUs at a Crossroads*, (Washington, DC: AGB Press, December 20, 2019), 1, https:// agb.org/reports-2/the-urgency-of-now-hbcus-at-a-crossroads.

9. John T. Bethell, *Harvard Observed: An Illustrated History of the University in the Twentieth Century* (Cambridge, MA: Harvard University Press, 1998), 22.

10. This popular story is told by Booker T. Washington in his autobiography, *Up From Slavery* (New York: Signet Classics, 2010).

11. Louis R. Harlan, Raymond W. Smock, and Geraldine McTighe, eds., *The Booker T. Washington Papers* (Urbana: University of Illinois Press, 1972–89), 2:108.

12. Harlan, Smock, and McTighe, *Booker T. Washington Papers*, 3:274.

13. Harlan, Smock, and McTighe, 3:85.

14. Harlan, Smock, and McTighe, 6:169–70.

15. Harlan, Smock, and McTighe, 1:164.

16. Harlan, Smock, and McTighe, 4:533.

17. Harlan, Smock, and McTighe, 1:165.

18. Harlan, Smock, and McTighe, 1:171.

19. Harlan, Smock, and McTighe, 5:293.

20. Harlan, Smock, and McTighe, 6:52.

21. William H. Watkins, *The White Architects of Black Education: Ideology and Power in America, 1865–1954* (New York: Teachers College Press, 2001).

22. Harlan, Smock, and McTighe, *Booker T. Washington Papers*, 5:643.

23. Emmett J. Scott and Lyman Beecher Stowe, *Booker T. Washington: Builder of a Civilization* (Garden City, NY: Doubleday, Page & Co., 1916), 257.

24. An analysis of the speech Washington delivered to provoke the transformational investment from Carnegie appears in chapter 8.

25. Harlan, Smock, and McTighe, *Booker T. Washington Papers*, 9:16. This endowment estimate was high, probably erroneous, and difficult to verify. It seems clear from other evidence that the Tuskegee endowment did not near or reach $2 million until 1915.

26. Scott and Stowe, *Builder of a Civilization*, 248.

27. Scott and Stowe, 249.

28. Harlan, Smock, and McTighe, *Booker T. Washington Papers*, 9:420.

29. "Choate and Twain Plead for Tuskegee: Brilliant Audience Cheers Them and Booker Washington," *New York Times*, January 23, 1906. Cleveland, McKinley, and Roosevelt helped Washington by cohosting fundraisers in New York City. In 1910, President William Howard Taft worked to connect Washington with Henry Clay Frick, one of the wealthiest men of the era; see Harlan, Smock, and McTighe, *Booker T. Washington Papers*, 10:360–61.

30. Harlan, Smock, and McTighe, *Booker T. Washington Papers*, 9:349–59, 10:51, 10:284–91, 12:131.

31. Harlan, Smock, and McTighe, 13:253.

32. Scott and Stowe, *Builder of a Civilization*, 248.

33. Samuel H. Williamson, "Seven Ways to Compute the Relative Value of a U.S. Dollar Amount, 1790 to present," MeasuringWorth, April 2022, https://www.measuringworth.com/calculators/uscompare/result.php?year_source=1915&amount=3000000.00&year_result=2015.

34. Grinnell College, "Grinnell College trustee, Joseph Frankel Rosenfield, dies," news release, June 8, 2000, https://web.archive.org/web/20060901102750/http://www.grinnell.edu/publicrelations/releases/2000/rosenfield.html.

35. John Silvanus Wilson, Jr., "Martin Luther King Jr. and the Educational Parity Revolution," HuffPost, January 16, 2012, updated March 17, 2012, https://www.huffpost.com/entry/martin-luther-king-jr-and_1_b_1208628.

36. Jason Zweig, "The Best Investor You've Never Heard Of," *Money*, June 2000.

37. Shane Jacobson, "The Case for Grinnell: Our Endowment," *Grinnell Magazine* 47, no. 3 (Spring 2015): 2, https://www.grinnell.edu/sites/default/files/docs/2019-09/Grin MagSpr15.web_.final_.pdf.

38. Barry Stavro, "Grinnell College's Quantum Jumps," *Forbes*, December 31, 1984.

39. Mark B. Schneider, "Endowments Can Become Too Much of a Good Thing," *Chronicle of Higher Education*, June 2, 2006, https://www.chronicle.com/article/endowments-can -become-too-much-of-a-good-thing.

40. Schneider, "Endowments."

41. Association of Governing Boards of Universities and Colleges, *An Anatomy of Good Board Governance in Higher Education* (Washington, DC: AGB Press, 2018), ii, https:// agb.org/wp-content/uploads/2019/12/Anatomy_Look-Inside.pdf.

42. US Department of Education, National Center for Education Statistics, "National Post-secondary Student Aid Study: Undergraduate, 2016," accessed from: https://nces.ed.gov /datalab.

43. US Department of Education, National Center for Education Statistics, Integrated Post-secondary Education Data System (IPEDS) student financial aid component final data (2001–02 to 2018–19) and provisional data (2019–20). NCES Trend Generator graph: https://nces.ed.gov/ipeds/TrendGenerator/app/trend-table/8/34?trending=cell&rvc= -1&cvc=4&f=59%3D1%3B2%3D1&cid=51.

44. George S. Day and Paul J. H. Schoemaker, *Peripheral Vision: Detecting the Weak Signals That Will Make or Break Your Company* (Boston: Harvard Business School Press, 2006), chap. 1.

45. Juan Williams, *Thurgood Marshall: American Revolutionary* (New York: Crown, 1998), 249.

46. George Day and Paul J. H. Schoemaker, "Scanning the Periphery," *Harvard Business Review* 83, no. 11 (November 2005): 135.

47. Glenn S. Johnson et al., "Historically Black Colleges and Universities (HBCUs) in the Twenty First Century," *Race, Gender & Class* 24, no. 3–4 (2017): 48, https://www.jstor .org/stable/26529222.

48. In addition to the aforementioned research, other noteworthy examples of the perception of HBCUs as nurturing include: Valerie Strauss, "Why Kamala Harris Chose Howard University," *Washington Post*, August 11, 2020, https://www.washingtonpost.com /education/2020/08/11/why-kamala-harris-chose-howard-university-what-she-did -weekends-there; and Skylar Mitchell, "Why I Chose a Historically Black College," *New York Times,* April 1, 2017, https://www.nytimes.com/2017/04/01/opinion/sunday /finding-growth-at-my-historically-black-college.html.

49. Globe Newswire, "Global Online Education Market Worth $319+ Billion by 2025," April 16, 2020, https://www.globenewswire.com/news-release/2020/04/16/2017102/0 /en/Global-Online-Education-Market-Worth-319-Billion-by-2025-North-America -Anticipated-to-Provide-the-Highest-Revenue-Generating-Opportunities.html.

50. Globe Newswire, "Online Education Market Study 2019: World Market Projected to Reach $350 Billion by 2025, Dominated by the United States and China," December 17, 2019, https://www.globenewswire.com/news-release/2019/12/17/1961785/0/en/Online -Education-Market-Study-2019-World-Market-Projected-to-Reach-350-Billion-by -2025-Dominated-by-the-United-States-and-China.html.

51. US Department of Education, National Center for Education Statistics, Integrated Postsecondary Education Data System (IPEDS) fall enrollment component final data

(2002–19) and provisional data (2020), accessed from: https://nces.ed.gov/ipeds
/datacenter.

52. US DOE, IPEDS fall enrollment data.

53. John Silvanus Wilson, Jr., "Assessing Infrastructural Health: Optimizing Return on
Investment in HBCUs," in *Investing in America's Workforce: Improving Outcomes for
Workers and Employers,* ed. Stuart Andreason, Todd Greene, Heath Prince, and Carl E.
Van Horn, vol. 1, *Investing in Workers* (Kalamazoo, Michigan: W. E. Upjohn Institute
for Employment Research, 2018), 205–18, https://www.investinwork.org/-/media/2D4A
43527C2E42919C5512A1D3A23B9E.ashx

Chapter 8

1. Benjamin E. Mays, "Financing of Private Negro Colleges," *Journal of Educational Sociology,* 19, no. 8 (April 1946): 466, doi: 10.2307/2263569. Note: Mays used data from a
1940 federal report.

2. Charles T. Clotfelter, *Unequal Colleges in the Age of Disparity* (Cambridge, MA: Harvard
University Press, 2017), 127.

3. Emmanuel Saez and Gabriel Zucman, "Wealth Inequality in the United States
Since 1913: Evidence from Capitalized Income Tax Data" (working paper 20625, National Bureau of Economic Research, October 2014), 1, http://www.nber.org/papers
/w20625.

4. The tie between the federal government's policies and charitable giving is best summarized here: Charles T. Clotfelter, "The Impact of Tax Reform on Charitable Giving: A
1989 Perspective" (working paper 3273, National Bureau of Economic Research, March
1990), https://www.nber.org/system/files/working_papers/w3273/w3273.pdf.

5. Donald Kennedy, "How Can We Look So Rich, Yet Feel So Poor?," *Campus Report*
(Stanford, CA: Stanford University Development Communications Office, March 19,
1986), 5.

6. The industry standard for capital campaigns was a seven-year counting period, with one
quiet-phase year, followed by five public-phase years, then one closeout-phase year.

7. Clotfelter, *Unequal Colleges,* chap. 5. Clotfelter refers to the popular interpretation of the
New Testament verse Matthew 25:29.

8. The six HBCUs that had conducted capital campaigns in excess of $100 million by 2020
are: Claflin University, Hampton University, Howard University, Morehouse College,
Spelman College, and Tuskegee University.

9. Lee A. Daniels, "A Black College Gets Cosby Gift of $20 Million," *New York Times,*
November 8, 1988.

10. Daniels, "Black College Gets Cosby Gift."

11. MacKenzie Scott, "116 Organizations Driving Change," Medium.com, July 28, 2020,
https://mackenzie-scott.medium.com/116-organizations-driving-change-67354c6d733d.

12. Samuel H. Williamson, "Seven Ways to Compute the Relative Value of a U.S. Dollar
Amount: 1790 to Present," MeasuringWorth, 2022, https://www.measuringworth.com
/calculators/uscompare/result.php?year_source=1903&amount=600000.00&year
_result=2015.

13. In Washington's first major address, entitled, "The Educational Outlook in the South,"
he positions education as the solution to the race problem; see Harlan, Smock, and
McTighe, *Booker T. Washington Papers,* 2:255.

14. Harlan, Smock, and McTighe, *Booker T. Washington Papers,* 3:583, 585–86.

15. Harlan, Smock, and McTighe, 7:113.
16. Harlan, Smock, and McTighe, 7:117.
17. Harlan, Smock, and McTighe, 7:116.
18. Harlan, Smock, and McTighe, 7:117.
19. Unsurprisingly, several speakers, including former US President Grover Cleveland and Edgar Gardner Murphy of the Southern Education Board, "laced their praise of BTW [Washington] and Tuskegee . . . with racist remarks," reflective of an abiding white supremacist mindset. Washington told a friend that this happened every time he "had a white man speak at a meeting." For a fuller statement, see Harlan, Smock, and McTighe, 7:118–19.
20. Harlan, Smock, and McTighe, 7:120.
21. Harlan, Smock, and McTighe, 7:120.
22. Other appeals to "the best class of Southern White people" include Harlan, Smock, and McTighe, 9:418 and 10:50; and Booker T. Washington, "The Case of the Negro," *The Atlantic*, November 1899, https://cdn.theatlantic.com/media/archives/1899/11/84-505/132120757.pdf.
23. Harlan, Smock, and McTighe, *Booker T. Washington Papers*, 7:114.
24. Harlan, Smock, and McTighe, 2:194. Washington also referenced how Jews emerged from slavery, 5:369.
25. Harlan, Smock, and McTighe, 7:116.
26. Harlan, Smock, and McTighe, 2:195.
27. Harlan, Smock, and McTighe, 5:480.
28. Charles Lemert and Esme Bhan, eds., *The Voice of Anna Julia Cooper* (Lanham, MD: Rowman and Littlefield, 1998), 248.
29. Harlan, Smock, and McTighe, *Booker T. Washington Papers*, 5:299.
30. Harlan, Smock, and McTighe, 5:355.
31. Harlan, Smock, and McTighe, 12:264.
32. Harlan, Smock, and McTighe, 13:347.
33. Victoria Earle Matthews, ed., *Black Diamonds: The Wisdom of Booker T. Washington* (Deerfield Beach, FL: Health Communications, 1995), 146. Originally titled *Black-Belt Diamonds* (New York: Fortune and Scott, 1898).
34. Examples of the power of federal and state policy changes controlling the fate of nearly all HBCUs (and many other colleges and universities) include shrinking Title IV aid, deliberately changing credit requirements (2012 Parent Plus Loans), steep cuts in state aid, and forced state system mergers or closures.
35. An example of a financial profile that removes precarity is one with an endowment/expense ratio above seven, modern facilities, zero deferred maintenance, well-paid faculty, well-aided students with zero debt, alumni giving above 50%, enlightened governance, and brand excellence.
36. Dambisa Moyo, *Dead Aid: Why Aid Is Not Working and How There Is a Better Way for Africa* (New York: Farrar, Straus and Giroux, 2009), 9.
37. Moyo, *Dead Aid*, 47.
38. Moyo, 8.
39. Moyo, 36.
40. Moyo, 14.
41. Moyo, 47.
42. Moyo, xviii.

43. Adam Harris, *The State Must Provide: Why America's Colleges Have Always Been Unequal—And How to Set Them Right* (New York: HarperCollins, 2021).

44. Krystal L. Williams and BreAnna L. Davis, *Public and Private Investments and Divestments in Historically Black Colleges and Universities*, Minority-Serving Institutions Series (Washington, DC: American Council on Education, January 2019), 2, https://www.acenet.edu/Documents/Public-and-Private-Investments-and-Divestments-in-HBCUs.pdf.

45. "Title III Part B, Strengthening Historically Black Colleges and Universities Program," US Department of Education, updated July 7, 2020, https://www2.ed.gov/programs/iduestitle3b/index.html.

46. Ilana Kowarski, "10 HBCUs with the Highest 4-Year Graduation Rates," *U.S. News & World Report*, February 22, 2022, https://www.usnews.com/education/best-colleges/the-short-list-college/articles/historically-black-schools-with-the-highest-4-year-graduation-rates.

47. Higher Education Act of 1965, Pub. L. 89-329; approved November 8, 1965, https://www.govinfo.gov/content/pkg/COMPS-765/pdf/COMPS-765.pdf.

48. Andrea Fuller, "Updates on Capital Campaigns at 36 Colleges and Universities," *Chronicle of Higher Education*, November 21, 2010, https://www.chronicle.com/article/updates-on-capital-campaigns-at-36-colleges-and-universities; Inside Higher Ed, Capital Campaigns database: https://www.insidehighered.com/capital_campaigns; William Logan Rhodes, "The Factors That Influenced the Decision to Enter into a $1 Billion Fundraising Campaign by Two Public Higher Education Institutions" (PhD diss., University of Tennessee, 2015), https://trace.tennessee.edu/utk_graddiss/3347.

49. A summary of the motivating factors behind philanthropy is provided by Russ Alan Prince and Karen Maru File, *The Seven Faces of Philanthropy* (San Francisco: Jossey-Bass, 2001).

50. Jessica Gunderson, *Mount Rushmore: Myths, Legends, and Facts* (North Mankato, MN: Capstone Press, 2015).

51. W. E. B. Du Bois, "The Future of Wilberforce University," *Journal of Negro Education* 9, no. 4 (October 1940): 559, doi: 10.2307/2292801; Herbert Aptheker, *The Education of Black People: Ten Critiques* (New York: Monthly Review Press, 1973), 182.

52. Melissa Repko, "As Black Buying Power Grows, Racial Profiling by Retailers Remains Persistent Problem," CNBC, July 5, 2020, https://www.cnbc.com/2020/07/05/as-black-buying-power-grows-racial-profiling-by-retailers-remains-a-problem.html; Bruce C. T. Wright, "Black Buying Power by the Numbers: History in the Making," NewsOne, February 10, 2020, https://newsone.com/3901998/black-buying-power-by-numbers-history-making; the notion is definitively debunked in Jared A. Ball, *The Myth and Propaganda of Black Buying Power* (Cham, Switzerland: Palgrave Macmillan, 2020).

53. Neil Bhutta et al., "Disparities in Wealth by Race and Ethnicity in the 2019 Survey of Consumer Finances," FEDS Notes, Board of Governors of the Federal Reserve System, September 28, 2020, https://www.federalreserve.gov/econres/notes/feds-notes/disparities-in-wealth-by-race-and-ethnicity-in-the-2019-survey-of-consumer-finances-20200928.htm.

54. Taylor Nicole Rogers, "There Are 614 Billionaires in the United States, and Only 7 of Them Are Black," Insider, updated September 4, 2020, https://www.businessinsider.com/black-billionaires-in-the-united-states-2020-2.

55. Peggy McGlone, "How the African American Museum Is Raising the Bar for Black Philanthropy," *Washington Post*, May 24, 2016, https://www.washingtonpost.com

/entertainment/museums/african-american-museums-fundraising-touches-deep-history
-among-donors/2016/05/23/bc2cbc94-1613-11e6-924d-838753295f9a_story.html.
56. Cia Verschelden, *Bandwidth Recovery* (Sterling, VA: Stylus Publishing, 2017).

Chapter 9

1. Ellen Daugherty, "Negotiating the Veil: Tuskegee's Booker T. Washington Monument,"
   American Art 24, no. 3 (Fall 2010): 52–77, www.jstor.org/stable/10.1086/658209.
2. John F. Callahan and Marc C. Conner, eds., *The Selected Letters of Ralph Ellison* (New
   York: Random House, 2019), 20.
3. Ralph Ellison, *Invisible Man* (New York: Vintage Books, 1995), 36.
4. Julian B. Roebuck and Komanduri S. Murty, *Historically Black Colleges and Universities:
   Their Place in American Higher Education* (Westport, CT: Praeger Publishers, 1993), 43.
5. "Ivy-plus" includes the 8 institutions of the Ivy League—Brown, Columbia, Cornell,
   Dartmouth, Harvard, Princeton, UPenn, and Yale—plus Stanford and MIT.
6. Samuel H. Williamson, "Seven Ways to Compute the Relative Value of a U.S. Dollar
   Amount: 1790 to Present," MeasuringWorth, 2022, https://www.measuringworth
   .com/calculators/uscompare/result.php?year_source=1915&amount=2000000&year
   _result=2015.
7. *Higher Education for American Democracy: A Report of the President's Commission on
   Higher Education*, vol. 1, *Establishing the Goals* (Washington, DC: US Government
   Printing Office, 1947), 5–8.
8. Margaret Spellings and Cheryl Oldham, *A Test of Leadership: Charting the Future of U.S.
   Higher Education* (Washington, DC: US Department of Education, 2006).
9. Robert M. Diamond, "Why Colleges Are So Hard to Change," *Inside Higher Ed*, September 8, 2006, https://www.insidehighered.com/views/2006/09/08/why-colleges
   -are-so-hard-change.
10. Laurence R. Veysey, *The Emergence of the American University* (Chicago: University of
    Chicago Press, 1965), chap. 5.
11. Veysey, *Emergence of the American University*, 338.
12. Charles Dorn, *For the Common Good: A New History of Higher Education in America*
    (Ithaca, NY: Cornell University Press, 2017), 4–11.
13. Craig S. Wilder, *Ebony and Ivy: Race, Slavery, and the Troubled History of America's Uni-
    versities* (New York: Bloomsbury, 2013), 212.
14. Wilder, *Ebony and Ivy*, 228.
15. David Levering Lewis, *W. E. B. Du Bois: Biography of a Race, 1868–1919* (New York:
    Henry Holt, 1993), 73.
16. Eric Foner, *The Second Founding* (New York: W. W. Norton, 2019), 1.
17. Foner, *Second Founding*. Foner argues that the Reconstruction Amendments (Thirteenth,
    Fourteenth, and Fifteenth) grafted the principle of equality onto the Constitution and,
    in so doing, marked the second founding of the United States.
18. Frederick Douglass, "Our Composite Nationality," in *The Speeches of Frederick Douglass:
    A Critical Edition*, ed. John R. McKivigan, Julie Husband, and Heather L. Kaufman
    (New Haven, CT: Yale University Press 2018), 278–303.
19. Douglass, "Our Composite Nationality," 280.
20. Douglass, 280.
21. Douglass, 295.
22. Douglass, 300.
23. Douglass, 285.

24. Douglass, 295.

25. Ian Bremmer, "The U.S. Capitol Riot Was Years in the Making. Here's Why America Is So Divided," *TIME*, January 16, 2021.

26. "Caroline Schoeder," Inspirational Quotations, https://inspiration.rightattitudes.com /authors/caroline-schoeder.

27. *Carbon Dioxide and Climate: A Scientific Assessment,* Report of an Ad Hoc Study Group on Carbon Dioxide and Climate (Washington, DC: National Academy of Sciences, 1979), viii (submitted to the Climate Research Board Assembly of Mathematical and Physical Sciences, Woods Hole, MA: July 23–27, 1979), https://geosci.uchicago .edu/~archer/warming_papers/charney.1979.report.pdf.

28. Nathaniel Rich, "Losing Earth: The Decade We Almost Stopped Climate Change," *New York Times Magazine,* August 1, 2018, https://www.nytimes.com/interactive /2018/08/01/magazine/climate-change-losing-earth.html.

29. Rich, "Losing Earth."

30. The US National Aeronautics and Space Administration (NASA) tracks the vital signs of global climate change, and they have already concluded that "there is unequivocal evidence that Earth is warming at an unprecedented rate. Human activity is the principal cause." See https://climate.nasa.gov/evidence/.

31. Michael D. Shear, "Trump Will Withdraw U.S. from Paris Climate Agreement," *New York Times,* June 1, 2017, https://www.nytimes.com/2017/06/01/climate/trump-paris -climate-agreement.html.

32. James Gustave Speth, *They Knew: The US Federal Government's Fifty-Year Role in Causing the Climate Crisis* (Cambridge, MA: MIT Press, 2021). Speth carefully describes the devastating climate change negligence of each US presidential administration from 1977 through 2020.

33. Ibram X. Kendi, *Stamped from the Beginning* (New York: Bold Type Books, 2017), 105.

34. MacKenzie Scott, "116 Organizations Driving Change," Medium.com, July 28, 2020, https://mackenzie-scott.medium.com/116-organizations-driving-change-67354c6d733d; MacKenzie Scott, "384 Ways to Help," Medium.com, December 15, 2020, https:// mackenzie-scott.medium.com/384-ways-to-help-45d0b9ac6ad8.

35. Scott, "384 Ways to Help."

36. Warren Buffett, Melinda French Gates, and Bill Gates, "About the Giving Pledge," https://givingpledge.org/about.

37. In 1889, Rockefeller invested $600,000 to launch the University of Chicago, the 2015 GDP equivalent of $781 million, and in 1903, Andrew Carnegie invested $600,000 to bolster the endowment of the Tuskegee Institute, the 2015 GDP equivalent of $417 million—both relative value estimates according to the calculation method employed by Samuel H. Williamson; see "Seven Ways to Compute," https://www.measuringworth .com/calculators/uscompare/index.php.

38. Jamie Merisotis, *Human Work in the Age of Smart Machines* (New York: RosettaBooks, 2020).

39. Goldie Blumenstyk, "Talking About Talent: Jamie Merisotis on the Role of Higher Education," *Chronicle of Higher Education,* September 24, 2015, https://www.chronicle .com/article/talking-about-talent-jamie-merisotis-on-the-role-of-higher-education.

40. Anand Giridharadas, *Winners Take All* (New York: Alfred A. Knopf, 2018), 170.

41. Darren Walker, *From Generosity to Justice* (New York: Ford Foundation/Disruption Books, 2019).

42. Kate Aronoff, *Overheated: How Capitalism Broke the Planet—and How We Fight Back* (New York: Bold Type Books, 2021), 11.

Chapter 10

1. Kenrick Cai, "These Eleven Colleges Have Produced the Most Billionaire Alumni," *Forbes*, April 14, 2021, https://www.forbes.com/sites/kenrickcai/2021/04/14/these-10 -colleges-have-produced-the-most-billionaire-alumni.
2. David O. Levine, *The American College and the Culture of Aspiration, 1915–1940* (Ithaca, NY: Cornell University Press, 1986), 43.
3. Juliana Menasce Horowitz, Ruth Igielnik, and Rakesh Kochhar, "Most Americans Say There Is Too Much Economic Inequality in the U.S., but Fewer Than Half Call It a Top Priority," Pew Research Center, January 9, 2020, https://www.pewresearch.org/social -trends/2020/01/09/trends-in-income-and-wealth-inequality; Tommy Beer, "Top 1% of U.S. Households Hold 15 Times More Wealth Than Bottom 50% Combined," *Forbes*, October 8, 2020, https://www.forbes.com/sites/tommybeer/2020/10/08/top-1-of-us -households-hold-15-times-more-wealth-than-bottom-50-combined.
4. "Eight Billionaires Own as Much as Poorest Half of Global Population," *Philanthropy News Digest*, January 28, 2017, https://philanthropynewsdigest.org/news/eight -billionaires-own-as-much-as-poorest-half-of-global-population; Deborah Hardoon, *An Economy for the 99%*, Oxfam Briefing Paper (Oxford: Oxfam GB, January 2017), https://oi-files-d8-prod.s3.eu-west-2.amazonaws.com/s3fs-public/file_attachments /bp-economy-for-99-percent-160117-en.pdf; Andre Damon, "Pew Report: 84 Percent of World Population Subsists on Under $20 per Day," World Socialist Web Site, July 11, 2015, https://www.wsws.org/en/articles/2015/07/11/poor-j11.html.
5. John Dewey, "The Need of an Industrial Education in an Industrial Democracy," in *The Middle Works*, 1899–1924, ed. Jo Ann Boydston (Carbondale: Southern Illinois University Press, 1980), 10:139.
6. Laurence R. Veysey, *The Emergence of the American University* (Chicago: University of Chicago Press, 1965), 338.
7. Alexander Meiklejohn, "What Does the College Hope to Be During the Next Hundred Years?," *Amherst Graduates' Quarterly*, no. 40 (August 1921): 336, https://www.amherst .edu/system/files/media/What_does_the_College_hope_to_be.pdf.
8. Frederick Douglass, "Our Composite Nationality," in *The Speeches of Frederick Douglass: A Critical Edition*, ed. John R. McKivigan, Julie Husband, and Heather L. Kaufman (New Haven, CT: Yale University Press, 2018), 278–303.
9. Benjamin Elijah Mays, "The Role of the Negro Liberal Arts College in Post-War Reconstruction," *Journal of Negro Education* 11, no. 3 (July 1942): 400–11, doi: 10.2307/2292678.
10. Mays, "Role of the Negro Liberal Arts College," 400.
11. Mays, 400.
12. Mays, 402.
13. Mays, 405.
14. Mays, 406.
15. Mays, 407.
16. Benson R. Snyder, *The Hidden Curriculum* (Cambridge, MA: MIT Press, 1970).
17. Mays, "Role of the Negro Liberal Arts College," 408.
18. Mays, 410.

19. Mays, 411.
20. Benjamin Elijah Mays, "The Unfinished Task," in *Dr. Benjamin E. Mays Speaks,* ed. Freddie C. Colston (Lanham, MD: University Press of America, 2002), 83.
21. Richard I. McKinney, *Mordecai, the Man and His Message: The Story of Mordecai Wyatt Johnson* (Washington, DC: Howard University Press, 1997), 266.
22. Charles Lemert and Esme Bhan, eds., *The Voice of Anna Julia Cooper* (Lanham, MD: Rowman and Littlefield, 1998), 261.
23. Chiazam Ugo Okoye, *Mary McLeod Bethune: Words of Wisdom* (Bloomington, IN: AuthorHouse, 2008), 153.
24. Audrey Thomas McCluskey and Elaine M. Smith, eds., *Mary McLeod Bethune: Building a Better World* (Bloomington: Indiana University Press, 2001), 246.
25. Marybeth Gasman, *Envisioning Black Colleges* (Baltimore: Johns Hopkins University Press, 2007), 44.
26. Kenneth B. Clark, "Higher Education for Negroes: Challenges and Prospects," *Journal of Negro Education* 36, no. 3 (Summer 1967): 198, doi: 10.2307/2294447.
27. Eric Anderson and Alfred A. Moss, Jr., *Dangerous Donations: Northern Philanthropy and Southern Black Education, 1902–1930* (Columbia: University of Missouri Press, 1999): 20.
28. Joy Ann Williamson, *Radicalizing the Ebony Tower: Black Colleges and the Black Freedom Struggle in Mississippi* (New York: Teachers College Press, 2008); see especially chap. 1.
29. Christopher Jencks and David Riesman, "The American Negro College," *Harvard Educational Review* 37, no. 1 (Spring 1967): 3–60, doi: 10.17763/haer.37.1.k3295 t48l48612h2.
30. Marybeth Gasman, "Salvaging 'Academic Disaster Areas': The Black College Response to Christopher Jencks and David Riesman's 1967 Harvard Educational Review Article," *Journal of Higher Education* 77, no. 2 (March/April 2006): 317–52, http://repository .upenn.edu/gse_pubs/12.
31. "Colleges: Academic Disaster Area," *Time*, March 31, 1967, https://content.time.com /time/magazine/article/0,9171,941091,00.html.
32. "'The American Negro College,' Four Responses and a Reply," *Harvard Educational Review* 37, no. 3 (Fall 1967): 451–68, doi: 10.17763/haer.37.3.t7l04u8g3576p776.
33. Kenneth B. Clark, *Prejudice and Your Child* (Boston: Beacon Press, 1955); especially chap. 1.
34. Clark, "Higher Education for Negroes," 202.
35. Clark, "Higher Education," 199.
36. Clark, "Higher Education," 199.
37. Clark, "Higher Education," 198.
38. Clark, "Higher Education," 200.
39. Clark, "Higher Education," 200.
40. Clark, "Higher Education," 201.
41. Kenneth B. Clark, "Intelligence, the University and Society," *American Scholar* 36, no. 1 (Winter 1966–67): 23–32, doi: https://www.jstor.org/stable/41209437.
42. Clark, "Higher Education," 198–99.
43. Clark, "Higher Education," 201.
44. Clark, "Higher Education," 201.
45. Clark, "Higher Education," 203.
46. Vincent Harding, "W. E. B. Du Bois and the Black Messianic Vision," in *Black Titan: W. E. B. Du Bois,* ed. John Henrik Clarke et al. (Boston: Beacon Press, 1970), 53.

47. Kenneth B. Clark, "The Present Dilemma of the Negro," *Journal of Negro History* 53, no. 1 (January 1968): 1.

48. W. E. B. Du Bois, *Dusk of Dawn* (New Brunswick, NJ: Transaction Publishers, 2009), 27. Reprint, citations refer to the Transaction edition.

49. Quoted in David Levering Lewis, *W. E. B. Du Bois: The Fight for Equality and the American Century 1919–1963* (New York: Henry Holt, 2000), 567.

50. Benjamin E. Mays, *Born to Rebel* (Athens: University of Georgia Press, 1971), 60.

51. Randal M. Jelks, *Benjamin Elijah Mays: Schoolmaster of the Movement* (Chapel Hill: University of North Carolina Press, 2014), 151, Kindle.

52. Jelks, *Benjamin Elijah Mays*, 144.

53. Benjamin E. Mays, *Quotable Quotes of Benjamin E. Mays* (New York: Vantage Press, 1983), 4.

54. Sanjiv Chopra and Gina Vild, *The Two Most Important Days* (New York: St. Martin's Press, 2017), xvii. This quote is popularly attributed to Twain, but some have disputed his authorship.

55. As a Morehouse student in 1979, when Mays often visited the campus, I heard countless stories about him from faculty and alumni. I also met him and had my own transformative experience under his influence.

56. Bronnie Ware, *The Top Five Regrets of the Dying* (New York: Hay House, 2012), chap. 1. Note that this story is also cited in Kate Aronoff, *Overheated: How Capitalism Broke the Planet—and How We Fight Back* (New York: Bold Type Books, 2021), 345.

57. "The Top 10 Crises the World Can't Ignore in 2022," International Rescue Committee, updated March 1, 2022, https://www.rescue.org/article/top-10-crises-world-cant-ignore-2022.

58. Ayi Kwei Armah, *The Healers* (Senegal: Per Ankh edition, 2016).

59. Walter Rodney, *How Europe Underdeveloped Africa* (London: Bogle-L'Ouverture Publications, 1972), chaps. 4 and 6.

60. Armah, *Healers*, 55.

61. Martin Luther King, Jr., *Strength to Love* (Boston: Beacon Press, 1963).

Epilogue

1. T. Thomas Fortune, "A Cathedral in the Black Belt," *The Sun* (Tuskegee, AL), April 3, 1898, 16.

Acknowledgments

The best books are not merely read. Those I have cherished above all the rest have never simply been an ordered collection of ideas. Instead of reading them, I have encountered them, and they have encountered me. I believe such books have the power to awaken citizens to a new and better world. And the best among them also stimulate a whole new mindset about how to journey to that world.

I am grateful to all the allies I developed while generating this book, especially those who understood the deeply personal nature of my task. I thank Jayne Fargnoli, my publisher at the Harvard Education Press, who never wavered in her firm belief in the importance of my message. I thank my key foundation funders, and a very special anonymous donor who believes in HBCUs. I thank Mitch and Freada Kapor, who provided me with a timely boost to get me over the finish line. I am grateful to my collection of "data gurus" who helped so much with the analysis phase of my work, including Resche Hines, David Lerch, Tafaya Ransom, and Kimberly Truong. Special thanks to Josh Kornblat who translated the tables and made them digestible.

A number of key people spent considerable time reviewing multiple draft chapters, with the understanding that I did not want this to be "just another book about HBCUs." They include Sulayman Clark, Suzanne Smith, and Joe Williams. Dr. Clark has been a true friend since graduate school, and he served as a critical muse, keeping my focus sharp. I encountered his book, *The Friends of Freedom*, as a transformative story of string shooters, written by a string shooter.

I am especially indebted to those who provided resources, information, and feedback to improve the quality of my thinking and writing. A number of them eased the toil of drafting in one thoughtful way or another, with grace. They include: Ryan Bean, Matthew Boulay, Barri Anne Brown, Javier F. Cevallos, Philip Clay, Julia Falkoff, Deanna Gordon, Katie Hebert, Keon Holmes, Thomas Hollister, Ann E. Kaplan, Walter Kimbrough, Tomasine Kirkland-Quamina, Patti Kunkle, Rick Legon, Katie McArdle, Darien Pollock, Colleen Previte, Gregory N. Price, Michael Rosenthal, Stephanie Saul, Folashade Solomon, and Barbara Stowe.

I thank those whose work I encountered and thereby received a deeper understanding of where I needed to go within myself to ever have a chance at getting this book to where my soul needed it to be. They include: Ayi Kwei Armah, Kate Aronoff, Charles Clotfelter, Leroy Davis, Carol Dweck, Ibram X. Kendi, David Levering Lewis, Donald Mathews, Dambisa Moyo, Khalil Gibran Muhammad, Robert J. Norrell, Adam Serwer, Alan Taylor, and Craig Steven Wilder. In addition to encountering their work, I had enormously helpful conversations with Lisa D. Cook, Marybeth Gasman, Randal Jelks, Robert W. Livingston, and Ruth Simmons.

David Kwabena Wilson, another special friend from graduate school, has executed a presidency at Morgan State University that is reflective of many of this book's most progressive themes. He has measurably shifted that campus toward optimization. A few of the other contemporary HBCU presidents whose measurable optimization work I have admired include: Mary Schmidt Campbell (Spelman College), Johnnetta B. Cole (Spelman College), Walter Kimbrough (Philander Smith College and Dillard University), Ronald Mason, Jr. (Jackson State University and the University of the District of Columbia), Ruth Simmons (Prairie View A&M University), Beverly D. Tatum (Spelman College), and Henry N. Tisdale (Claflin University).

A constellation of Morehouse guys kept me strong in recent years, and I am indebted to them each, but especially to that special set of eleven brothers known as "The Kosmic Benediction."

Robert Lee Mallett and I attended Morehouse and Harvard together. He encouraged me to finish writing this, especially when things went south at our alma mater. More than most, he knows I am merely writing what we knew my team and I needed and intended to do.

Speaking of my team, I am convinced that I hired and converged, at Morehouse, the best-ever team at any college! Of special note were Garikai Campbell (phenomenal provost and leader), Lacrecia Cade (stellar general counsel and chief of staff), David Lerch (financial guru), John Brown (advancement seer), Tafaya Ransom (data sage), Clifford Russell (technology genius), Christine Trotman (energy guardian), Cathy Tyler (messaging virtuoso), Ralph Johnson (truth shark), and Chief Valerie Dalton (safety and security expert). Yet others were super special, too, and they include Bennie Cade, Tim Sams, and Kasi Turner. And the very special faculty who "got it," included Jann Adams, Andrew J. Douglas, Vickie Edmondson, David Wall Rice, and Ulrica Wilson. There are a few others I could list, but you know who you are, and so do many others . . . because you were and remain string shooters!

Special thanks to my brother, Lucas Bernard Wilson, who attended Morehouse two years behind me and who has always made me see what I needed to see, especially about Morehouse, HBCUs, and string shooters. Lucas is an economics professor, and I have been consistently nourished by his wisdom and advice about economics, African American history, American higher education, family, and so much else. Thank you, bro!

Two Morehouse-made professors did much to help set my pathway to both the Morehouse presidency and this book. They are Drs. William V. Guy and Charles Vert Willie. Each mentored me early on and remain the spiritual wind beneath my wings. Sadly, Dr. Willie transitioned as I completed this book. It would have been my high honor to personally hand him a signed copy, just as he handed me a signed copy of his book on HBCUs years ago.

As I am the son, grandson, and great-grandson of preaching ministers, I must acknowledge those clergy who have had much to do with my overall spiritual health, my pathway to this book, or both. They include: Revs. Robert Johnson Smith (a Morehouse man who had the congregation believing that Jesus graduated from Morehouse); Joseph S. Ratliff (whose sermons were invariably real, powerful, and brief); William V. Guy (who kept my signal-to-noise ratio high during my student days at Morehouse . . . and ever since); Howard Haywood (the most authentic follower of the religion of Jesus I ever knew, and nobody even comes close); Donald Kelly (good heart, good message, good man); Jonathan Walton (brilliant preacher, solid scholar, walks his talk); Richard W. Wills, Sr. (refreshing theology, great pastor, rare honesty and integrity); and Howard-John Wesley (a living example of the phrase "I'd rather see a sermon than hear one." But with him, you can see and hear a great sermon each and every time).

I acknowledge, too, my friend and mentor in and beyond graduate school, the late Reverend Peter J. Gomes, Harvard's longtime Plummer Professor of Christian Morals and Pusey Minister in the Memorial Church. By the Sparks House fireside, he told me countless stories about spending the first two years of his career teaching on the campus of the Tuskegee Institute. He would be relieved to discover that I finally learned to truly hear and appreciate Booker T. Washington.

Providing key encouragement and consistently keeping my spirits high was Ali Abdule'as'Salaam. I wish him all the best as he and Christina continue to do a great job raising their son, Tahjia "Taco" Jordan! May Taco's focus and discipline reward him and the world with a life of "string shooter consequence," akin to that of Densu in *The Healers*.

I have known Heather Andrea Williams since graduate school at Harvard. What a string shooter! After completing Harvard College, she handled Harvard Law School with ease, practiced law only briefly, but then she had her second day: destiny decided that she needed to earn a PhD and become a world-class historian. Since then, my encounters with her books have invariably lifted me, especially *Help Me to Find My People*, which brings tears every time I revisit or even think about it.

Last, and most, I thank my family. At age ninety-five, my mother, Genester Nix Miller, an author herself, has maintained the measured yet lofty expectations to which only mothers can encourage and challenge their children. As a huge fan of HBCUs, she urged and willed this book out of me. Relatedly, her pride in being among Morgan State University's oldest living graduates is exceeded only by her seventy-four years of beaming as Morgan's proudest living graduate!

Equally powerful, yet in a different way, is my wife's abiding confidence, expectation, and love! Carol's eager patience as this book took years to emerge from me is akin to my eager patience as our three children took months to emerge from her. She has been a wonderful mother, a brilliant professor, a successful entrepreneur, and an incomparable wife. I am blessed that she and our children were consistently loving, supportive, encouraging, confident, and at peace with the time I spent on this project. Their great sacrifice makes it their work, too, although each and every mistake is mine.

Finally, only by stepping back from this completed work have I truly sensed the high stakes of it all. I have become convinced that the best way to ensure that there is a new day in store for America and the world is to elevate, enrich, and scale key elements of the HBCU approach to shaping better citizens. And the best way to unveil the dawn of that new day envisioned by the original HBCU architects is to shape string shooters by the millions. As Rev. Gomes would often thunderously proclaim, "Nothing more is required, and nothing less will do!"

About the Author

John Silvanus Wilson, Jr., serves as the executive director of the Millennial Leadership Initiative, a program of the American Association of State Colleges and Universities that is designed to diversify and bolster the American college presidency. He has spent his entire career in higher education, including serving as an advancement director at the Massachusetts Institute of Technology, an associate professor and executive dean at the George Washington University, president of Morehouse College, and senior advisor and strategist to the president of Harvard University. He directed the White House Initiative on HBCUs in the Obama administration and served as a trustee of Spelman College and an overseer at Harvard University. He holds a BA from Morehouse College, a master of theology from Harvard University, and both master's and doctoral degrees in administration, planning, and social policy, also from Harvard University.

Index